THE GOSPEL AND PLURALISM TODAY

Reassessing Lesslie Newbigin in the 21st Century

Edited by
SCOTT W. SUNQUIST
and AMOS YONG

An imprint of InterVarsity Press
Downers Grove, Illinois

InterVarsity Press
P.O. Box 1400, Downers Grove, IL 60515-1426
ivpress.com
email@ivpress.com

InterVarsity Press® is the book-publishing division of InterVarsity Christian Fellowship/USA®, a movement of students and faculty active on campus at hundreds of universities, colleges and schools of nursing in the United States of America, and a member movement of the International Fellowship of Evangelical Students. For information about local and regional activities, visit intervarsity.org.

While any stories in this book are true, some names and identifying information may have been changed to protect the privacy of individuals.

Cover design: David Fassett
Interior design: Beth McGill
Images: Lesslie Newbigin: James Burke/The Life Picture Collection/Getty Images
white paper: ©tomograf/iStockphoto

ISBN 978-0-8308-5094-5 (print)
ISBN 978-0-8308-9899-2 (digital)

Printed in the United States of America ♾

As a member of the Green Press Initiative, InterVarsity Press is committed to protecting the environment and to the responsible use of natural resources. To learn more, visit greenpressinitiative.org.

Library of Congress Cataloging-in-Publication Data

The gospel and pluralism today : reassessing Lesslie Newbigin in the 21st century / edited by Scott W. Sunquist and Amos Yong.
pages cm.—(Missiological engagements)
Includes bibliographical references and index.
ISBN 978-0-8308-5094-5 (pbk. : alk. paper)
1. Newbigin, Lesslie. The Gospel in a pluralist society. 2. Christianity and culture. 3. Christianity—20th century. 4. Apologetics. 5. Missions—Theory. 6. Evangelistic work—Philosophy. I. Sunquist, Scott W. (Scott William), 1953- editor.
BR115.C8N46834 2015
261—dc23

2015027324

P 23 22 21 20 19 18 17 16 15 14 13 12 11 10 9 8 7 6 5 4 3 2 1
Y 35 34 33 32 31 30 29 28 27 26 25 24 23 22 21 20 19 18 17 16 15

We dedicate this volume to the past deans of
Fuller Seminary's School of Intercultural Studies (formally the
School of World Mission and Institute of Church Growth) who have
encouraged mission engagement in global contexts,
including in the West:

Donald A. McGavran (1965–1971)

Arthur F. Glasser (1971–1980)

Paul E. Pierson (1980–1992)

J. Dudley Woodberry (1992–1999)

Sherwood G. Lingenfelter (1999–2003)

C. Douglas McConnell (2003–2011)

This first volume in the Missiological Engagement Series derives from the
2014 Missiology Lectures, which have been held annually at SWM/SIS
since 1965 under the oversight of these innovative leaders in
global mission. We are indebted to all of them.

Contents

Acknowledgments

This volume emerged out of the annual Missiology Lectures at Fuller Seminary's School of Intercultural Studies. Most of the chapters in this volume were first heard and discussed at the 2014 Missiology Lectures, which were held November 13–15. We are grateful to the following people for their part in making these lectures happen:

- President Mark Labberton and Provost C. Douglas McConnell for their support of the School of Intercultural Studies and its various initiatives;
- Wendy S. Walker, Allison Norton, Johnny Ching, Caroline Kim, and others in the School of Intercultural Studies and its Center for Missiological Research for their behind-the-scenes and more obviously evident efforts in making the lectures a success;
- Abigail Cook, Victoria Smith and those on the events team of Fuller Theological Seminary for their roles in organizing the logistics of the lectures;
- Mike Karim and Ryan Seow, two great teaching assistants, for their work on the conference, and other PhD students who filled in admirably to attend to various tasks related to the conference and book project;
- Johnny Ramírez-Johnson for his role in emceeing the sessions at the lectures;
- Tod Bolsinger, Mark Lau Branson, Paul Yonggap Jeong and Steve Yamaguchi for offering elective sessions on various aspects of Newbigin's life and/or theology;
- Kevin K. Haah, Josi Hwang Koo, Mike Karim, Enoch Jinsik Kim, Mark Labberton, Daniel D. Lee, Jonathen Lew, Joy J. Moore, Diane Obenchain and Johnny Ramírez-Johnson for their responses to the presentations that stimulated revisions toward the final version of papers now included in this book.

Thanks also to each of the presenters at the lectures and others who wrote specifically for the book, some at very short notice.

We are also grateful to the staff at InterVarsity Press for many reasons: their interest in the book series of which this is the inaugural volume, their professionalism in working on the series as a whole and this book in particular in its various production phases, and their vision for publishing more in missiology and mission theology. David Congdon has been especially efficient in brokering multiple conversations that have resulted in the series and the book you now hold in your hands.

Last but not least, our wives, Nancy Sunquist and Alma Yong, deserve special recognition; neither of us would be the scholars, editors or persons we are without their support.

Abbreviation Note

GPS—Lesslie Newbigin, *The Gospel in a Pluralist Society*, in its various editions; chapter authors will provide the full publication information in the first instance for the edition of the book they are using, after which the *GPS* abbreviation will be used in the notes.

1

Introduction

The Legacy of Newbigin for Mission to the West

Scott W. Sunquist

J. E. Lesslie Newbigin (1909–1998) was a missionary. He had many other titles—reverend, bishop, ecumenist, general secretary of the International Missionary Council—but he was always a missionary. His conversion to orthodox Christianity came from a vision of the cross reaching from heaven to earth and embracing the world.[1] This image, along with Jesus' high priestly prayer (Jn 17), would guide his theological writing for the rest of his life. Seldom has a life been so focused from such an early age, and at the same time so acutely aware of cultural changes that influence that focus. Major events, key personalities, important writings and family shaped him relentlessly and providentially. Yet the image and the prayer remained a steady guide.

Born into a devout and politically alert Northumbrian family December 8, 1909, Newbigin straddled English and Scottish cultures. His mother was of Scottish background, his father English, and he studied in Cambridge, served in Glasgow, and was ordained in the Church of Scotland. The contrast for North Americans may seem small, but for a Scot to be mistaken for an Englishman is more than grounds for a feud. Newbigin embraced the divide as he did many other liminal spaces in his life. As a college student he straddled the divide between ecumenical and evangelical fellowship

[1]As described in his autobiography, Lesslie Newbigin, *Unfinished Agenda: An Updated Biography*, 2nd ed. (Grand Rapids: Eerdmans, 1993), p. 11.

groups. He worked in the summers with the Quakers, providing some relief for the coal miners in south Wales, another culture. In India he continued to straddle the divide between church traditions and worked very hard to make sure that union and unity were central concerns for gospel fidelity. He learned Tamil well enough to speak, teach, write, preach and even to carry on theological discourse with some of the best Tamil Hindu scholars. He embraced India, with all of its many gods and castes, and returned to England alert to the gods and castes of postmodern Europe. He understood bridging, engaging and remaining faithful to the Christian tradition in the midst of competing plural norms and values.

In between his missionary and pastoral work in South India and his work in England upon "retirement" in 1974, he had a very fruitful ministry as an ecumenical leader in both the International Missionary Council and the Faith and Order Movement. His ecumenical leadership actually began in South India with the forming of the Church of South India. A year later he attended the first Assembly of the World Council of Churches in Amsterdam where, at the age of thirty-nine, he helped to draft the statement that came out of that assembly. This ecumenical period is very important in Newbigin's life, but we focus here on the last and most fruitful chapter of his life, his return to the West in 1974.

The major theme of Newbigin's scholarship upon his return to England might be described as the proper understanding of the missionary nature of the church and the need for thoughtful missionary engagement in the post-Christendom and pluralist West. This may be a little inelegant, but I believe it is accurate. He was always the missionary, but at the same time he was always the *thoughtful* missionary who studied cultures more as a theologian and philosopher than as an anthropologist. As early as 1952, in his Kerr Lectures (later published as *The Household of God*), Newbigin wrote about the importance of ecclesiology in light of the breakdown of Christendom. He realized that ecclesiology was the key and Pentecostal ecclesiology was an important new voice in framing missiology and ecclesiology for the future. As much as any other theologian, Newbigin was both early and profound in his description of what the end of Christendom meant for Christianity.

The West as the new missionary context was most clearly illustrated in the experience Newbigin had in 1979 when, at the age of seventy, he was asked to chair his local church council meeting (United Reformed Church). On the docket was the proposal to close a 120-year-old church located in the slums across from Winson Green Prison. The local URC pastors reasoned that since the area had become mostly South Asian through immigration, there was no reason to keep the church alive. This, of course, was a Christendom understanding of church as chaplain to Christian society. Newbigin the missionary who had worked in South Asia, armed with the same facts, reasoned the exact opposite. Since the church was in the midst of a mission field, it was right where it was supposed to be. He argued that the church should be kept open, and he would pastor it with a South Asian pastor working with him. Newbigin and his new colleague, Hakkim Singh Rahi, began their ministry by visiting all the houses in the region.

> Together they went door to door in the run-down neighborhood, and Newbigin got a ground-level introduction to how far from Christian his England had become. While Asian immigrants almost always welcomed him and Rahi in for tea, Anglo neighbors often slammed the door in their faces. When the two pastors did get inside, they found lives formed by the omnipresent television, not the Bible. Religion was seen as a matter of personal taste, a private concern about which no one should trouble another.[2]

Thus, the decline of Christianity in England, the privatized nature of Western life and belief, along with the loss of missionary zeal in the church all came together for Newbigin in Winson Green. *The Gospel in a Pluralist Society*, along with other titles written in the 1980s and 1990s (well into his retirement), focus on understanding the Western predicament, and helping the church to re-engage in God's mission at all levels, in each cultural context.[3] This led us at Fuller Theological Seminary to look again at *The Gospel in a Pluralist Society* after twenty-five years. This volume is a collection of papers that reflect on the ongoing meaning and value of *The Gospel in a Pluralist Society* for the twenty-first century. But first we need to remember the book itself.

---

[2]Tim Stafford, "God's Missionary," *Christianity Today*, December 9, 1996, pp. 24-33.

[3]See, for example, *The Other Side of 1984* (1983), *Foolishness to the Greeks* (1986) and the important essay "Can the West Be Converted?," *Princeton Seminary Bulletin* 6, no. 1 (1985): 25-37. In this essay he lays out his concern: "Surely there can be no more crucial question for the world mission of the Church than the one I have posed. Can there be an effective missionary encounter with this culture—this so powerful, persuasive, and confident culture which (at least until very recently) simply regarded itself as 'the coming world civilization.' Can the West be converted?"

THE BOOK: *THE GOSPEL IN A PLURALIST SOCIETY*

I find it interesting that Newbigin identifies himself in *The Gospel in a Pluralist Society* not as a professor (which he was), nor as a missionary (which he had been), nor as a bishop (which he had also been), but as a pastor.[4] In his mind he is writing a book to help pastors and other church leaders re-imagine what it means to be a pastor in a post-Christendom world. Context is not everything, but it is more than most things when it comes to interpreting a document. The context of these lectures, as Wilbert Shenk reminds us in chapter one, was a confused one. Newbigin was invited to give the Alexander Robertson "lectures" at Glasgow, which he came prepared to deliver. However, when he arrived he found out that he was actually teaching a course to university students of all stripes. Many came to his lectures as post-Christendom cynics, but others came as pre-ministerial students. His lectures had to be expanded and reshaped to meet his diverse audience. Thus, there is a very strong apologetic nature to the lectures, as if he is trying to convince his largely nominal Christian audience of the veracity of the Christian faith itself, not just describe the problem of belief in the West.

Although written with such a diverse audience in mind, *The Gospel in a Pluralist Society* became one of the most important mission books of the last half of the twentieth century. Oddly enough it is one of the few mission books that has been read by theologians (both practical and systematic), pastors and seminary students with great zeal. Theologians read the book but are troubled by its lack of notation and cross-referencing. Pastors read it but are often troubled by the philosophical bent of much of his argument. (Most pastors are reading books on mission and ministry, but few read philosophy.) Seminary students usually read it because they have to. But once they are introduced to Newbigin through *The Gospel in a Pluralist Society*, many want more.[5] Since 1996 over 40,000 copies have been sold. Before that, the publisher does not have records. I think it is safe to say that it has sold close to 100,000 copies. Why the popularity of such a strange book, a book on epistemology, history, mission, culture and ecclesiology?

---

[4]Lesslie Newbigin, *The Gospel in a Pluralist Society* (Grand Rapids: Eerdmans, 1989).

[5]I used *GPS* in teaching introductory missiology courses and was soon asked to teach a course only on Newbigin as a missiologist. I relented and have done so for fifteen years now.

In brief, I think it is because his words rang true to the experience of the Western church.

Newbigin was not the first person to observe the global transformation of Christianity in his lifetime,[6] but he was the first person to analyze what it meant for the Western church and how Christians in the West must now think and act differently to be faithful to God's mission. A few decades before *The Gospel in a Pluralist Society*, the Roman Catholic scholar Walbert Bühlman wrote *The Coming of the Third Church*.[7] He was one of the earliest to observe what was taking place in global Christianity as the Western church was in decline and the "southern" church (Third Church) became stronger and more numerous. The transformation that was taking place in the world Christian movement was more than just a matter of counting Christian noses in each country or region. More significant were the changes that were taking place in Christian identity (within) and in cultural perceptions of Christianity (from without). The dramatic changes in Christianity that Newbigin recognized can be illustrated by two events in New York City, which were just 101 years apart.

In 1900 the largest and most influential mission conference, called the 1900 Ecumenical Conference on Foreign Missions, was held. Speakers included the president of Columbia University and three presidents of the United States: Teddy Roosevelt (governor of New York at the time), former president Benjamin Harrison and President William McKinley. The meetings were held in Carnegie Hall and in various churches in New York. To give us a sense of how thoroughly the idea of Protestant missionary work to the world was supported by the larger society, here are a few of the words from the president of Columbia University:

> I think men have also grown to realize that God has not left Himself without witnesses, even in lands that we are accustomed to think of as heathen lands. And yet, what can Christians do better, in such a time as this, than to bear

[6] A number of books have described some of this "great reversal" that occurred in the twentieth century. See, for example, Scott W. Sunquist, *The Unexpected Christian Century: The Reversal and Transformation of Christianity in the Twentieth Century* (Grand Rapids: Baker Academic, 2015); Dyron Daughtery, *The Changing World of Christianity* (New York: Peter Lang, 2010); Wesley Granberg-Michaelson, *From Times Square to Timbuktu: The Post-Christian West Meets the Non-Western Church* (Grand Rapids: Eerdmans, 2013); and, among others, Philip Jenkins, *The Next Christendom: The Coming of Global Christianity* (Oxford: Oxford University Press, 2002).

[7] Walbert Bühlman, *The Coming of the Third Church: An Analysis of the Present and Future of the Church* (Maryknoll, NY: Orbis, 1977).

> their unshaken testimony to their belief that there is no other Name under heaven, whereby men must be saved, but the Name of Jesus Christ?[8]

The best and the brightest, the political and most academic leaders all supported Protestant Christian missions for the world's ills. Twenty-five hundred delegates and 115 mission societies attended and heard three US presidents give their support for foreign missions. American was Protestant, and its growing global engagement was a political, military and missionary engagement woven together.[9] The Philippines is probably the clearest example of this manifestation of twentieth-century Christendom. In the Philippines, the Spanish Catholic rulers were ousted and the United States came in with the support and encouragement of Protestant missionaries to help rebuild the Philippines as a Protestant nation. Newbigin was born into this type of Christendom.

One hundred and one years later, New York experienced violence on its own shores from what had been called "heathen lands." September 11, 2001, stands as a symbol of many global changes, but I would like to suggest here that the responses to 9/11 also symbolize something else as well. Instead of a call to missionary work (what we might expect in 1900 and what happened after the Boxer Rebellion), there was a national reevaluation of our place in the world. In the final months of 2001 there were many gatherings calling for national repentance. A brief rise in church attendance was then followed by decline in both church attendance and membership in the West. Western missions continued to decline. Many Western Christians had accepted the crusading missionary discourse that identified Christian missions with imperialism and the Crusades. Rather than a declaration ("Let's go into all the world proclaiming Christ"), there was a question in Western souls ("Did we bring this on ourselves?"). The place of the church, and certainly of the church in mission, had completely changed in a century.

Newbigin's understanding of the change in the West came from his life as a missionary; a missionary who was deeply embedded in south Indian Hindu culture. In India, he walked with and talked to common people as

[8]From the library of Columbia University (accessed December 15, 2014): http://library.columbia.edu/content/dam/libraryweb/locations/burke/fa/mrl/ldpd_4492656.pdf.

[9]Just months after this largely celebratory conference was the Boxer Rebellion in China where anti-foreign and anti-Christian sentiments spilled out across many eastern provinces. The response of missions was largely to increase their efforts to bring the best of the Christian West to China.

well as the best scholars of Tamil Hindu literature. His *South India Diary* reveals a man who walked from village to village encouraging local evangelists and preachers, visiting parishioners in their homes, and catechizing new converts.[10] He was a student of South Indian languages and cultures. But he was a student of cultures in order to be a more faithful missionary presence. He was the same missionary when he returned to England, only then he had to learn another new culture. He had to study the declining Christian culture, a culture which had lost its meaning and its nerve. But he also had to study the broader intellectual culture, a culture that no longer seemed to have a place for Christian truth.

Because of the missionary nature of his investigation, *The Gospel in a Pluralist Society* appeals to different people for different reasons. First, the book is appealing to Christian philosopher–types who are trying to make sense of the epistemological age in which we live and move and have our being. Newbigin offers them the lens of Michael Polanyi to help explain that the modernist divide between fact and belief is a false one. All knowledge is personal and therefore relational. Newbigin finds such contemporary philosophy helpful in making his case that there is, and must always be, a place for religious belief in the public square; that is, there must be a place for all religious belief, not just Christian belief, for he is a true pluralist.

Second, the volume is appealing to those involved in interreligious dialogue or those who are living among people of different faiths. Newbigin again brings his Indian experience, a missionary life, into Western discourse. The same attitudes, respect and convictions that guided him in India (a truly pluralist society) guide this discussion in *The Gospel in a Pluralist Society*. His strong affirmation of public exchange of ideas and public convictions of Christian belief are held together not in tension but in harmony. Like his discussion of epistemology he pushes against the modern, or Enlightenment, propensity to dichotomize, as if the church must choose between hospitality or evangelism. Another way of looking at this is that he refuses to give in to the modern Western propensity to reductionism, as if we must reduce interreligious relations to dialogue. Again, Newbigin embraces pluralism for the sake of mission.

---

[10]Lesslie Newbigin, *A South India Diary* (London: SCM Press, 1951).

Third, the volume is particularly helpful for pastors who are watching their church decline as the older members age and die and fewer young people join the church. These pastors of all ages are looking for a way to recover the purpose and mission for their local church and also the universal church. Newbigin provides a way to begin to talk about Christian belief in the new arena where Christian belief is not respected. For centuries there were basic Christian assumptions in the public square: God created the heavens and the earth, Jesus was sent by God to save us, the Bible is a book to be respected and followed, and so on. Most Christian leaders in the West have not made the transition from speaking about the church in a Christendom culture to speaking about Jesus in a post-Christian culture. Newbigin found out that a post-Christian culture is more resistant to the gospel than a pre-Christian village, and he guides the reader to understand what it means for the church to be a foretaste of the kingdom and what it means for the church to be a hermeneutic of the gospel.

Finally, the volume has become valuable for younger people interested in new ecclesiologies and planting new forms of churches. I am sure this was not one of the intended goals (if Newbigin even had any intended goals in publishing *The Gospel in a Pluralist Society*), but many of these leaders are looking to Newbigin to guide them in these areas. Newbigin's call to engage cultures and to develop forms of Christianity that speak the local language in ways that connect with local communities is a call that has taken on a life of its own. Church-planting networks and new ecclesial movements find much of their inspiration in Newbigin's call to missionary engagement in the West.

Personally, as a historian, I am cognizant that in describing how Christians must now think about our missional presence in the West, Newbigin bases his argument first on the nature of knowledge as personal and then second on the understanding that our knowledge concerns the "fact of the Jesus" of history. What Newbigin means by this is that we must center our presentation of the faith around the historic life of Jesus Christ. We are to argue not on the basis of feelings or therapy (Christians are happier), but on historic facts. Christian belief is rooted in a true incarnation, not an avatar or a myth. Jesus is a historic figure who can be studied alongside other historic figures. It is important, therefore, that Christians do not abandon history in their witness to Jesus Christ, but that they engage with historians in the study of a particular historical figure. Four chapters near the middle of the book discuss history,[11] and I would suggest that the argument of the book hinges on history. In the history section he discusses the life of Jesus, the nature of the Bible and the meaning of election. One might say that he enters straight into major debates about the reliability of Christian faith in these four chapters.

Through all of this reasoning about the nature of the church in the post-Christendom world, we must remember that Newbigin led the church in this discussion from a deep personal spirituality. For example, in most all settings, he knew the Scriptures better than all others.[12] His prayers and his own spiritual attentiveness were genuine, attractive and palpable when he entered a room. His concern for mission came from his deep love of Christ and therefore deep love for those whom Christ loves. He knew that mission must be carried out in humility and spiritual communion. One story may help illustrate his spiritual attentiveness.

After becoming bishop of the church in South India, he would often receive new missionaries from the West. One young college graduate came to work under Newbigin, and he described to me his first encounter. "At the appointed time I came into the bishop's study. He was sitting erect behind his desk, and a single chair was across from him at his desk. He asked me to sit down. We looked directly at each other, and then his first words came to me. I remember them to this day: 'Tell me, John, about the state of your soul.'" All ministry and missionary work must begin with an awareness of the state of our own soul in relation to Jesus Christ. Newbigin's writings came from a deep spiritual well, and it is important to remember this when we read him today.

The Conference

The Missiology Lectures that were held at Fuller Theological Seminary November 13–15, 2014, were designed to hold up this twenty-five-year-old treatise (*The Gospel in a Pluralist Society*) as if it were a lens and to look through it from a number of angles as we gaze into the twenty-first century. The theme of the conference and the issues in *The Gospel in a Pluralist Society* were first introduced in chapel with a sermon by Dr. William Burrows,

---

[11]Chapters six through nine: "Revelation in History," "The Logic of Election," "The Bible as Universal History," and "Christ, the Clue to History."

[12]From a conversation with Wilbert Shenk (October 2014), who knew Newbigin.

who worked for twenty years as editor for Orbis Books. Burrows set the tone for the conference by preaching from the Gospel of John (1:1-14), the one book of the Bible for which Newbigin wrote a commentary.[13] Along with the lectures, the school offered a course for credit, so fifteen students came to the conference having read more than *The Gospel in a Pluralist Society* and having already turned in papers and begun thinking of topics for papers applying the book's insights for today. This concern—the relevance of *The Gospel in a Pluralist Society* for the twenty-first century—was a driving theme in lectures, responses and audience questions.

The particular plenary addresses will be discussed in the next section, but it is important to explain here that a "conference culture" developed over our time together. People from distant regions and diverse backgrounds came together and developed a new culture and discourse about the value of *The Gospel in a Pluralist Society* for ministry and mission in the West. Our moderator for the event was a new faculty member who had experience as a missionary in Central America and Lebanon, and who was involved in church planting in the United States. Johnny Ramírez-Johnson, himself a product of local missionary outreach (in this case, children evangelizing children) and conversion in the West (Puerto Rico), represented something of Newbigin's insights. After each presentation, Ramírez-Johnson introduced respondents who had come prepared with brief statements. The respondents included professors representing all three schools at Fuller,[14] pastors and PhD students. After respondents gave their observations and critiques the session was opened up for the audience to ask questions. The audience included pastors, lay leaders, students, faculty, and staff in Pasadena and others who watched via Polycom from other Fuller campuses. There was never need to prod the audience, for the topics were close to the hearts of most all who attended. The topic that raised the greatest number of comments and questions was the application of Newbigin (who we must remember worked in Asia) to church and missionary work in Asia today. The audience included a large percentage of Asians who had come for the very purpose of asking about the relevance of Newbigin's ideas for ongoing Asian missionary work.

---

[13]Lesslie Newbigin, *The Light Has Come: An Exposition of the Fourth Gospel* (Grand Rapids: Eerdmans, 1987).

[14]Theology, Intercultural Studies and Psychology.

Another element that added to the diversity of the event was the separate track and course for credit that was run in the Korean language by our Korean faculty, since many of Newbigin's books have been translated into Korean. All of the lectures, responses and questions were translated into Korean. Some of the questions were even asked in Korean and then translated into English for the benefit of our speakers!

In the concluding session a panel of six speakers each made summary comments in light of the two days of presentations. These comments all proved very enlightening and set an agenda for future work. Although a number of comments are worth discussing here, I mention only one. Esther Meek challenged the idea of the West being truly pluralist. Her reasoning is explained in chapter five. During the conference we discussed that Christianity has lost a place, or a voice, in the marketplace of ideas. Secular universities are not pluralist places where many ideas can be voiced and compared. Christian groups and Christian assumptions are often not welcome in the classrooms of many universities. Thus, our future in the West, and the new context for the church in the West, may be more contentious than pluralist. Pluralism has devolved or has been pulled back into the Enlightenment with its strong dichotomies and its rejection of religious faith as a place for truth claims. Meek talked about the possibility that the Enlightenment was not overcome by post-Enlightenment critiques (notice the past tense), and so the struggle is not for the church to find a place in the marketplace of ideas but to just have a place at the table (to mix metaphors). Thus, Newbigin's approach and much of his apologetic may still be applicable, but the situation is perhaps much more extreme than he thought twenty-five years ago.

This Book

This volume includes the lectures from the missiology conference, plus a few additional chapters to fill in issues and themes that time did not allow for. The opening chapter by Wilbert Shenk places Newbigin in the context of the late-twentieth-century decline of Christianity in the West and the growth of the church in the non-Western world. Shenk, who knew Newbigin fairly well, is uniquely qualified to write this chapter. A historian with a special concern for the post-Christendom Western context, Shenk explains many of the formative influences on Newbigin, including Christian leaders, institutions, social trends and conferences. After hearing some of Shenk's stories about Newbigin at the conference we were tempted to have him write another chapter on the Newbigin he knew.

The next chapter gives another view of Newbigin, from the perspective of a Roman Catholic missionary and editor of mission books. William Burrows places Newbigin's ideas in the context of the post–Vatican II Catholic world and suggests how Newbigin's project can be understood as parallel to and complementary with the work of *aggiornamento* precipitated by the council, helpfully reorienting central theological impulses in the Roman Catholic tradition (such as the nature-grace construct) in an even more robustly biblical direction. Although some Roman Catholic theologians might politely decline to receive "assistance" from a Protestant source such as Newbigin, Burrows's perceptive analysis confirms the ecumenical character of the bishop of South India's contribution and demonstrates its potency twenty-five years later and looking ahead into the middle of the twenty-first century.

In chapter three ecumenical theologian Veli-Matti Kärkkäinen and missiology student Michael Karim take a look at Newbigin's relationship to postmodernism. They note that for Newbigin the archenemy of the church has been modernity, and it could be assumed from his attack of modernity that he had strong affections for postmodernity. But such an assumption is wrong. Newbigin did not need postmodern threads to weave a more coherent fabric of Christian existence for the West. This article neatly describes Newbigin's approach, which we might follow today and which provides a more coherent and responsible way to reason after the collapse of Enlightenment hubris, but without succumbing to the nihilist trajectories of postmodern thought.

Chapter four by Steven B. Sherman, a philosophical theologian by training, is a paper that was not presented at the conference but has emerged as nicely situated between the Kärkkäinen-Karim essay and Esther Meek's that follows. The exposition of Newbigin's theological method and epistemology, particularly the holism that informs and organically connects both aspects of Newbigin's thinking, mediates between the more contextual analysis of the former and the more detailed and constructive analysis of the bishop's theory of knowing in the latter. Sherman's added contribution is a succinct elaboration of the performative aspects of Newbigin's method and epistemology for a pluralistic context. The rest of the chapters in the book can also be read as filling out the details of this.

Esther Meek's chapter does an excellent job explaining the importance of Michael Polanyi's philosophy to Newbigin's analysis of Western culture. She explains how Polanyi's philosophy opens up Christian witness for Newbigin, breaking apart the Enlightenment logjam. As someone who has done extensive work in epistemology, including engaging with and extending Polanyi's ideas, she also explains how both Polanyi and Newbigin move beyond the subjective-objective dichotomy by the use of what Polanyi calls "subsidiary-focal integration." This understanding of the two-level nature of knowing, says Meek, is central to Newbigin's argument, even though it is embedded rather than on the surface. Meek's chapter surfaces this and other concepts that are germane to Newbigin's thesis.

Also not part of the conference but written specifically for this volume, Amos Yong, a Pentecostal theologian, picks up Newbigin's strongly trinitarian themes in missiology and looks further at the pneumatological dimensions. Although well developed pneumatologically in comparison with other late-twentieth-century efforts in trinitarian theology and missiology, much of Newbigin's contributions can be considered to have laid the groundwork for the renaissance of pneumatology and pneumatological theology in the last two decades. Drawing particularly from recent Pentecostal scholarship, Yong explains how an even more robust pneumatological mission theology can invigorate Christian engagement with the scientific and technological domains of a pluralistic and secularized Western culture than an otherwise one-sided reading of Newbigin might inspire.

In chapter seven, Carrie Boren Headington, an evangelist with the Episcopal Church in Texas, asks what it means to be an evangelist in a pluralist society, guided by the thinking of Newbigin. Many of the discussions from other chapters turn to practical matters, but Headington focuses from the start on the practice of evangelism. Her chapter engages us with real questions that our post-Christendom neighbors are asking, and then she shows how Newbigin's analysis can be used as an apologetic in particular contexts. Her opening story of public witness in modern Oxford shows that Newbigin's experience in Winson Green nearly forty years ago is still very real today.

Barth scholar John Flett focuses his chapter on one chapter from *The Gospel in a Pluralist Society*, chapter eighteen, "The Congregation as a Hermeneutic of the Gospel." Flett builds his essay around the misunderstanding that usually develops when people read that the congregation, the local expression of Christian community in a particular parish, is a hermeneutic of the gospel. This does not mean that the local congregation somehow interprets the gospel for those around. In fact, hermeneutics is not interpretation or explanation, but has to do with rules or method for interpretation. The key to this discussion may be Newbigin's oft-repeated phrase that Jesus did not write a book but formed a community.

The last chapter looks at Newbigin from more of a global perspective, not specifically from the perspective of the audience to which it was originally written. Allen Yeh brings Newbigin's context and concern back to Asia where it all began. He asks, from his background with expertise in Latin American Christianity and a growing scholarly interest in Asian Christianity, what it means to bring Newbigin's ideas back to the pluralistic contexts of Asia. In addition, he asks what Christianity has to offer Asia, the continent that is the home of so many world religions. Next, Yeh turns the tables and asks what Asia has to offer to Christianity. The multicultural and incarnational nature of Christianity make both questions important for the development of Christianity in Asia.

Newbigin did not live to see the images of 9/11 on television or to hear about the restructuring of Arab societies around Islam and the struggles for greater democracy. The world has changed greatly in the twenty-five years since Newbigin argued for the Western church to engage Western societies. The ongoing debates about immigration and the acceptance of Islamic customs in the West have become more important since Newbigin's passing, although he was aware of them in the 1980s. Christianity in the West has continued its decline, even with helpful books like *The Gospel in a Pluralist Society*. We do not know how he might respond to these and many other newer issues that face the church, but I would suggest we have some hints. In his last lectures he was very strong in denouncing the unfettered reign of the free market that continues to oppress the poor and pollute the environment.[15]

[15]See a discussion of his understanding of the perils of the free market economy in Geoffrey Wainwright's *Lesslie Newbigin: A Theological Life* (New York: Oxford University Press, 2000), pp. 261-65.

His vision was always much broader than most people's and, at the same time, much deeper. This volume is not written by prophets but by committed Christians looking into the twenty-first century with the advantage of Newbigin's *The Gospel in a Pluralist Society* as our guide. The important themes discovered will help leaders to better serve not only the Western church but the worldwide church in the coming decades.

2

Newbigin in His Time

Wilbert R. Shenk

Lesslie Newbigin came of age as the West was in the grips of deep and prolonged crisis: the Great War, 1914–1918, had devastated Europe, an ill-conceived peace settlement among European countries had become the breeding ground for messianic ideologies that were paving the way for yet another global conflict, and the world economy collapsed in 1929. During his first year at university Newbigin became a committed Christian and identified with the Student Christian Movement, which was dedicated to nurturing in its members a strong sense of Christian vocation. He learned the importance of being attentive to the issues that were defining human existence. This was an essential element of Christian discipleship. To be a Christian meant living responsibly in God's world.

As the twentieth century progressed, Newbigin decried the way Christian faith in the West had become enfeebled, with Christians ceding control of public life to secular ideology, permitting secularism to establish itself as the authoritative plausibility structure by which women and men ordered their lives. Western Christians had acquiesced to these powerful secular forces, retreating to the margins of public life. For Newbigin this constituted a betrayal of the gospel. The central act in redemptive history—the cross and resurrection of Jesus Christ—was a public act, carried out by the political and religious establishments of the day. That victory of God in Jesus Christ remains the essential claim of the gospel. Faithfulness requires that Christians never retreat from proclaiming this good news to the world. Newbigin pleaded passionately that Christians in the West recover their apostolic nerve and boldly witness to God's gracious saving action on behalf of all people.

To understand the significance of Newbigin's witness, I review the way he continually engaged with the changing times and thoughtfully adapted to each new situation in which he found himself. What gave his witness extraordinary power was his intelligence, gift for communication, rich experience of serving more than three decades in India and extensive travel to all continents. Lesslie Newbigin disdained fads, but he was equally concerned not to be trapped in blinkered thinking that prevents one from seeing the present as clearly and discerningly as possible. Essential to effective communication and relationship is informed understanding of the culture of the other. This was a lesson he learned in a profound way when he went to India and threw himself into learning the challenging Tamil language and studying Indian history, culture and religion so that he might be an effective Christian servant in that land. He developed a deep appreciation for Indian people and their cultures and felt indebted for the privilege he had of living and serving in that great land.

At Cambridge, Newbigin's world was expanded. The Student Christian Movement (SCM) engaged distinguished guest speakers, including John R. Mott, J. H. Oldham, William Paton and Archbishop William Temple, who were informed and perceptive observers of the world situation and challenged students to take up their Christian responsibility in the world. He was especially drawn to J. H. Oldham, whom he held in high esteem. Oldham was endowed with prophetic ability to "discern the times." He observed that Oldham intuited the next burning issue that would capture world attention, and he would then focus his energy on addressing that concern through research, writing, speaking, study groups and conferences. From Oldham he learned that leadership requires knowing where the frontier lies and learning to understand it. People must be equipped to witness to the reign of God in this emerging new reality.

As founding editor of the *International Review of Missions,*[1] Oldham had effectively used the journal as a platform for addressing a series of these

[1]In 1969 the journal title changed to *International Review of Mission.*

frontline issues. Early on he saw the importance of breaking out of the Eurocentrism that characterized Western Christianity. He solicited contributions from Asian and African church leaders. Oldham felt special urgency to address the issue of racism, and published articles by articulate international Christian leaders. He wrote a major book, *Christianity and the Race Problem,* published in 1924. He set the problem of modern racism in the context of more than four centuries of Western colonization of other peoples. He wrote penetrating critiques of colonialism. Oldham recognized early that Hitler's ideology of National Socialism was insidious and would wreak havoc on the world. Always his restless energy impelled him to stay focused on the future of Christian witness and responsibility.

Throughout his life Lesslie Newbigin continued to rely on the insights and example of J. H. Oldham. He never forgot that it was Oldham who first drew attention to the looming spiritual crisis of Western Christianity.

Student Christian Movement

Upon completing his studies at Cambridge in 1931, Newbigin joined the staff of the SCM and was appointed a field secretary in Scotland. He was soon called on to help organize national student conferences and was one of two delegates the British SCM sent to a conference organized by the International Student Service, which was hosted by Germany in 1932. Delegates were drawn from various fields: politics, the academy and other professions. The crisis in Germany dominated the atmosphere. While the conference was in session President Hindenburg dissolved the German Reichstag. Among the German delegation Newbigin was most impressed by the National Socialist delegates, who showed a sense of direction. They had political momentum on their side. Indeed, their leader Adolf Hitler became chancellor of Germany in January 1933.

That summer Newbigin went on holiday in Europe. While worshiping in an Austrian church on a Sunday morning, the service was suddenly interrupted by the drumbeat call "Heil, Hitler! Heil, Hitler!" as a company of "Brownshirts" marched by. He was immediately overwhelmed with a sense of the idolatrous character of what he had just heard. For the rest of his life he was haunted by his failure to discern the nature of this movement at the conference in Germany in 1932. Ever after he would be skeptical when he heard a social or political movement acclaimed as "God at work in the world."[2]

One of SCM's important initiatives was to bring together students of diverse backgrounds. In January 1933 the SCM hosted the Edinburgh Quadrennial. Several thousand students from some fifty countries were challenged to give themselves to Christian world mission. Remarkably, this conference gave priority to the crisis of Christendom. The rise of Communism generated considerable discussion. But Oldham addressed the convention on the way the philosophy of the Enlightenment had set Europe on a path away from the Christian faith. Newbigin does not record his own reaction to Oldham but reports that the next day the *Scotsman* carried letters condemning what Oldham had said.[3] It would be another fifty years before Europeans were willing to acknowledge that their culture was steadily being reclaimed by paganism; Europe was indeed a mission field.[4] Through SCM, Newbigin got acquainted with students from Africa and Asia who were studying in Great Britain, some of whom became lifelong friends. Among these students were future leaders such as (Sir) Francis Akanu Ibiam,[5] physician and distinguished Christian leader who became governor of the Nigerian Eastern Region upon independence in 1960. These friends made him aware of the irrepressible aspirations among these peoples to free themselves from the control of a colonial power. Justice demanded that colonialism be ended.

INDIA

The summer of 1936 Lesslie Newbigin completed his theological studies at Westminster Theological College, Cambridge; was ordained by the Church of Scotland for missionary service; married Helen Henderson, an SCM staff colleague; and together they sailed for India. Never one to squander time,

---

[2]Lesslie Newbigin, *Unfinished Agenda*, rev. ed. (Edinburgh: St. Andrew Press, 1993), p. 24, and conversation with Newbigin in 1991.

[3]Ibid., p. 25.

[4]W. A. Visser 't Hooft, "Evangelism in the Neo-Pagan Situation," *International Review of Mission* 63 (January 1974): 81-86; W. A. Visser 't Hooft, "Evangelism Among Europe's Neo-Pagans," *International Review of Mission* 66 (October 1977): 349-60.

[5]Ibiam renounced his knighthood in 1967 when Great Britain backed the central government of Nigeria in the civil war, 1967–1969.

Newbigin used the four-week voyage from Liverpool to Madras to complete the writing of a book, *Christian Freedom in the Modern World.*[6] This was the twenty-five-year-old Newbigin's reply to John Macmurray, an influential philosopher and Christian writer whose book *Freedom in the Modern World* he had found to be theologically inadequate because Macmurray seemed to posit that true human freedom was possible independent of the atoning work of Jesus Christ.[7]

Already while traveling on the *S.S. City of Cairo* the Newbigins encountered the contempt with which fellow Europeans held the peoples of the Middle East and India. Their sense of disquiet would only grow. Upon arrival at Madras on October 22, they were taken by car to the rural town of Singleput and the large missionary bungalow that was to be their home while they studied Tamil. The adjustment was not easy. They were shocked by what they "saw of the relations between missionaries and their Indian colleagues," he recalled.[8] They observed that the majority of their missionary colleagues seemed to be quite content with the status quo. Some firmly resisted any attempt to dismantle the colonial mission structures that had been in place for decades. These missionaries seemed frozen in time. In his diary Newbigin wrote:

> I must say I couldn't help being horrified by the sort of relation that seems to exist between the missionaries and the people. It seems so utterly remote from the New Testament. There seems to be no question of getting alongside them and sharing their troubles and helping them spiritually. . . . We drive up like lords in a car, soaking everybody else with mud on the way, and then carry on a sort of inspection. . . . They all sort of stand at attention and say "Sir." It's *awful*. . . . But one thing is as sure as death: surely they won't stand this sort of thing from the white man much longer.[9]

Fortunately, Newbigin soon discovered he was not alone. Among other recently arrived missionary colleagues he found those who shared his deep disquiet. Charles W. Ranson, who had come to India several years earlier and became a close friend, was similarly disturbed by the colonialist attitude

---

[6]Lesslie Newbigin, *Christian Freedom in the Modern World* (London: SCM Press, 1937).
[7]Newbigin, *Unfinished Agenda*, p. 37.
[8]Ibid., p. 39.
[9]Ibid.

of disdain for the Indian people.[10] During this time Newbigin also discovered the writings of Roland Allen. Years later he recalled, "I retain vivid memories of my own reading of Allen's work, when I was beginning missionary service in India."[11] Allen delivered a devastating critique of the modern mission establishment, stirring plenty of resentment among the old mission guard. Consequently, many mission leaders and missionaries dismissed Allen as idealistic and unfair. Late in life Newbigin would say: "Allen's ideas are sound. I know because I've tried them and they work!"[12]

IMC Tambaram Assembly 1938

Because the Newbigins were forced to return to Great Britain in 1937 for medical treatment following a serious traffic accident that left Lesslie with a complicated fracture of his left leg, he did not attend the 1938 International Missionary Council (IMC) Assembly at Tambaram, near Madras.

During his years as IMC's general secretary (which ended in 1927; William Patton succeeded him that year), Oldham had emphasized three priorities that the Christian movement faced worldwide: *indigenous agency*, *racism*, and *secularization*. While Oldham had raised consciousness of the importance of these issues, World War I and the turmoil of the post-war years distracted the mission agencies from taking constructive action. Meanwhile, the independence movements in the European-held colonies in Asia and Africa had grown steadily in strength. By the late 1930s Dutch mission agencies were taking steps in the Dutch East Indies (that is, Indonesia) to grant mission-founded churches their independence and transfer programs and leadership responsibilities to the Indonesians. Respected scholars and churchmen like Hendrik Kraemer and J. H. Bavinck had been lobbying for more than a decade for this action. But in India things were stalled.

A priority issue addressed at the Tambaram Assembly was the training of leaders for the growing churches in Asia and Africa. Not only had training facilities not been given the attention required, they also needed to consider thoroughly the type of training that was appropriate for churches in African

[10]Charles W. Ranson, *A Missionary Pilgrimage* (Grand Rapids: Eerdmans, 1988), pp. 46, 69, 75-76.

[11]Lesslie Newbigin, foreword to Hubert J. B. Allen, *Roland Allen: Pioneer, Priest, and Prophet* (Grand Rapids: Eerdmans, 1995), p. xiii.

[12]Lesslie Newbigin, in conversation with the author, 1991.

and Asian cultures. Until then it had been assumed the Western model of theological education was standard. Models appropriate to the churches of Asia and Africa had not been envisaged. But in a vigorous statement the IMC Study Committee called for the development of training programs suited to the needs and culture of each church. Yet in spite of the solid work that went into the background documents and the quality of the debate at the assembly, implementation would be deferred until the 1950s.

Upon their return to India in 1939 the Newbigin family moved to Kanchipuram, regarded as one of the seven most holy cities in India and a center of Hindu studies. He comments cryptically in his autobiography on what they found upon arrival: "There was a vast amount of learning to be done."[13] One can only be impressed with the multiple means Newbigin used to refine his knowledge of Tamil, to meet a wide range of local people and to establish relations with community leaders. In addition, he was invited by members of the Ramakrishna mission to come to their monastery for weekly study of Hindu and Christian scriptures: one week they would study a passage from the Svetasvatara Upanishad and the next week from the Gospel of John. This opened up to Newbigin the world of Hindu thought in a way few Westerners ever experience. He also established lasting friendships with the monks of the monastery and worked to break down the social barriers that had kept the missionaries separated from their fellow Christians in the local church community. For example, by traveling on foot or bicycle one was much more likely to stop and chat with people whom you met on a footpath. He did this as much as possible.

Training for Ministry in India

By the early 1940s Newbigin had developed a critique of modern missions that informed his response to a range of issues, including training for ministry. His assignment as a missionary included relating to rural villages where most people were not yet literate, poverty was endemic and opportunity for advancement was limited. But he observed that these village Christians were quite capable of sharing their faith, were faithful in stewardship, and participated regularly in worship. He was convinced that these

[13]Newbigin, *Unfinished Agenda,* p. 50.

humble Christians had resources that were being overlooked or discounted when criteria from the West were employed to test their maturity and potential contribution. His critique can be summarized in terms of five observations, which are both descriptive and prescriptive: (1) To accurately gauge ecclesial reality one must go to the *local church.* (2) This reality is most accurately displayed in the *rural areas.* (3) A local Christian congregation has the resources essential to nurture growth in discipleship, witness and service of its members. (4) Each congregation must be allowed to grow from within its own environment; this insures it will be owned and supported by its members. (5) Training for ministry must start in the *vernacular language.* Each of these points can be elaborated at great length; taken together they formed a grid to be used in evaluating the work being done.

In 1942 the British signaled that they were preparing to grant India its national sovereignty within five years (that is, 1947). Most mission agencies had made no preparation for such a step in relation to the churches to which they related. This was not because Indian Christians had not been pleading for a new relationship in which they would assume full leadership of their churches, with missionaries playing supporting roles. For many missionaries, it seemed their only concern was how to preserve their positions into the future. Newbigin retorted with the truism if democracy is good for the British, it is good for the Indians too.[14]

Meanwhile the National Christian Council of India, Burma and Ceylon decided to take up the 1938 IMC recommendation on theological training for ministry. Early in these discussions it was decided that a vernacular, medium-high level theological training school in each of the main languages used in India must be a priority. In 1942 Newbigin was asked to chair the committee that would develop such a school in the Tamil-speaking area. Nearly thirty years later the Tamilnadu Theological Seminary in Madurai was opened. The NCC also authorized an empirically based survey of ministerial training in all their constituent churches during 1943–1944. Charles W. Ranson directed the study and wrote the report, *The Christian Minister in India: His Vocation and Training.* Though much praised and widely read, its main recommendations were not implemented.

[14]Ibid., p. 73.

At this time the editor of the *International Review of Missions* requested Newbigin to write an article on the position of the missionary in the Indian church. It was published as "The Ordained Foreign Missionary in the Indian Church."[15] He developed his argument by describing how the role of the missionary had evolved over time. Typically, the missionary began as an evangelist in a rural village. As churches were established, the missionary became the pastor, and Indians were deployed as Bible women and evangelists. Subsequently, the mission established institutions and the missionary became the administrator. The missionary guided the entire development process, thus insuring that the missionary retained control. The power structure of the typical mission formed a pyramid, with the administrator—holding the purse strings—at the top. Even in cases where the mission had assigned responsibility to an Indian to serve as pastor, for example, it was understood that the mission retained effective control through its treasurer. Predictably, Newbigin's article stirred considerable controversy, especially in India.

If this pattern were to be fundamentally changed, as surely it must, Newbigin argued, the missionary had to give up all administrative positions, thus making way for Indians to assume these responsibilities. Naturally, this raised the question, what would be left for the missionary to do? Newbigin's prescription was a strong tonic. First, the missionary required a reorientation that started with deep change. Second, a new "spirituality" had to be developed based on a willingness to accept whatever assignment the church saw fit to give a missionary. Third, the missionary should be present as a servant of the church. To demonstrate the seriousness of his proposal, Newbigin and two Church of Scotland missionary colleagues placed themselves under the administrative authority of the Indian church, rather than the mission. In the process they gave up their rights as missionaries. A flurry of correspondence between these missionaries and the home office ensued.[16] The Church of Scotland Mission Office was caught off guard.

---

[15]Lesslie Newbigin, "The Ordained Foreign Missionary in the Indian Church," *International Review of Missions* 34 (1945): 86-94. William Patton, editor until his death in 1943, had also served in India and was a critic of "colonial" missions. He was known as an advocate of Indian independence and was likely the one who commissioned Newbigin to write the article.

[16]The General Administration Committee, Inter-Church Relations and Foreign Missions Committee consulted and brought a report to the General Assembly for decision (Minute 7279, 3/21/1944, NLS:Dep298/Box 191). Newbigin gives a rather oblique account of this episode in *Unfinished Agenda*, p. 67. My thanks to Dr. Mark T. B. Laing for the Minute citation.

CHURCH UNION

Lesslie Newbigin was propelled to international prominence because of the role he played in the founding of the Church of South India (CSI) in 1947. Negotiations had started in 1918 when the South India United Church (SIUC), the Wesleyan Methodist Church and the Anglican Church agreed to explore the possibility of uniting to form a single church. The SIUC itself was formed in 1908 when Presbyterian and Congregational churches formed a federation. The Church in South India process had been slow and stalled repeatedly. In 1943 Newbigin was elected convener of the SIUC committee responsible for church union and took an active role from that point on in CSI negotiations. He made a strategic contribution in getting agreement from all three parties to the final basis for the union.

A main sticking point had been Anglican insistence on apostolic succession, which would have required that pastors ordained in SIUC and Methodist Churches be reconsecrated at the hands of an Anglican bishop. Newbigin himself rejected this solution. He was finally able to finesse the situation so that Anglicans agreed—some reluctantly—that the ordinations of all pastors of the uniting churches would be recognized and that in the future the bishop would officiate at all consecrations.[17]

In the spring of 1947 Newbigin was relieved of other furlough duties in order to devote himself to the writing of *The Reunion of the Church*.[18] This book was an exposition of the Basis of Union of the Church in South India and an exploration of the unity and continuity of the church. This unprecedented union brought together episcopal and non-episcopal bodies in a polity that respected the traditions of the uniting bodies, and yet allowed for the formation of the Church of South India.

The Church of South India was inaugurated September 27, 1947. Six Anglican bishops were commissioned as bishops in the Church of South India, and they, in turn, consecrated another nine men as bishops to lead the dioceses of the new church. Newbigin was among the new class of bishops and,

[17]An influential group of British Anglicans strongly disapproved and worked to overturn the inclusion of Anglicans in the CSI. Newbigin engaged in dialogue with these critics over a considerable time without success. Finally, the archbishop of Canterbury, with the backing of the Anglican bishops in India, put the matter to rest by overruling the opponents.

[18]Lesslie Newbigin, *The Reunion of the Church* (London: SCM Press/New York: Harper & Row, 1948; 2nd rev. ed., London: SCM Press, 1960).

at age thirty-seven, the youngest of the sixteen CSI bishops.[19] He was assigned to lead the southernmost diocese, Madura and Ramnad.

From that point on Newbigin was present at most major international ecumenical events sponsored by the Protestant and Orthodox churches through the 1980s. He was given a leave from the Church of South India from 1959 to 1964 to oversee the merger of the International Missionary Council into the World Council of Churches and then to serve as director of the Commission on World Mission and Evangelism of the WCC for four years following the merger.

Lesslie Newbigin as Bishop

Newbigin had played a strategic role in bringing together three church bodies, two of which had non-episcopal polities. The third, the Anglican Church, was committed to the traditional concept of apostolic succession, which Newbigin rejected on theological and historical grounds, and because he knew there was no way union could be achieved if this view of episcopacy was retained.[20] He had embraced a view that recognized the value of the "historic episcopate" and episcopacy as a suitable way of governing the church. But he was at great pains to redefine the role of the bishop long associated with hierarchical church government. In the final stage of negotiations toward union, Newbigin wrote to a group who remained concerned that acceptance of episcopacy would result in a church led by bishops who were primarily church bureaucrats. To allay these fears he asserted:

> I agree that the ultimate control should rest with the Diocesan Council [which the bishop chaired]. But I am very anxious to emphasize at the outset that I do not regard the Bishop as therefore mainly an administrator. You will remember that the Scheme is very clear about the function of a bishop: he is to be a pastor, an evangelist, a teacher of the faith, and a leader in worship. I am holding to that definition with both hands![21]

In all discussions of the nature of episcopacy thereafter, he would reiterate and elaborate this vision. But more important was the way in which

---

[19]When the Church of South India celebrated its fiftieth year in 1997, Newbigin was the only surviving bishop from the original group of fifteen. His health was failing and he declined to make the trip.
[20]See Newbigin, *Reunion of the Church*, pp. 82-83, 107-9.
[21]Newbigin, *Unfinished Agenda*, pp. 86-87.

he attempted to follow this model in his own ministry. Immediately upon leaving Madras to take up his work as bishop, he made it his first priority to "get into personal touch with the congregations," of which there were some 550. Many congregations were isolated and rural. But he knew "the union will mean nothing unless there can be personal contact. . . . It must be clear from the outset that a bishop is primarily a pastor, not a bureaucrat."[22] During the following years he spent on average three days per week visiting congregations. No matter how distant or humble, he went to them: evangelizing, catechizing, baptizing, helping resolve disputes, encouraging the local pastor and leading in worship. As much as possible he traveled on foot, by bicycle, bullock cart and bus. His charming little book *That All May Be One: A South India Diary* is a series of vignettes of these visits to congregations during the first three years of his service as bishop of Madura and Ramnad.[23]

The Household of God

In November 1952 Newbigin delivered the Kerr Lectures at Trinity College, Glasgow. It was natural that he would address some aspect of ecclesiology given the role he had played in the formation of the CSI. The focus here is not the way he treated the topic, although the published lectures were widely read, discussed and studied on all continents.[24] Rather, we want to note how, in 1952, he situated the problem of ecclesiology historically. He began with an examination of the doctrine of the church in the light of three developments: (1) the ending of historical Christendom, (2) the impact of the modern missionary movement outside of Europe and North America, and (3) the emergence of the ecumenical movement in the twentieth century, which was a direct outgrowth of the missionary movement. For the rest of his life he would emphasize the indissoluble relationship between mission and unity.

Dissolution of Christendom. The *corpus Christianum* in Europe had been forged over a period of a thousand years so that Christianity became the folk religion of the continent. Sixteenth-century Reformation theologies took this for granted. This was not a missionary situation. The people and culture of

---

[22]Ibid., p. 28.

[23]Lesslie Newbigin, *That All May Be One: A South India Diary* (New York: Association Press, 1952). British edition: *A South India Diary* (London: SCM Press, 1951).

[24]Published as *The Household of God* (London: SCM Press, 1953; New York: Friendship Press, 1954).

Europe were asserted to be "Christian." Over the past four centuries this religio-cultural synthesis had broken down. But this process did not happen suddenly. The first European-sponsored missions sent to other continents mistakenly attempted to transplant "Christendom" wholesale in those cultures. This proved to be wholly ineffective. The "Christendom" was deeply European and inflexible, and it required that the new church be separated from its indigenous culture and grafted into the culture of Christendom. This, of course, impaired its ability to evangelize. "Eventually, it was recognized that a new kind of line had now to be drawn, a line dividing the Church from the world without separating the Christian community from the local culture."[25] This was but a precursor of what was also taking place in the West. In old Christendom, that is, Europe, the scope of the church's authority and influence was steadily shrinking. It was becoming laughable to claim that the church had authority in the wider culture. Instead, the church had to learn to think of itself vis-à-vis culture, a body distinct from culture but dynamically related to it. Consequently, it was urgently necessary to rethink the nature of the church in light of its changing context. Traditional ecclesiologies were of little value in the new situation around the world.

Not only was the place of the church in culture being drastically redefined; the way personhood was understood was also being radically altered. The traditional view of the *person* as an interdependent member of the *group* had given way to the *autonomous self*. The nature of modern industrial society, the breakdown of the old social structures and webs of relationship—all these forces were redefining the meaning of the human. An atomized society had increasing difficulty relating to what we call the body of Christ. If it was to have a future, the church had to reclaim its self-understanding as a body distinct from society as a whole.

The missionary movement beyond Europe and North America. The majority of people who heard Newbigin's initial lecture had little capacity to understand existentially what he was saying about the importance of the Christian mission for reforming their understanding of ecclesiology. Yet increasing numbers of Westerners were now Christian in name only; many were embarrassed by the foreign mission movement of the past 150 years. Increas-

---

[25]Ibid., p. 2.

ingly, the institutions responsible for the academy, economy and public life were completely secular. Christians were allowed to work within these agencies so long as they kept their faith commitment private. The churches were expected to care for their own affairs and not interfere in public life. Even within the churches the experience of deep fellowship and solidarity had increasingly been supplanted by the cultural emphasis on the individual.

Modern Christian missions had been directed to peoples and cultures where previously there had been no Christian presence. Among these were lands of other great religious traditions that generally did not welcome attempts by Christians to establish churches in their midst. Those individuals who heard the gospel message and embraced it were usually cut off from their birth family and community. From the early days of the mission movement, the missionaries realized that the church had to become an alternative community in solidarity with these people who, as Christians, were cast out of their indigenous cultural homes. This placed the question of ecclesiology front and center. It was urgent, and it had to be practical as well as theological. In this situation the church had to provide for its members the social support and discipline that are taken for granted in the natural community.

In spite of official and cultural sanctions, Christians in these lands were finding ways of living out their faith and witnessing to Jesus Christ. The West needed to learn from the experience of these new churches in non-Christian cultures the meaning of *ekklesia*. Being a Christian in a non-Christian context called for recovery of a biblical ecclesiology.

The ecumenical movement. The ecumenical movement was born from the modern missionary movement beyond historical Christendom. Early on, missionaries became aware that Christian disunity was a scandal. The sight of multiple varieties of Christians coming to Asia or Africa, vying with one another for territory and adherents was disgraceful. It was not surprising that missionaries were leading advocates of Christian unity. However, that originally *oikoumenē* referred to the whole inhabited world into which the church was sent to announce the gospel was overlooked. Newbigin cautioned, "There is a real danger at the present time of a false sort of ecumenism, an attempt to find consolation amid the wreckage of the old Christendom in the vision of a new and wider Christendom, yet without the acceptance of the hard demands of missionary obedience."[26] The integrity of the church's witness depends on the church demonstrating that it actually lives this new life in Christ. Disunity is a counter-witness. Newbigin was under no illusion as to the difficulty of realizing this unity in the present age, but he refused to accept the status quo. The Lord of the Church desires "that all may be one." We must strive to honor Christ's prayer.

The main premise. Newbigin draws this introductory discussion to a conclusion: "The Church is the pilgrim people of God. It is on the move—hastening to the ends of the earth to beseech all men to be reconciled to God, and hastening to the end of time to meet its Lord who will gather all into one."[27] The church ought to be understood as a dynamic organism, not a staid institution. Structures and forms should always be understood as temporary. When they do not facilitate missionary faithfulness, they must be abandoned or reformed in light of the new situation toward which the church is inexorably moving. Only in this way will the church continue to engage each culture where it is located as the instrument of God's mission.

Interlude

Newbigin's years of service with the International Missionary Council—implementing its merger with the World Council of Churches, and then as the first director of the Commission on World Mission and Evangelism—had not been entirely satisfactory. In January 1965 the CSI called Lesslie Newbigin to return to India to serve as bishop of the Madras diocese. He welcomed the call to return to India and take up duties in this dynamic metropolis and found this fulfilling. Then in 1974, at age sixty-five, he retired as bishop, having served the CSI in that role for twenty-seven years. The Newbigins returned to Great Britain, and in September they settled in Birmingham where he would lecture on theology of mission at Selly Oak Colleges the next five years. They became active in the United Reformed Church.[28]

Returning to Great Britain after a long absence required considerable adjustment. The visible erosion of "Christian Britain" was widely evident.

---

[26]Ibid., p. 10.

[27]Ibid., p. 18.

[28]Newbigin was reared in the English Presbyterian Church. This church and the Congregationalists formed the United Reformed Church in 1972.

The palpable loss of hope on the part of younger people was deeply disturbing. What was to be the future of Christian faith in Europe? This was the nagging question. Newbigin seemed to have accepted that historical Christendom was finished and there was little value in discussing it further.[29] But he remained deeply concerned about the future of the church.

Unfinished Agenda

In his seventy-second year Lesslie Newbigin completed writing his autobiography, presciently titled *Unfinished Agenda*. A decade later a new edition of the autobiography was released with a twenty-page postscript. There Newbigin remarks, "When I finished the writing of the preceding chapters in 1982, I had no idea that there were still ten years ahead which would turn me in a new direction and present new tasks."[30]

In early 1981 the latest report on the state of the churches in Great Britain was published. Faced with the dispirited findings of the continuing decline of the churches in Great Britain, various people urged that something be done to address the situation. Meeting in July, the executive committee of the British Council of Churches (BCC) considered, and approved, a proposal to convene a large national conference in 1984 on the theme of the gospel and culture.[31] It was quickly apparent this action did not meet with the approval of a number of people, including some who were not present at the meeting but heard about the BCC action. This included Lesslie Newbigin. The opponents reminded the Council that this was by no means the first time such a national meeting had been held for this purpose. Most notably, the 1943 Assembly of the Church of England called for appointment of a commission "to survey the whole problem of modern evangelism with special reference to the spiritual needs and prevailing intellectual outlook of the non-worshipping members of the community, and to report on the organization and methods by which such needs can most effectively be met."[32] Addressing the first meeting of this special commission the following

[29]See Geoffrey Wainwright, *Lesslie Newbigin: A Theological Life* (New York: Oxford University Press, 2000), pp. 99, 177, 211, 238, 256, 296, 354, 368, 404.

[30]Newbigin, *Unfinished Agenda*, p. 242.

[31]The year was deliberately chosen because of George Orwell's book *1984*.

[32]Commission on Evangelism, *Towards the Conversion of England* (London: Press and Publications Board of the Church Assembly, 1945), p. vi.

autumn, Archbishop William Temple emphasized two points: (1) "The message of the church is the eternal gospel," and (2) "The first need in evangelism is for a strengthening and quickening of spiritual life within the church." The report issued in 1945 was widely acclaimed but resulted in no action to reverse the decline.

The BCC agreed that before convening a large-scale conference, more thorough preparation was required, starting with a careful and clear definition of the problem. At this point the Council turned to Lesslie Newbigin to prepare this programmatic statement. He quickly drafted a statement that was then circulated to a number of BCC leaders. They were impressed and offered their comments. Newbigin then reworked the manuscript and it was circulated to BCC members. Soon it was suggested that this programmatic statement should be fully published. The result was the small book *The Other Side of 1984: Questions for the Churches.*[33] It quickly attracted wide attention around the world, going through multiple printings. The impact of this small book was as surprising to Newbigin as anyone. It would set the course for the rest of his life.

In view of the range of suggestions the British Council of Churches received for next steps, it appointed a task force to organize an initiative to lead the churches in responding to the present situation. Newbigin was named to this task force and drew directly on what he had learned from J. H. Oldham. Instead of the usual one- or two-day consultation, the task force recommended a six-year initiative that would be launched in 1986 and end in July 1992: The Gospel and Our Culture Programme. The goal was to enlist the participation of lay Christians active in academia, the professions, business, politics and industry, plus pastors. Several regional conferences were held to prepare for the national conference in July 1992. The goal was to create a movement that would engage a cross-section of lay Christians. Eight theme study groups were organized consisting of specialists in each area—history, science, the arts, epistemology, economics, education, health and healing, and the media—with the task of preparing an essay. These essays were compiled and edited by Hugh Montefiore as the study volume

[33]Lesslie Newbigin, *The Other Side of 1984: Questions for the Churches* (Geneva: World Council of Churches, 1983).

The Gospel and Contemporary Culture.[34] It was used at the national conference of several hundred Christian leaders at Swanwick in July 1992.

Throughout the six years *The Gospel and Our Culture Newsletter* appeared regularly. Each issue featured a lead article by Newbigin, as director of the Programme. He traveled throughout the British Isles, the European continent and North America speaking at conferences and lecturing. In 1984 he gave a talk to a group of German church leaders meeting in Stuttgart titled "The Cultural Captivity of Western Christianity as a Challenge to a Missionary Church."[35] That year he also delivered the Warfield Lectures at Princeton Theological Seminary.[36] In these lectures he developed and elaborated ideas that were adumbrated in *The Other Side.* He encouraged parallel "Gospel and Our Culture" initiatives in other countries.[37] In 1990 he delivered the Osterhaven Lectures at Western Theological Seminary, Holland, Michigan. These were published as *Truth to Tell: The Gospel as Public Truth.*[38] But the Alexander Robertson Lectures for 1988, published subsequently as *The Gospel in a Pluralist Society,* were the most substantial of his writings after 1983.

The Gospel in a Pluralist Society

Fall term 1988 Lesslie Newbigin delivered the Alexander Robertson Lectures at Glasgow University. However, the way the lectureship was carried out was something of a surprise.[39] Newbigin had been to Glasgow frequently over the years. As already noted, in November 1952 he delivered the Kerr Lectures in Trinity College, Glasgow, on the nature of the church, published as *The Household of God.* So when the invitation came to present the Alexander Robertson Lectures for 1988, Newbigin was confident he knew what to

---

[34]Hugh Montefiore, ed., *The Gospel and Contemporary Culture* (London: Mowbray, 1992).

[35]Published in *A Word in Season: Perspectives on Christian World Missions,* ed. Eleanor Jackson (Grand Rapids: Eerdmans, 1994), pp. 66-79.

[36]Published as *Foolishness to the Greeks: The Gospel and Western Culture* (Geneva: World Council of Churches, 1986).

[37]For report of a spin-off from the British Programme, see Wilbert R. Shenk, "A Missiology of Western Culture: Background and Development of a Project," in *Mission in Context,* ed. John Corrie and Cathy Ross (Farnham, UK: Ashgate, 2012), pp. 169-85. The Gospel and Our Culture Network was formed in North America and the Deepsight Trust in New Zealand.

[38]Lesslie Newbigin, *Truth to Tell: The Gospel as Public Truth* (Grand Rapids: Eerdmans, 1991).

[39]The account in the following two paragraphs was given to me personally by Newbigin in 1990. He did not indicate why he had not included this information in the preface to *The Gospel in a Pluralist Society* (Grand Rapids: Eerdmans, 1989). One may conjecture he felt it inappropriate to speak so frankly so soon after the event. He recounted the experience with warm appreciation.

expect. He proceeded to prepare several lectures and went to Glasgow with the lectures already in typescript.

Professor George Newlands met the Newbigins upon their arrival at the Glasgow station. Rather matter-of-factly Newlands informed Newbigin that he would be giving the lectures as a course for some twenty first-year students in the regular academic term. Newbigin had assumed he would be lecturing to a general audience. But his years of missionary service stood him in good stead. The first rule in mission: expect the unexpected! Newbigin set about immediately reorganizing and expanding his material to fit the kind of students enrolled in the class.

When he met the class for the first time, he observed that the students ranged in age from new university graduates to men and women in their thirties who had left professional careers because of a call to Christian ministry. Newbigin soon realized that this class represented a microcosm of contemporary European culture: secularized and skeptical, distrustful of religion and disillusioned with the church, searching for meaning but unsure where to find it. It was a living laboratory of contemporary culture. Throughout the term he met with the students in small groups weekly as well as for individual tutorials. It proved to be immensely rewarding and fruitful.

Given the circumstances in which these lectures were delivered, and the creative process that Newbigin used with the class, there is no doubt that his final draft was enhanced by the results of the lively interaction between professor and students. The topics included were calculated to connect with that diverse group. The fact that *The Gospel in a Pluralist Society* continues to resonate and reverberate with a wide range of people, twenty-five years on, surely owes a good deal to the provenance offered by that Glasgow classroom.

3

Newbigin's Theology of Mission and Culture After Twenty-Five Years

Attending to the "Subject" of Mission

William R. Burrows

In 1985, during the heyday of liberation theology, Sharon Welch made an observation, the wisdom of which I have been impressed with ever since. I sometimes turn it into a question, and the chapter that follows is an extended exercise in pondering the legacy of Lesslie Newbigin in the light of that question. Welch's observation seems unremarkably straightforward until you begin to ask it of every call to carry on the mission of the church as a bearer of the Spirit's witness. First her observation:

> The type of humanity envisioned by liberation theologians does not come about naturally; it has to be achieved. This type of human community is not a given; it must be fought for. . . . Liberation theology is part of a struggle for the establishment of a particular kind of subjectivity, not a declaration of the a priori existence of that subjectivity.[1]

Exchange the words "liberation theologians" and "theology" in that quotation with the words "missiologists" and "missiology," and one immediately runs into the importance of a certain kind of community, academic and spiritual disciplines, and missionary agent if mission is to achieve the new creation imaged in Scripture and missiological reflection.

---

[1]Sharon Welch, *Communities of Resistance and Solidarity: A Feminist Theology of Liberation* (Maryknoll, NY: Orbis, 1985), p. 66.

The question I have often asked is this: *To what extent are we taking seriously the necessity of the personal transformation of the subjects—that is, the human agents—of mission?* Or, put another way: *In mission studies, are we paying adequate attention to developing the kind of human beings who can embody the kind of mission envisaged in our reflections and who live the gospel in the pluralist society Lesslie Newbigin speaks of?*

To go deeper, I find my orientation toward mission in a famous text of Irenaeus, "For the glory of God is a living human being, and the life of a human being consists in beholding God" (from *Against the Heretics* IV, 20, 7). The first part of that text is often translated freely as "the glory of God is a human being *fully* alive," but the way it is translated, "glory" is commonly not attended to or is reflexively considered a mere synonym for God being honored. Instead, "glory" (from the Hebrew *kabod* and the Greek *doxa*) means "manifestation [of the hidden God]," especially in Johannine theology. And the second part of Irenaeus's sentence is often omitted—"and the life of a human being consists in beholding God." In scholastic theology that "beholding" of God was spoken of as contemplation.

I am fully aware that a talk about missiology does not often get into the area of contemplation. Please bear with me. In putting the emphasis I do on this point, I should say I am returning to the beginning of my own academic life in 1966 when my BA paper at Divine Word College in Epworth, Iowa, was titled "Contemplation as the End of Human Life." Forty-eight years later, I would probably be embarrassed to read it (although I need not worry, since it was long ago lost in one of my many moves and, in a fortunate coup de grâce, shredded in a weeding of the Epworth library).

Contemplation, as I learned while wrestling with the concept in the writings of Thomas Aquinas and Jacques Maritain, is not some sort of neo-Platonic ecstasy wherein the soul of a spiritual virtuoso escapes the body to "see" God in the heavens. Instead, contemplation is the culmination of a process begun as the individual discovers the divine depths of all things—including one's self and one's fellow human beings—and begins to live fully alive to the presence of God in the world. Yes, contemplation sometimes takes place in solitary, mountaintop or desert moments, but it can also occur when a person is moved to tears by a hymn in a worship service, watching the tenderness of a mother nursing her baby, or when one beholds the mystery of a loved one as *thou.*

What is one seeing in such moments? Simply this: *things as they really are* as one enters for a moment into an understanding of reality in its ontological depth, as the great chain of being proceeding from the Creator-God-YHWH, whom Jesus calls Abba. And by participating in this reality consciously, one becomes Godlike to the extent the Spirit offers entrée into this state of heightened consciousness wherein one *participates* in the mystery of creation and its consummation. I stress the word *participation* because I want to stress the difference between a lived and felt presence of the divine in the ordinary, not merely having ideas about the divine learned in books, including the Bible.

The premise of everything that follows is a view of Christian anthropology's take on human nature, especially the anthropology revealed in what the Orthodox call the process of *theosis*, for becoming Godlike is another name for becoming a mature Christian, a life that begins in faith and ends in vision, living in the presence of God who is all in all. In Thomistic anthropology, as retrieved and updated for our own age by Juan Alfaro, SJ, "the internal activity of grace affects the entire human being in both his or her intellect and will; it affects the depth of the person, which is what is meant by the biblical use of the term 'heart.'" Alfaro goes on to say that "this internal activity of grace calls the human being to union with God through faith and love, ultimately through the vision [of God]." This occurs to the extent that "'the knowledge of God' spoken of in the New Testament, which faith brings about, includes both communion with and personal intimacy with God."[2]

Our participation in mission, accordingly, must be a sharing of the church's and our own communion and intimacy with God as revealed by Christ and mediated in our inmost depths by the Spirit. This is also what I believe is implicit in Newbigin's theology and will enrich us if we bring it from background to foreground.

Encounters with Newbigin

The first and most significant book by Lesslie Newbigin for me was his

---

[2]Juan Alfaro, *Fides, Spes, Caritas: Adnotationes in Tractatum de Virtutibus Theologicis*, 9th ed. (Rome: Gregorian University Press [*ad usum privatum auditorium*]), pp. 292-93, my translation.

Honest Religion for Secular Man,[3] which I read in 1970 when I was student in Rome, at the suggestion of Luis Rodriguez, a Chilean Divine Word missionary who had taught me philosophy in the United States from 1964 through June 1966. Luis was in Rome in 1970 for a renewal course. We met and talked often. Sometimes, as Luis and I took several long hikes in the Apennine Mountains near L'Aquila west of Rome, we reminisced over a 147-mile canoe trip that we and four others took down the Mississippi River one summer. Listening to my views on the modernization of the church and the Society of the Divine Word, of which I was then a member, Luis feared I was losing my way and forgetting what I had learned about communion with God as the proper end of human growth. I remember him saying that a book by Lesslie Newbigin would be a good antidote to my fascination with a popular book by Harvey Cox and two books by Rudolf Bultmann that I quoted frequently.[4] Mentioning Cox and Bultmann, of course, suggests what was influencing me in the years immediately after the Second Vatican Council. Our search was to be relevant and to catch up with Protestant advances in studies of Scripture. In regard to the latter, we Catholics were attempting—in a five-year smorgasbord—to digest developments that had taken place since Friedrich Strauss (1808–1874) started historians searching for an academically respectable biography of Jesus.

Many Catholics developed indigestion in trying to gain nourishment from modern authors such as Cox and Bultmann. To give an idea of movements that exemplified the problem, let me rehearse one aspect of what was occurring during my two years studying theology at St. Mary's Divine Word Seminary in Techny, Illinois. What became most important for most of us seminarians was engagement in an intense two-year process of group therapy utilizing a confrontation-disclosure model. Each participant was encouraged to bare his soul in weekend group sessions that aimed for a breakthrough to emotional and intellectual honesty about both our hang-ups and aspirations. For me, certainly, as well as for most of my confreres, these marathons and their follow-up sessions were dramatic. They resulted

[3]Lesslie Newbigin, *Honest Religion for Secular Man* (London: SCM Press, 1966).

[4]Harvey Cox, *The Secular City: Secularization and Urbanization in Theological Perspective* (New York: Macmillan, 1965), and Rudolf Bultmann, *Theology of the New Testament*, 2 vols., trans. Kendrick Grobel (New York: Scribners, 1951–1955); *Jesus Christ and Mythology*, trans. L. P. Smith and E. H. Lantero (New York: Scribners, 1958).

in a new way of looking at life. The way they operated revealed a sort of escapism in my upbringing and regarded traditional Catholic piety and religious life as both otherworldly and unrealistic about human nature. In the end, the marathon process made me think that my attempts to dwell prayerfully in the Spirit were escape mechanisms. To replace traditional christological orthodoxy and spirituality, our psychologist offered us a chance to embrace then-popular strands of theology that envisioned Jesus as someone calling us to genuine existence beyond conventional thinking.

In essence what we were illustrating was the case made in Philip Rieff's *The Triumph of the Therapeutic.*[5] Rieff's book was an analysis of the cultural crisis in the West as stemming from the destruction of traditional cultural "control and release" mechanisms undergirded by the Jewish and Christian story, controls that served for centuries as the foundation of morality and social order in the West. In the popularized vision of Rieff's therapeutic in our seminary's confrontation-disclosure encounters, such abstractions were absent. I cannot speak for all my confreres, but I believe that the biblical vision of Christian discipleship was often replaced by an amalgam of ideas clustered around the notion that a person needed to become emotionally free of the hang-ups that were impeding him from becoming his authentic self. Where Christ stood in all this was unclear, but we were presented with him as an example par excellence of someone who had achieved authenticity, one who had broken through and become transparent.

A major theme in Newbigin's *Honest Religion for Secular Man* brought exactly this sort of thinking into question and set me on a new course. When I went back to reread *Honest Religion* in preparation for the Fuller conference that occasioned the chapter you now read, the following words of Newbigin struck as forcefully in 2014 as they had in 1970. Newbigin spoke of the insufficiency of attempts to use existentialist—Bultmannian—interpretations of the Scriptures to answer the challenges posed by our secularizing culture:

> The Bible speaks of God's calling of the individual in the context of his purpose for all the nations. No one can doubt that the Bible takes seriously the individual and his responsibility for decision. No existentialist could complain that the solitary responsibility of each man to give his answer to

[5]Philip Rieff, *The Triumph of the Therapeutic: Uses of Faith After Freud* (New York: Harper, 1968).

> God is not fully acknowledged. But if one thinks of the great moments of the Bible where an individual is confronted with the calling of God, the question at issue is never just his own destiny; it is God's purpose for his people and through them for mankind. Abraham's call is to be the founder of the nation through which all the nations will bless themselves. Moses is called to be the liberator of an enslaved people. The great prophets are all called to be God's messengers to the people and politicians of their time. The apostles are called by Jesus to be his messengers to the nations. The calling of the individual is not simply for the acceptance of his own personal destiny; it is for the fulfilment of his role in God's plan for the salvation of mankind. It is a calling to responsible participation in the events which are the key to world history.[6]

Post–Vatican II Catholicism and Newbigin

In *Honest Religion,* Newbigin characterizes Christian life as a response to a call to bring a message to the nations. It is not a private message to assuage the loneliness of the mildly neurotic. Nor is it a political action plan to please either conservatives or liberals. Even less is it a program to save a failing church. Instead, it is a radical vision of a universe unfolding within the arc of God's purposes and promises, in the light of which both the individual's and the church's role receive their meaning. That theme reverberates in different ways in *The Gospel in a Pluralist Society,*[7] but the differences between the two books only serve to underline the notion that Christianity is nothing if not a message about God's promises and the election of Jesus' followers to embody and proclaim that promise.

In the period in my life when I first encountered Newbigin, the Society of the Divine Word was attempting to grapple with the issue of its missionary identity in implementing three Vatican II decrees: *Lumen Gentium* (on the nature of the church); *Ad Gentes* (on the mission of the church); and *Gaudium et Spes* (on the church and modernity). Its superior general from 1958 through 1969, Johannes Schütte, was one of the main promoters of *Ad Gentes,* and in a long conversation with me not long before his death in 1971, he told me that his principal concern was to make mission the animating concern of the

---

[6]Newbigin, *Honest Religion,* p. 44.

[7]Lesslie Newbigin, *The Gospel in a Pluralist Society* (Grand Rapids: Eerdmans, 1989).

entire church, not just something that was farmed out to missionary orders. In his judgment, that attempt had failed.

I took part in the debates over the Society of the Divine Word's missionary identity, but as I look back on it today, my focal image of the life of faith was to characterize Christian life as a means to attain authenticity by becoming myself, and serving others. These were the hallmarks of genuine religious life, and in contradistinction to the early Newbigin, they had almost nothing to do with Christ. In effect, Jesus had become a model and teacher in a perspective influenced by (a) Bultmann's contention that New Testament studies and Christology could no longer rely on the presuppositions of "supernatural" interpretations of Christianity; and (b) the typically Catholic belief that the relation between God and humanity is best expressed in the adage "Grace perfects nature." As I look back on that outlook and, even more, as friendships with several Lutherans have unfolded, I have become convinced that the grace-nature paradigm—although a useful metaphor for understanding aspects of the Christian message—is dangerous if it becomes the focal image of Christian life. Why? Because it occludes the radical nature of the challenge addressed to us both in Word and worship as an invitation to trust the promise of the gospel in the person of Jesus. "Sin-grace" and "sin-forgiveness" encapsulate the interpersonal drama of the God-human relationship much better than "nature-grace." If grace is merely some thing perfecting nature, however, and if one took clues on what nature is from contemporary society, then our major task was to modernize the church.

And, although Vatican II's document on the church in the modern world, *Gaudium et Spes* (1965), attempted to show how Catholicism was not hostile to modernity, its reasons for witnessing *gaudium* ("joy") and *spes* ("hope") had more of an optimistic, formulaic quality and more this worldly optimism than gospel hope.

By contrast, Newbigin's work is anchored in a biblical worldview that complemented Catholic doctrine, in particular the documents of Vatican II, which owed much to the ideas of Oscar Cullmann and Karl Barth on the centrality of Christ, ideas that were eclipsed after the council was over and we began arguing about church structures. As I read Newbigin, I was reminded of the early fathers of the church. Concretely I saw Newbigin offering an *apologia* for Christianity and the ways of God in a manner analogous to Augustine's *City of God*—an alternate theology of history to replace that which was shattered by the invasion of Rome in 410 by the Visigoths under Alaric. On the other hand, was Newbigin, I wondered, taking account of the challenge of contemporary science and philosophy in the way Justin Martyr did in his *Apologies* and Origen in his *On First Principles*? Especially in Origen one finds the beginnings of spiritual exercises and traditions aimed at helping Christians understand their call to internalize the message and convert culture to Christ.

NEWBIGIN'S CENTRAL ORIENTATION

It is clear that Newbigin himself had internalized the truth of Galatians 2:19-20: "I have been crucified with Christ; and it is no longer I who live, but it is Christ who lives in me. And the life I now live in the flesh I live by faith in the Son of God, who loved me and gave himself for me." In the first chapter of his monumental biography of Newbigin, Geoffrey Wainwright quotes Newbigin and makes an observation on Christ as the center of his life:

> "Faith is the hand that grasps what Christ has done and makes it my own"; but first "Christ has laid hold of me." That expresses the intensely personal character of the faith within which Lesslie Newbigin's own life was lived and in which all his more technical discussions must be situated.[8]

The Newbigin I encountered in the early 1970s was addressing the results of a century and a half reduction of Christianity's nature on the part of Christians who had tried to articulate a vision of Christian self-understanding

> in which the boundaries of what is possible to believe were firmly fixed by the axioms of the Enlightenment, [a culture] in which it was taken for granted that the modern scientific world-view provides the only reliable account of how things really are, and that the Bible has to be understood only in terms of that account. This required a reconstruction of biblical history on the lines of modern historical science. It required the elimination of miracle. It dictated that while the crucifixion of Jesus could be accepted as a fact of real history, his resurrection was a psychological experience of the disciples. Insofar as the biblical scholar recognized religion as an authentic fact of human experience,

---

[8]Geoffrey Wainwright, *Lesslie Newbigin: A Theological Life* (Oxford: Oxford University Press, 2000), p. 29; Wainwright is quoting from Newbigin's *Sin and Salvation* (London: SCM Press, 1956), pp. 62, 99.

> he could find in the Bible testimony to religion, perhaps to the supreme and definitive experience of the religious spirit. But intellectual integrity required that the Bible must be understood in terms of what it is possible for a modern person to believe.[9]

In both *Foolishness to the Greeks* and *The Gospel in a Pluralist Society*, Newbigin entered deeply into a critique of the fundamental shifts of Western consciousness and its relegation of faith to the realms of indemonstrable, private beliefs. He succeeded in retrieving the *historical* nature of the central teaching of the New Testament. Christianity is much more than a grounding for morals in the way that the trajectory of liberal theology from Kant onward would make it. Instead, as Newbigin knows, Israel, Christ and the followers of Christ are about the promise of God to bring the world to its destiny as revealed and accomplished in the teaching, death and resurrection of Jesus.

Newbigin knew that the church and the Christian movement it represents are founded in the notion that the world is God's and that Jesus reveals its meaning, shape and destiny. Faith involves a basic orientation toward history as the manifestation of God. And the Christian vocation in that context is not primarily concerned with the mere "salvation" of its individual members but with its mission in the world, a mission based on a truth that seems foolish to those wise in the way of the world.[10]

Newbigin, Mission and Christianity as Christomorphic

As we shift into the next section of this chapter, I want to suggest that the whole of Newbigin's theology of mission and Christian identity is christomorphic in the sense that H. Richard Niebuhr finds christomorphism in the thought of F. D. E. Schleiermacher.[11] First, let us recall what Niebuhr says about the christomorphic dimension in Schleiermacher's thought:

> His theology is Christomorphic in two senses. First of all, it asserts that Jesus of Nazareth objectively exhibits what human nature ideally is, although Schleiermacher does not on this account counsel Christians to imitate Jesus

[9]Lesslie Newbigin, *Foolishness to the Greeks: The Gospel and Western Culture* (Grand Rapids: Eerdmans, 1986), p. 45.

[10]A view presented in Newbigin's 1984 lectures at Princeton Seminary, later edited, expanded and printed as *Foolishness to the Greeks*.

[11]H. Richard Niebuhr, *Schleiermacher on Christ and Religion: A New Introduction* (New York: Charles Scribner's Sons, 1964), pp. 212-19.

> in any naïve way. . . . In this sense, then, the redeemer is the measure of human nature. And in the second place the redeemer is the historical person whose presence mediated through Scriptures, preaching and the Holy Spirit becomes the abiding occasion for the reorganization and clarifying of the Christian's consciousness of his absolute dependence, of his identity in the world, and of his appropriate actions toward and responses to others.[12]

University of Chicago historical theologian and my teacher Brian Gerrish often noted in his lectures that Schleiermacher is sometimes presented by his critics as someone who compromised the truth claims of theology and collapsed theology into anthropology.[13] By contrast, the heart of Schleiermacher's work is a profound realization that subjective appropriation of dynamic religious truth is an essential aspect of whatever objectivity that truth discloses. In addition, like both Calvin and Barth, Schleiermacher's theology cannot be said to have a single center, something that I believe can also be said about Newbigin. Third, it is appropriate to remind ourselves that Newbigin is Reformed in the contours of his missiology. In that framework, the sole reliable source of knowledge of God is Scripture, but Scripture requires careful exegesis under the inspiration of the Spirit, and theology cannot ignore what humanity learns in the book of nature. Fundamentalism, in other words, finds no true home in the Reformed tradition. Indeed, as Brian Gerrish has often remarked, Calvin was deeply influenced by the new learning of the Renaissance and was among the very earliest to approach the Bible with something like a modern sense of the hermeneutic task; yet that notwithstanding, for Calvin, "Word and Spirit are united by an 'inviolable bond,' and the ultimate norm is Scripture plus Spirit. The Word has become the instrument by which the illumination of the Spirit is dispensed."[14]

The Word-cum-Spirit, if I may use that term, is for Calvin a sacrament making Christ present in the church and in the heart of the believer. Newbigin exhibits this same sensitivity.[15] Preaching is not mere instruction but

---

[12]Ibid., pp. 212-13.

[13]B. A. Gerrish, *The Old Protestantism and the New: Essays on the Reformation Heritage* (Chicago: University of Chicago Press, 1982), see chap 10, "The Reformation and the Rise of Modern Science: Luther, Calvin, and Copernicus," pp. 163-78.

[14]Gerrish, *Old Protestantism and the New*, pp. 66-67.

[15]Lesslie Newbigin, *Trinitarian Faith and Today's Mission* (Richmond, VA: John Knox Press, 1964), pp. 32-33, 78.

the instrument utilized by the Spirit to make us participants in Jesus' obedience to the Father in our own social and historical context and—within that context—enabling us to trust in God, for: "we also boast in our sufferings, knowing that suffering produces endurance, and endurance produces character, and character produces hope, and hope does not disappoint us, because God's love has been poured into our hearts through the Holy Spirit that has been given to us" (Rom 5:3-5).

Always a pastor, Newbigin develops his missiology as he is asked to address concrete questions. And the context in which he reflects after his return to Europe from 1959 to 1965 and again from 1974 till his death in 1998 was the decline of the church and the growing implausibility of being an active Christian throughout Europe.[16] In attempting to understand this recession from Christian life and faith, Newbigin takes from his toolbox of wide reading, knowledge of Scripture and personal experience to offer reflections that both throw light on the question and often reframe it. Concretely, the axis around which *The Gospel in a Pluralist Society* and *Foolishness to the Greeks* revolve is the deteriorating situation of Christianity in the West and the question of its reconversion. Moreover, what another of my teachers, Langdon Gilkey, was fond of saying—admiringly—of Barth is also true of Newbigin. Both are masters at outflanking modern reductionists, whether their reductionism came in the form of scriptural literalism and fundamentalism, on the one hand, or higher criticism of Scripture or scientism's scorn of faith as a way of truly knowing anything important, on the other hand. Newbigin refuses to be confined by contemporary Western culture's pigeonholing of Christianity on the subjective value side of an opinion/values versus fact divide. It is a theme he returns to often.[17] His refusal to let modernity set the terms of faith becomes, in my view, an important but perhaps too seldom attended to dimension of what Catholics in these same years were pursuing under the rubric of *aggiornamento*.

Newbigin and *Aggiornamento*

In recent years an influential group of Catholic theologians has pursued the question of what *aggiornamento* is about under the rubric of the French word

---

[16]Wainwright, *Lesslie Newbigin*, pp. 72-75.

[17]See, for example, Newbigin, *Foolishness to the Greeks*, pp. 42-64, and Newbigin, *GPS*, pp. 27-38.

ressourcement (literally "re-sourcement").[18] *Ressourcement* points to the necessity of retrieving the dynamic dimensions of the biblical, patristic and high medieval heritage as resources for interpreting Scripture and for creating theology that is critical in the modern sense but also, and more importantly, is not reduced to categories of modern science and academic vogues. In short, *ressourcement* is a search for a path around the barren deserts of post-Kantian moralism and reductionism, on the one hand,[19] and what Pope Benedict XVI calls the postmodern "dictatorship of relativism" on the other hand.[20]

Honest Religion for Secular Man can be distilled to a short formula—namely, that the gospel is not properly interpreted by modernity so much as all history must be interpreted by the gospel. The problem is how one can make sense of this for modern, Western men and women. Simply asserting it seems preposterous and arbitrary, and not just to cultured despisers of religion. For we are faced with a multitude—including perhaps a majority in our pews—for whom Jesus has been demoted to the status of a personal Savior (at one end of the theological spectrum) or to that of a great teacher (at the other end of the spectrum). For both, the most important thing is interpreting the gospel for political ends, such as the need to uphold traditional morality or create a just society by means of politics.

For Newbigin, the key to the gospel is Jesus, who embodies and discloses the good news and the goal of human history. Mission, for Newbigin, revolves around sharing the story of Jesus, in which is revealed the true story about ourselves.[21]

As is well known, Newbigin served in India from 1936 to 1959, when he became general secretary of the International Missionary Council (IMC) and oversaw the amalgamation of the IMC (some might call it a "takeover") into

---

[18]A good resource to understand *ressourcement* in its depth and breadth is David Schindler, ed., *Love Alone Is Credible: Hans Urs von Balthasar as Interpreter of the Catholic Tradition*, vol. 1 (Grand Rapids: Eerdmans, 2008), a collection of essays on aspects of Balthasar's theology as an exemplar of a retrieval of the depths of Catholic tradition that is rooted in its total aesthetic, not merely its doctrinal formulae.

[19]In a memorable quip at a meeting I attended, the Maryknoll theologian William Frazier defined moralism as "the reduction of Christian life to the axiom 'do good and avoid evil'" and charted how that attitude had eroded the theological foundations of mission.

[20]See Pope Benedict XVI, *General Audience*, December 16, 2009, http://w2.vatican.va/content/francesco/en/speeches/2014/november/documents/papa-francesco_20141125_strasburgo-parlamento-europeo.html (accessed on May 14, 2015).

[21]Newbigin, *GPS*, pp. 124-27.

the World Council of Churches (WCC). The WCC itself had been founded eleven years earlier in the aftermath of World War II, bringing together two major currents of Protestantism ("Life and Work" and "Faith and Order"), which had been active after World War I. The IMC itself was the direct descendant of the International Missionary Conference at Edinburgh in 1910. The birth of the WCC was complex, occurring as it did during the reconstruction of Europe and the beginnings of the United Nations after World War II. The Life and Work stream that flowed into the new WCC represented the energies of churches organizing to bring relief to millions of refugees. The Faith and Order stream was concerned with achieving church unity by means of patient dialogue aimed at clarifying theological and practical obstacles standing in the way of both cooperation and communion among Christians. The IMC stream that joined the WCC represented missionary organizations in Europe and North America whose concern was mission understood primarily as explicit evangelization of non-Christians.

The leaders of the IMC, whom Newbigin was representing in 1959, were primarily learders of missionaries and missionary societies, but they were dealing with the maturation of indigenous churches throughout Africa, Asia and Oceania. If IMC voiced the concerns of Western missionaries, indigenous church leaders were in the ambiguous position of depending on these societies for financial support and personnel while feeling the need to assume leadership roles—in the decolonization terminology of the day—"nationalizing" and "indigenizing" their churches. Indigenous church leaders found in the WCC an organization that shared their opinion that the colonial-era structures of the missionary societies needed to be tamed. The IMC's relationship to the European colonial powers is complex, but one area in which both the foreign missionary and colonial leaders shared a problem was difficulty in giving up power.

In that context, Newbigin's credentials were impressive and gave promise for integrating a vigorous understanding of evangelism into the WCC's concerns for social justice and ecumenical dialogue. In his missionary life he had been, after all, one of the major figures in the effort to erase the denominational boundaries between churches founded by European Methodists, Anglicans, Presbyterians and Congregationalists and their unification into what became known as the Church of South India. He was also not interested in missionary societies retaining power, but my sense is that he found himself caught in a three-way argument between the WCC, the IMC and local church leaders. Without attempting to assign blame to anyone, the integration of the IMC into the WCC was not smooth and did not satisfy any of the parties, especially the missionary societies. What is important is to understand that Newbigin was a committed ecumenist, on the one hand.[22] On the other hand, the Faith and Order and Life and Work movements defined the culture of the WCC, and they found allies among indigenous church leaders who felt the need to throw off, as I have said above, what many perceived to be the heavy hand of colonial-minded missionaries and missionary societies.

Nothing epitomizes this spirit of the day better than the Kenyan Presbyterian leader John Gatu's speech in Milwaukee in 1971, in which he argued for "a withdrawal of foreign missionaries from many parts of the Third World, that the churches of the Third World must be allowed to find their own identity, and that the continuation of the present missionary movement is a hindrance to this selfhood of the church."[23] Gatu spoke in 1971, but he referred to events that were going on precisely when Newbigin was in Geneva and unhappily watching the marginalization of the idea that evangelism was at the heart of mission. Although the passage I cite next from Newbigin's *Unfinished Agenda* was written in 1968 at the Uppsala, Sweden, Fourth Assembly of the WCC (thus before Gatu's speech), we find in it Newbigin's growing disenchantment with the regnant theology of WCC-affiliated churches:

> The mood [at Uppsala] was one of anger. The well-drilled phalanx of students in the gallery [this is the year of the European student revolt against the "establishment"] ensured that the emotional temperature was kept high. . . . We were corporately shaken over the pit of hell. The word of the Gospel was hardly heard, except, in a muted way, when a little band of Salvationists sang to us. More characteristic was the evening when Pete Seeger sang the well-

---

[22]This is brought home by Wainwright in his biographical study, *Lesslie Newbigin*, chap. 3, "The Ecumenical Advocate," pp. 81-134.

[23]John Gatu, "Missionary Go Home," *The Church Herald* (November 1971): 4. See "Moratorium: Retreat, Revolt or Reconciliation," in *IDOC International Documentation Project, The Future of the Missionary Enterprise, No. 9* (New York: IDOC International, 1974), pp. 49-86. This section of *IDOC* contains a variety of perspectives on Gatu's speech and is the essential resource for understanding his so-called "Moratorium" proposal.

> known mockery of the Christian Gospel which affirms that "there will be pie in the sky when you die," and the assembly sat in rapt silence and then applauded as though it were a new relation of truth. How, I couldn't help wondering, could such a group be so easily brainwashed?[24]

Newbigin returned to India in 1965, deeply disappointed by the WCC's adoption of a point of view espoused by William Earnest Hocking (1873–1966) on Christian identity vis-à-vis the world and world religions. For Hocking, according to Wilbert Shenk, faith is "an individual experience of timeless reality," while for Newbigin, "in the Bible the living God takes the initiative in creating a new social reality."[25] It can be said of the WCC that, like Hocking, its evolving theology was diffident about Christ, who for Newbigin was the ultimate revelation of God's initiative to enlighten humankind. Newbigin's gospel is vastly more than an expression of eternal truth that can be found in other religions; instead,

> It is the declaration of God's cosmic purpose by which the whole public history of mankind is sustained and overruled, and by which all men without exception will be judged. It is the invitation to be fellow workers with God in the fulfilment of that purpose through the atoning work of Christ and through the witness of the Holy Spirit. It calls men to commitment to a worldwide mission more daring and more far-reaching than that of Marxism. And it has—what Marxism lacks—a faith regarding the final consummation of God's purpose in the power of which it is possible to find meaning for world history which does not make personal history meaningless, and meaning for personal history which does not make world history meaningless.[26]

A Catholic Appreciation of Newbigin's Theology of Mission

I do not know if Pope John Paul II was acquainted with Newbigin's writings, but it is clear that both he and Newbigin were concentrating on healing the same spiritual illness that beset European society and Christianity. Indeed,

---

[24]Lesslie Newbigin, *Unfinished Agenda: An Autobiography* (Grand Rapids: Eerdmans, 1985), pp. 231-32.

[25]Wilbert Shenk, "Lesslie Newbigin's Contribution to the Theology of Mission," *The Bible in TransMission: A Tribute to Lesslie Newbigin (1909–1998)*, special edition 1998, p. 4.

[26]Newbigin, *Honest Religion*, p. 46.

I believe that any fair-minded Protestant who reads John Paul II's encyclical letter on the permanent validity of the church's mission will find a kindred spirit, especially in the following citation in which, mutatis mutandis, the pope is stating what is at the core of Newbigin's thought:

> Proclamation is the permanent priority of mission. The Church cannot elude Christ's explicit mandate, nor deprive men and women of the "Good News" about their being loved and saved by God. "Evangelization will always contain—as the foundation, center and at the same time the summit of its dynamism—a clear proclamation that, in Jesus Christ . . . salvation is offered to all people, as a gift of God's grace and mercy" [John Paul quotes Pope Paul VI, *Evangelii Nuntiandi*, § 27]. All forms of missionary activity are directed to this proclamation, which reveals and gives access to the mystery hidden for ages and made known in Christ (cf. Eph 3:3-9; Col 1:25-29), the mystery which lies at the heart of the Church's mission and life, as the hinge on which all evangelization turns.[27]

The principal difference between the two men, I believe, stems from John Paul's identity as an academically trained philosopher, whose preoccupations lay with developing a Christian anthropology that would speak to the spiritual depths of humanity—depths that define the whole person and which John Paul believed were occluded in secular ideologies. John Paul's anthropology, however, is not empirical but philosophical, rooted in Thomism and permeated by Husserl's phenomenology.[28] If one spends time with John Paul, the theme that unites everything is Christ the concrete universal, the revealer of God's riches bestowed on those who will embrace him in faith, the perfect exemplar of humanity in its fullness. Newbigin uses biblical language to express this reality; John Paul the language of the perennial philosophy transfused by Husserl's philosophy.

John Paul's and Lesslie Newbigin's adversaries are also very similar. John Paul believed that the West had lost its moorings in Christian faith and that the progressive wing of Western Catholic theology had imbibed too deeply historical studies that did not deal adequately with the transcendent mystery of humanity and the way in which Christ and the Spirit revealed humanity's

---

[27]Pope John Paul II, *Redemptoris Missio* §37 (1990), www.vatican.va/holy_father/john_paul_ii/encyclicals/documents/hf_jp-ii_enc_07121990_redemptoris-missio_en.html.

[28]The best entrée in Pope John Paul's overview is found in his *The Acting Person*, Analecta Husserliana 10 (Berlin: Springer Verlag, 1979); the original Polish edition was titled *Osoba i Czyn*, published in 1969.

potential. It is no accident that the pope's most significant encyclicals dealt with (1) Christ as the redeemer of humankind, (2) the Spirit as the bearer of true life, and (3) theological reductionism's weakening of a full grasp of the church's mission.[29] John Paul saw himself primarily as a teacher, but at least in passing, I must also observe that in my many visits to Rome as an editor working for Orbis Books, a constant refrain was the judgment of Roman insiders that John Paul was so taken up with his own writing and international trips that he was neglecting administration. Problems were allowed to fester, my conversation partners said, and the crisis represented by clergy's sexual abuse of minors was not faced.

When I read Newbigin, I find myself reading a man whose career as a missionary bishop in India led him to concentrate on the essentials, because he was forced to translate the message into Indian languages. This gave him a pastoral perspective that John Paul lacked, since his challenge was outfoxing a Communist government and preserving space for his church to operate. He carried on that ministry among a people for whom practicing Catholic faith was a way to demonstrate disaffection with that regime. When Communism fell, in no small measure because of John Paul's efforts, Catholicism enjoyed immense prestige in Poland. It did not take long, however, for the bishops and clergy to overplay their hand, and Catholicism began to suffer the same—albeit less pervasive—recession it had in the rest of Europe as Poles strove to modernize their economic, educational and legal systems. John Paul was used to commanding and being obeyed in a situation of oppression. He confronted a different situation as pope, and his critics doubted he understood that culture.

Newbigin's career brought him face to face with the same kind of reductionism that John Paul encountered in Western Catholicism in 1978, but neither John Paul nor Lesslie Newbigin was able to overcome what Bernard Lonergan diagnoses as the challenge of our age, confronting "a problem of evil that demands the transformation of self-reliant intelligence into an *intellectus quaerens fidem* ["understanding seeking faith"]."[30] Lonergan is quite conser-

[29]*Redemptoris Hominis* (1979), *Dominum et Vivificantem* (1986) and *Redemptoris Missio* (1990), respectively.

[30]Bernard J. F. Lonergan, *Insight: A Study of Human Understanding* (New York: Philosophical Library, 1957), p. 731.

vative in matters of doctrine. There would be little disagreement between him, Newbigin and John Paul on the core of faith, but I find him quite radical in his grasp of what ails the church in its attempts to retrieve and propagate the gospel. In the following passage, he speaks explicitly of Catholicism, but the same problems confront Protestants in the Western world, that is to say,

> a crisis not of faith but of culture. There has been no new revelation from on high to replace the revelation given through Christ Jesus. There has been written no new Bible and there has been founded no new church to link us with him. But Catholic [or Protestant] philosophy, and Catholic [or Protestant] theology are matters, not merely of revelation and faith, but also of culture. Both have been fully and deeply involved in classical culture. The breakdown of classical culture and, at least in our day, the manifest comprehensiveness and exclusiveness of modern culture confront . . . philosophy and . . . theology with the gravest problems, impose upon them mountainous tasks, invite them to Herculean labors.

In that context, he goes on to say:

> There is bound to be formed a solid right that is determined to live in a world that no longer exists. There is bound to be formed a scattered left, captivated by now this and now that new development, exploring now this and now that new possibility. But what will count is a perhaps not numerous center, big enough to be at home in both the old and the new, painstaking enough to work out one by one the transitions to be made, strong enough to refuse half-measures and insist on complete solutions even though it has to wait.[31]

Lonergan is not a missiologist in the way both Newbigin and John Paul were, but he has three issues in hand that complement Newbigin's and John Paul's analysis and lead us forward: his identification of the "human problem" within humanity, the need to recognize evil, and the need for conversion or transformation if evil is to be overcome and God's victory over it *in principle* in Christ is to be realized de facto in history.

And here we return to the challenge with which we began, the question of *how to form the agents who will bring the gospel to the nations*. Yes, I realize that Newbigin and John Paul both employ great rhetorical art that exhorts men and

---

[31]Bernard J. F. Lonergan, *Collection: Papers by Bernard Lonergan, S.J.*, ed. F. E. Crowe, S.J. (New York: Herder and Herder, 1967), pp. 266-67.

women to put the gospel into practice, but do they put us in touch with the spiritual disciplines that the Christian tradition teaches us are necessary if the Spirit's work of making us new selves in Christ (Eph 4:22-24) is to occur?

It is one of the truisms of modern biblical hermeneutics that Christ promised to usher in the kingdom but left us with a church. It was the genius of the apostle Paul, as N. T. Wright's marvelous body of work has shown, to translate kingdom language into the reality of the Spirit ushering the believer into an entirely new dimension of life.[32] From Wright's perspective, the experience of the Spirit is our entrée into beginning to feel and live in the mystery of the kingdom. When one grasps that the Gospels were written in the light of the primitive Jesus movement's growing understanding of what it means for Jesus to be *Messiah/Christos*, the stories of the life, teaching, ministry, death and resurrection of Jesus as told in the Synoptics and John take on new meaning. The details of the narratives recorded fifty and more years after his death and resurrection are shaded by the Evangelists to illustrate the dimension of Jesus' that any given Gospel is bringing attention to. Taken together they offer a kaleidoscopic image of the gospel as the promise that God will deal with humanity and the cosmos as Jesus is transformed in the power of the Spirit after his crucifixion.

The Lutheran shorthand for what the gospel *is* is helpful in this regard: the gospel is the *promise* to whose veracity and trustworthiness the Spirit testifies in our inmost being.[33] A promise of what? That sins will be forgiven, that mortal flesh will be transformed, that the universe is moving toward the day when all discord will be reconciled and God will be "all in all" (1 Cor 15:28) through the reconciling activity of the cosmic Christ, an activity that we now experience as the "first fruits" of what is to come (Rom 8:20-26).

What I have been driving at is fairly simple. The splendid insights that Newbigin brings forth concerning the need to become a missional church

---

[32]Not a Scripture scholar myself, I have found two of N. T. Wright's shorter books immensely important for taking me beyond the dead ends of both the old and new searches for the historical Jesus. See N. T. Wright, *Jesus and the Victory of God* (Minneapolis: Fortress Press, 1996); also, *Paul in Fresh Perspective* (Minneapolis: Fortress, 2005).

[33]See Jukka A. Kääriäinen, *Mission Shaped by Promise: Lutheran Missiology Confronts the Challenge of Religious Pluralism* (Eugene, OR: Pickwick Publications, 2012), pp. 29-78, for an up-to-date summary of the Lutheran confessional doctrine of the gospel as promise and what happens when the Christian participation in the mystery of salvation is retrieved as "mission shaped by promise" (pp. 177-225).

and face up to the end of Christendom will come to nothing if our congregations and formation programs are not first and foremost entrées into the promise of the gospel mediated to individuals through community life, study, prayer, worship, contemplation and a grasp of the depths of life by the Spirit.

Toward an Inconclusive Conclusion

I was once an invited participant in a series of seminar events convened at Princeton Theological Seminary by Andrew F. Walls to discuss various aspects of the reality often called—without, I fear, clear definition—"world Christianity." There were many wonderful papers presented and discussed, but the one that struck me most strongly was presented by Professor Moonjang Lee. Several years later he would publish his main ideas in an Orbis book.[34] In his presentation and the spirited dialogue that followed, Lee advanced the notion that a Korean candidate for ministry is invariably disappointed, sometimes severely so, during his first year in seminary. He or she comes with the Korean cultural expectation that the candidate is being led into a transformative experience of the *Tao* of Jesus—the moment in which "knowledge" moves from the theoretical, academic level to living harmony in the heart of the Christian. That expectation, of course, comes from Korea's history of involvement with the great religions and life systems of East Asia—in particular, Buddhism, Taoism and Confucianism as they are added to a fundament of Korean sensitivity to the presence of ancestor and nature spirits. Skillful teachers lead novices to breakthrough moments when the shape and nature of the "Whole" are experienced as Tao. To meet Korean expectations, theological education must immerse the candidate for ministry to the Tao of Jesus.

What happens when students come to Christian seminaries and other schools or departments of theology—and not just in Korea—however, is an encounter with a theological curriculum that is more a non-aggression pact between academic disciplines and fields than a vehicle for dwelling and being transformed by divine *Sophia*/Wisdom. Each field competes for the maximum number of lecture hours to introduce students to what professors believe is

[34]See Moonjang Lee, "Theological Education as Embodiment of Jesus," in *Understanding World Christianity: The Vision and Work of Andrew F. Walls*, ed. William R. Burrows, Mark R. Gornik and Janice A. McLean (Maryknoll, NY: Orbis Books, 2011), pp. 79-88.

essential to master in his or her field, be it history, systematic or doctrinal theology, Scripture, ethics, counseling and pastoral theology, preaching and worship, or management skills. Integration is left to the student, and many fail at the task.

In this age of recognizing the need to acknowledge the reality of cultural and religious pluralism, are we capable of seeing the challenge that this Korean theologian presents us? Seeking to meet this challenge is, of course, not something completely alien to Western tradition, for in Catholic reform movements of the thirteenth century (in orders founded by St. Francis and St. Dominic) and in the sixteenth (in the order founded by St. Ignatius), immersion in the Tao of Jesus was exactly what was involved.

Moonjang Lee points to the need to transform the formation of men and women for mission in a secularizing world with the courage to embody the wisdom that heart speaks to heart, and that the only way to measure up to Newbigin's challenge to be communities that embody the gospel in pluralistic, secularizing societies is immersion in the transforming Spirit.

4

Community and Witness in Transition

Newbigin's Missional Ecclesiology Between Modernity and Postmodernity

Veli-Matti Kärkkäinen and Michael Karim

Introduction: Setting Newbigin in the Context of Postmodernism

It has been noted recently that it was only during the last decade of his productive life that Newbigin intentionally and explicitly started addressing the challenge of postmodernism.[1] Paul Weston, in his important essay on Newbigin's relation to postmodernism, mentions that all references to that concept occur after 1991 when he was already eighty-two years old.[2] Had he lived longer, Newbigin's engagement with postmodernism would have loomed large in the horizon of his cultural critique. At the same time—and this is the key to our investigation—as Weston rightly notes, "Newbigin can be shown to have developed a missiological approach that effectively anticipates many of the questions raised by contemporary postmodern perspectives."[3] We attempt to show in this essay that the English bishop's engagement of postmodernism goes way beyond the year 1991. Indeed, we

[1]This chapter was originally delivered as two lectures at the Newbigin Centenary gatherings in Birmingham and Edinburgh, UK, in 2009 and subsequently published in *Mission and Postmodernities*, ed. R. Olsen (Oxford: Regnum, 2011), pp. 83-108, and *Theology in Missionary Perspective: Lesslie Newbigin's Legacy*, ed. M. Laing and P. Weston (Eugene, OR: Pickwick, 2012), pp. 125-54. With minor revisions, it is reprinted here by permission of Regnum Books, Pickwick Publications, and the editors of both volumes.

[2]Paul Weston, "Lesslie Newbigin: A Postmodern Missiologist?," *Mission Studies* 21, no. 2 (2004): 229.

[3]Ibid., p. 230.

set forth an argument according to which Newbigin's cultural critique of modernity offers a fruitful and a fresh way of considering the church's relation to the postmodern condition. However, what is ironic is that the bishop himself neither attempted a response to postmodernism nor was by and large conscious of it.

We hesitate regarding the judgment of those who consider Newbigin "A 'Postmodern' before Postmodernity Arrived."[4] Rather than considering him a "crypto-postmodernist," we argue that a careful analysis of his writings over a longer period of time reveals that while he saw in some features of postmodernism orientations that helped clarify the critique of modernity, by and large he was extremely critical of key features of what he thought comprises postmodernism. At no point did Newbigin consider the program of postmodernism as a whole an ally to his own pursuit of "the gospel as public truth." We fear that one of the titles Newbigin would absolutely eschew having attached to his legacy is "postmodern." The reason for this assessment is simply the fact that, in the bishop's understanding, postmodernism represented to him everything destructive, almost as much as his archenemy, modernity.

Our approach in this investigation is based on the methodological conviction—or, at least, a hypothesis—according to which Newbigin's thinking reveals a remarkable integrity and consistency throughout the period of his mature life, beginning from the late seventies or early eighties, when he began focusing on the critique of the church's mistaken "contextualization" strategy into the Western (European American) culture. This is not to say that his thinking was systematic or even always tightly ordered, and he himself was often the first one to acknowledge it.[5] It is simply to

[4]Ibid., p. 243.

[5]As a preacher rather than an academic scholar, Newbigin often used ideas and movements as heuristic "talking points" and examples rather than as showcases of detailed academic analysis. His writing style was occasional rather than systematic. To take up obvious examples: his tracing of the prehistory and development of modernity from antiquity (in terms of the two narratives of Christian faith and Hellenistic philosophy) or his treatment and contrasting of Augustine and Aquinas, which in its details hardly stands the scrutiny of rigorous academic investigation. Similarly, his preference for "good guys" in history such as Athanasius and Augustine and disdain for "bad guys" such as Aquinas and Descartes reflect much more their role in the unfolding intentionally biased reading of history than anything else. While for the purposes of academic scholarship the acknowledgment of those kinds of biases should not go unnoticed, in our opinion, they should not blur the significance of Newbigin's critique and constructive proposal. In many ways, it can be said that his innovative and bold proposal can stand on its own feet even if it can be shown—unfortunately—that not all the historical and philosophical judgments do.

say that upon his return from India, in a relatively short period of time, the key theses of a missionally driven postcritical thinking emerged. Therefore, methodologically, the best way to determine his relation and contribution to postmodernism is to look broadly at the writings of the whole of his mature career. Indeed, his critique—as well as the occasional affirmation—of postmodernism is to a large extent unspoken and tacit in the texture of the cultural critique whose main target was modernity.[6] Consequently, those who critique Newbigin for the lack of a nuanced understanding of postmodernism[7] not only miss the point but expect of him something he never set out to do.

In Newbigin's judgment, postmodernism had no independent existence: it was both parasitic on and an offshoot of modernity. He didn't see postmodernism as a "savior" to the church, but rather another challenger along with modernity—even when occasionally he affirmed some elements of this new epistemological approach.

Our discussion is composed of two main parts. In part one we will attempt a diagnostic assessment of Newbigin's view of postmodernism. Quite apart from whether Newbigin's vision of postmodernism was correct or even balanced, our task is simply to analyze his view. Part two then advances what would be the key aspects of Newbigin's constructive proposal with regard to the church's mission under the postmodern condition. Not surprisingly, in light of our methodological remarks above, we contend that Newbigin's response to postmodernism is not radically different from his response to modernism. To both modernists and postmodernists, he offered as an alternative the view of the gospel as public truth.

Needless to say, all of the essay is necessarily reconstructive from our point of view, particularly in view of our stated purpose above: rather than searching for the term *postmodern* in his writings or even trying to de-

---

[6]One of the many contributions of the essay from Weston is that it outlines the key aspects of Newbigin's indebtedness to Michael Polanyi, the philosopher of science from whom the bishop borrowed well-known ideas such as "universal intention," testimonies "from within the tradition," and so forth. These are concepts that helped the mature Newbigin to construct his cultural critique and point the way toward his view of "the gospel as public truth."

[7]Elaine Graham and Walton Heather, "Walk on the Wild Side: A Critique of *The Gospel and Our Culture*," *Modern Churchman* 33, no. 1 (1991): 5-7.

termine veiled references to postmodernism, we reconstruct Newbigin's viewpoint on the basis of his overall missional thinking and epistemology.[8]

Newbigin's View of Postmodernity

As will soon become apparent, we will attempt a description of postmodernism "from below."[9] We will do our best to discern from Newbigin's own writings the way he discerned the effects and implications of the transition underway in the cultures of the West as the Enlightenment was slowly giving way to a new way of thinking and being. The term *transition* in the subheading below is intentional and important: it seems to us that the best way—and to a large extent, the only way—to generate what Newbigin opined about postmodernism appears in the contexts in which he is discussing the move away, the transition, from modernity to postmodernism. Thus, seeking for and counting terms such as *postmodernism* is to miss the point. Without often naming what this "post-" or "late-" was, he focused his reflections on the implications of the transition away from modernism to church's mission.

The epistemological challenge of the transition from modernity to late modernity. We will divide Newbigin's diagnosis of postmodernism into two interrelated themes: epistemology and lifestyle. The first one gets the lion's share in this discussion, and is further divided into two segments. While interrelated, epistemology and lifestyle can also be distinguished for analytic clarity.

The key to properly understanding Newbigin's diagnosis of postmodernism is to acknowledge its parasitic nature. As mentioned above, for Newbigin, postmodernism had no independent existence; rather it was an extension of and offshoot from modernity. This may also help explain the lack

[8]In my (VMK) investigation of many aspects of Newbigin's thinking I am indebted to the published doctoral dissertation submitted to the faculty of theology at the University of Helsinki by Jukka Keskitalo. That careful study is the most comprehensive theological analysis of Newbigin's thinking. Unfortunately, it is written in Finnish and has only a brief English summary. Therefore, I do not give references to it unless there is a direct citation or otherwise important reason in terms of academic integrity. Jukka Keskitalo, *Kristillinen usko ja moderni kulttuuri: Lesslie Newbigin käsitys kirkon missiosta modernissa länsimaisessa kulttuurissa* [The Christian Faith and Modern Culture: Lesslie Newbigin's View of the Church's Mission in Modern Western Culture], Suomalaisen Teologisen Kirjallisuusseuran Julkaisuja 218 (Helsinki: Suomalainen Teologinen Kirjallisuusseura, 1999).

[9]Any attempt at a generic description of postmodernism flies in the face of an intellectual movement that intentionally opposes any generalizations.

of sustained analysis of postmodernity.[10] It only came to the fore as Newbigin was reflecting on the transition away from modernity. This state of affairs is reflected in his choice of terminology, although one does find designations such as "postmodern culture" or "postmodernity,"[11] "the postmodern development of modernism,"[12] as well as "postmodern reaction."[13] I believe the term "*late* modern" might best characterize Newbigin's view, which builds on the idea of continuity, and we will use such a phrase to emphasize his view.[14] In keeping with his idea of the parasitic nature of postmodernism, one of the key observations of Newbigin was that the advent of postmodernism, if such has already happened, does not mean a complete shift in terms of replacement of the old for new but rather a cohabitation of a sort. This cohabitation includes both intellectual and lifestyle issues, as the discussion will show.

There are a number of internal dynamics, even contradistinctions, in postmodernism in Newbigin's analysis. On the one hand, there are many who have grown very suspicious of the project of the Enlightenment, with its search for Cartesian indubitable certainty. On the other hand, this is only one side of contemporary Western intellectual culture. Among the ordinary folks—and in many ways among the educated as well—there is still a firm trust in the facts of science and modernity. This confidence in the project of modernity is greatly aided by the economic and scientific-technological globalization process.[15]

Over against this continuing confidence in the Enlightenment, there is a definite shift that, for the bishop, signals the transition away from modernity: for "an increasing number of people . . . there is no longer any confidence in the alleged 'eternal truths of reason' of . . . Lessing."[16] The

---

[10]Keskitalo, *Kristillinen usko*, p. 214, notes that Colin Gunton's view of postmodernity is similarly.

[11]Among other items, Lesslie Newbigin, *Proper Confidence: Faith, Doubt and Certainty in Christian Discipleship* (Grand Rapids: Eerdmans, 1995), pp. 27, 51; Lesslie Newbigin, *Truth and Authority in Modernity*, Christian Mission and Modern Culture Series (Valley Forge, PA: Trinity Press International, 1996), p. 82.

[12]See, for example, Newbigin, *Proper Confidence*, p. 83.

[13]See Newbigin, *Truth and Authority*, p. 7.

[14]So also Keskitalo, *Kristillinen usko*, p. 214.

[15]Lesslie Newbigin, "Modernity in Context," in *Modern, Postmodern and Christian*, ed. John Reid, Lesslie Newbigin and David Pullinger (Carberry, Scotland: Handsel Press, 1996), p. 8.

[16]Newbigin, *Truth and Authority*, p. 77.

following "working definition" of postmodernism by Newbigin is as illustrative of his perception of that movement as any:

> Its main feature is the abandonment of any claim to know the truth in an absolute sense. Ultimate reality is not single but diverse and chaotic. Truth-claims are really concealed claims to power, and this applies as much to the claims of science as to those of religion. The father of this whole movement is the German philosopher F. W. Nietzsche. Nietzsche was the one who foresaw, in the closing years of the 19th century, that the methods of the Enlightenment must in the end lead to total scepticism and nihilism.[17]

At the heart of Newbigin's analysis of postmodernity is thus the loss of confidence in any kind of universal truth of reason (AKA the Enlightenment),[18] a feature he also calls "the sickness of our culture."[19] In Newbigin's mind, the "foundationalism" of the Enlightenment, with its belief in grandiose truths, has been replaced in postmodern culture with the idea of "regimes of truth," which stand next to each other in a pluralist society:

> In the last decades of this century, the intellectual leadership of Europe has begun to turn its back on modernity. We are in the age of postmodernity. The mark of this is a suspicion of all claims to universal truth. Such claims have to be deconstructed. The "metanarratives" told by societies to validate their claim to global power are to be rejected. There are no privileged cultures and no privileged histories. All human cultures are equally entitled to respect. There are only different "regimes of truth" (Michel Foucault) which succeed one another. . . . There are no overarching criteria by which these regimes can be judged.[20]

---

[17]Lesslie Newbigin, "Religious Pluralism: A Missiological Approach," *Studia Missionalia* 42 (1993): 231.

[18]E.g., Newbigin, *Truth and Authority*, p. 77.

[19]Lesslie Newbigin, "Religious Pluralism and the Uniqueness of Jesus Christ," *International Bulletin of Missionary Research* 13, no. 2 (1989): 50. Newbigin refers several times to the well-known ideas of the Jewish-American philosopher Alan Bloom, who in his influential work *The Closing of the American Mind* (New York: Simon & Schuster, 1987) sees a total relativism as the dominant feature of Western culture; see, e.g., Lesslie Newbigin, *A Word in Season: Perspectives on Christian World Mission*, ed. Eleanor Jackson (Grand Rapids: Eerdmans/Edinburgh: Saint Andrews Press, 1994), pp. 105-6.

[20]Newbigin, *Proper Confidence*, p. 27. Newbigin distinguishes himself in his comprehension of "metanarratives" (Fr, *grand récits*), an elusive term in English. Cf. Jean-François Lyotard, Geoffrey Bennington and Brian Massumi, *The Postmodern Condition: A Report on Knowledge* (Minneapolis: University of Minnesota Press), 1984.

In order to properly understand the parasitic nature of postmodernity, one needs to acknowledge the bridge from Descartes via Friedrich Nietzsche—the "spiritual father" of all postmodernists—to contemporary elimination of the original Enlightenment dream of the certainty of knowledge.[21] Ironically, the method of doubt—which was viewed as the main way of achieving indubitable certainty—was changed in the hands of Nietzsche into the main weapon against modernity, which in turn paved the way for the total loss of confidence manifested in postmodernity. "The Cartesian invitation to make doubt the primary tool in search for knowledge was bound to lead to the triumph of skepticism and eventually of nihilism, as Nietzsche foresaw."[22] Nietzsche replaced rational argument as the means of arbitrating between competing truth claims with "will to power."[23] Terms such as "true" and "untrue" have simply lost their meaning;[24] what remains is simply different "narratives," themselves historically conditioned.[25] Even science—believed by the Enlightenment pioneers to be the source of indisputable truths—becomes yet another expression of the will to power.[26]

Not surprisingly, Newbigin did not tire himself with highlighting this built-in irony of the line of development from the dream of indubitable certainty coupled with the method of doubt from Descartes to Nietzsche's rejection and replacement of all such "uncritical" attitudes for historization of all knowledge, which finally led to the total loss of confidence of postmodernity. "It is deeply ironic that this method has led us directly into the program of skepticism of the postmodern world."[27] Ultimately, the fact that postmodern culture doesn't allow us to know which God really is the "true" God is for Newbigin a sign of a "dying culture."[28]

A pluralist society. A virtual synonym for Newbigin for "postmodern culture" is "pluralist culture." While pluralism as such is nothing new to Christian faith, which was born in a religiously pluralistic environment, what is new is the form of contemporary pluralism: "The kind of western

[21]E.g., Newbigin, *Proper Confidence*, pp. 26-27.
[22]Newbigin, *Truth and Authority*, p. 8.
[23]Ibid.
[24]Newbigin, *Personal Choice*, p. 26.
[25]Ibid., pp. 73-74.
[26]Ibid., p. 27.
[27]Ibid., pp. 27, 36, 105; *Truth and Authority*, p. 9.
[28]Newbigin, "Religious Pluralism and the Uniqueness of Jesus Christ," p. 52.

thought which has described itself as 'modern' is rapidly sinking into a kind of pluralism which is indistinguishable from nihilism—a pluralism which denies the possibility of making any universally justifiable truth-claims on any matter, whether religious or otherwise."[29]

An important aid to Newbigin in his analysis of the nature and effects of the late modern pluralism is offered by Peter Berger's *Heretical Imperative*,[30] with which he interacted extensively in several writings.[31] Berger's well-known thesis is that, whereas in premodern societies heretical views were discouraged at the expense of communal and cultural uniformity, in contemporary[32] Western culture there is no "plausibility structure," the acceptance of which is taken for granted without argument and dissent from which is considered heresy. "Plausibility structure" simply means both the ideas and the practices in a given culture that help determine whether a belief is plausible or not. To doubt these given beliefs and believe differently makes a heresy. Understandably, the number of those in pre-modern society who wanted to be labeled heretics was small, whereas in the contemporary culture, formulating one's own views—apart from given plausibility structures or even in defiance of them—has become an imperative. Consequently, all are heretics! The corollary thesis of Berger is that in this situation Christian affirmations can be negotiated in three different ways: in terms of choosing one's belief from a pool of many views, or making a distinction between beliefs that are still viable and ones that are not in light of current knowledge, or finally, building one's beliefs on a universal religious experience that precedes any rational affirmation.[33] Berger himself opts for the last one, coming from Friedrich Schleiermacher.

---

[29]Newbigin, "Religious Pluralism," pp. 227-28 (227). We would also direct the reader to the chapter in this book by Esther Meek for an intriguing proposal for the enduring influence of an ancient question that counters the notion of pluralism, i.e., the question of "the one and the many."

[30]Peter Berger, *Heretical Imperative: Contemporary Possibilities of Religious Affirmation* (London: Collins, 1980).

[31]Lesslie Newbigin, "Can the West Be Converted?," *International Bulletin of Missionary Research* 11, no. 1 (1987): 2-7; Newbigin, *The Gospel in a Pluralist Society* (Grand Rapids: Eerdmans, 1989), pp. 39-40, 53.

[32]Berger uses the term *modern* when speaking of contemporary Western culture. We have changed it to "contemporary" to avoid confusion; obviously, what Berger is describing is the culture of postmodernity, which encourages each individual have his or her own beliefs.

[33]Berger has named these three options deductive (Karl Barth as an example), reductive (Bultmann's demythologization program as a paradigm) and inductive (Schleiermacher, as mentioned, as the showcase).

While Newbigin appreciates Berger's analysis and affirms its basic idea concerning the radically widening array of choices in late-modern culture,[34] he also critiques it for lack of nuance. First, Newbigin complains that the pluralism of Berger's scheme is selective and does not include all areas of culture:

> The principle of pluralism is not universally accepted in our culture. It is one of the key features of our culture . . . that we make a sharp distinction between . . . "values" and . . . "facts." In the former world we are pluralists; values are a matter of personal choice. In the latter we are not; facts are facts, whether you like them or not. . . . About "beliefs" we agree to differ. Pluralism reigns. About what are called "facts" everyone is expected to agree.[35]

This takes us to another main dilemma of late-modern culture of the West, which—ironically—is also the malaise of the whole culture of the Enlightenment, as repeatedly lamented by Newbigin.[36] This irony couldn't be more pointed, and highlighting its significance takes us to the heart of the highly dynamic and tension-filled nature of postmodernism in the bishop's thinking. Briefly put: the fatal distinction between values and facts—as Newbigin believes—is not only the undergirding weakness of the culture of modernity; this very same difference also characterizes late-modern culture. Consequently, the culture of modernity would not be cured by the transition to postmodernism (any more than postmodern culture would be cured with the shift to the modernity). Both are plagued by the distinction that makes any talk about the gospel as public truth meaningless!

The second complaint against Berger's analysis of contemporary culture is Newbigin's incisive observation that while "the traditional plausibility structures are dissolved by contact with this modern world-view, and while . . . the prevalence and power of this world-view gives no ground for believing it to be true, he [Berger] does not seem to allow for the fact that it is itself a plausibility structure and functions as such."[37] In other words, the pluralist postmodern culture has not done away with plausibility structures but instead has replaced the traditional for another one, namely, the presupposition that

---

[34]See, e.g., Lesslie Newbigin, *Foolishness to the Greeks: The Gospel and Western Culture* (Grand Rapids: Eerdmans, 1986), p. 13.

[35]Newbigin, *GPS*, pp. 14-15.

[36]E.g., chapter 2, "Roots of Pluralism," in ibid.

[37]Newbigin, *Foolishness to the Greeks*, pp. 13-14.

individual choices only apply to certain aspects of reality—to values but not facts. This is a selective heretical imperative. The person who sets him- or herself against this plausibility structure—in other words, attempts to be a heretic in relation to established "facts"—is called just that, the *heretic.* Here Newbigin sides with Alasdair MacIntyre, who argues that "'fact' is in modern culture a folk-concept with an aristocratic ancestry," "aristocratic" referring to the Enlightenment philosopher Bacon's admonition to seek for "facts" instead of "speculations."[38] For Newbigin, modernity and postmodernism do not represent two different species, but rather, both represent the Enlightenment project.[39]

The effects on lifestyle of the transition to late modernity. With regard to lifestyle and cultural ethos, the transition to late modernity is causing "nihilism and hopelessness."[40] Along with the loss of confidence in truth, postmodern society has also lost hope and optimism of progress, so typical of modernity.[41] This loss of confidence not only in reason but also in the future can be discerned both in the lives of individuals and the society as a whole:

> In the closing decades of this century it is difficult to find Europeans who have any belief in a significant future which is worth working for and investing in. A society which believes in a worthwhile future saves in the present so as to invest in the future. Contemporary Western society spends in the present and piles up debts for the future, ravages the environment, and leaves its grandchildren to cope with the results as best they can.[42]

Newbigin painfully found that out when he returned to his homeland after a considerable period of missionary work in Asia. When asked what might have been the greatest difficulty in his homecoming, his response was the "disappearance of hope"[43] and the increase of "pessimism."[44] All this in turn has led

---

[38]Alasdair MacIntyre, *After Virtue: A Study in Moral Theory* (London: Duckworth, 1981), p. 79. For references to this phrase, see Newbigin, *Foolishness to the Greeks*, pp. 76-77; *Proper Confidence*, p. 55.

[39]Keskitalo, *Kristillinen usko*, p. 230.

[40]Newbigin, *Proper Confidence*, p. 47 (in reference to Carver Yu's phrase, cited on p. 46).

[41]Lesslie Newbigin, *The Other Side of 1984: Questions to the Churches* (Geneva: WCC Publications, 1984), pp. 1-2, 6; *GPS*, p. 112; *Proper Confidence*, pp. 46-47.

[42]Newbigin, *GPS*, pp. 90-91.

[43]Newbigin, *Other Side of 1984*, p. 1.

[44]Lesslie Newbigin, "The Secular Myth," in *Faith and Power: Christianity and Islam in "Secular" Britain*, ed. Lesslie Newbigin, Lamin Sanneh and Jenny Taylor (London: SPCK, 1998), p. 13.

particularly the young generation to the culture of "instant gratification." Whereas in the past people invested in the future, contemporary people in the West live only for today and do not see it meaningful to think of the future.[45]

While this kind of perception can be—and has been—critiqued as a function of reverse culture shock,[46] there is no denying the fact that these negative effects of postmodernity play a significant role in Newbigin's cultural analysis. The main point we want to make here is that in Newbigin's cultural analysis there is a direct link between the transition away from modernity, with its loss of confidence in reason, and the lifestyle of people living under those transitional forces. The implications for the church's mission are, of course, obvious: Should the church attempt a proper response, which would entail both epistemological and lifestyle-driven reorientation of thinking and practices?

Missional Response to the Culture in Transition Between Modernity and Late Modernity

Having looked at Newbigin's diagnosis of postmodernism through the lens of the effects of the transition away from modernity, the second part of this essay attempts to discern the main responses of Newbigin. To repeat our intent from earlier: rather than focusing on themes related to postmodernism, we will continue gleaning widely from Newbigin's writings in order to show that his response to late modernity can only be reconstructed from his response to modernity.

In order to bring to light the dynamic nature of Newbigin's thinking, we wish to reconstruct his response to late modernity along the lines of several polarities. Clearly, the bishop envisioned the mission of the church in this transitional period being faced with a number of dynamic tensions. While the notion of a safe middle ground hardly does justice to his radical program, in many ways we hear him calling the church to locate itself at the midpoint of various polarities, such as the following:

---

[45]Newbigin, *GPS*, pp. 90-91; see also pp. 111-12.

[46]Werner Ustorf, *Christianized Africa—De-Christianized Europe? Missionary Inquiries into the Polycentric Epoch of Christian History*, Perspektiven der Weltmission, Wissenschaftliche Beiträge Band 14, Herausgegeben von der Missionsakademie an der Universität Hamburg (Ammersbek bei Hamburg: Lottbeck Jensen, 1992), pp. 108-10; for Newbigin's response, see "The Secular Myth," pp. 6, 13.

- calling the church to be "relevant" while declining to explain the gospel in terms of late modernism
- adopting fallibilistic epistemology while resisting the nihilism of post-modernism
- standing on a particular tradition while rejecting subjectivism
- holding on to the gospel as public truth while critiquing the "timeless statements" of modernity
- affirming "committed pluralism" while condemning "agnostic pluralism"
- trusting the power of persuasion while abandoning any notion of the will to power[47]

Calling the church to be "relevant" while declining to explain the gospel in terms of late modernism. For the church to fulfill its mission in any culture, Newbigin argues, it has to be relevant on the one hand, and confront the culture, on the other hand.[48] One of Newbigin's recurring complaints against the church of modern Western culture is its unapologetic and uncritical desire to be only relevant, thus avoiding confrontation. This is the crux of the mistaken contextualization strategy of the church vis-à-vis modernity: the church has completely accommodated itself to the culture of modernity. At the heart of this mistaken strategy is the apologetic defense of the rationality of Christianity to the Enlightenment mind. The only way this strategy of "tactical retreat" may defend the "reasonable" nature of Christian faith is to stick with the standards of the rationality of modernity.[49] But those standards are, of course, not in keeping with the "Christian worldview." Among other deviations from the Christian view, those standards operate with the fatal split between values and facts, as explained above.

The reason the church of modernity attempts to accommodate itself to the strictures of the Enlightenment is the need to be "relevant." The church that is

[47]Space precludes consideration of the proposals of van Huyssteen and Shults for a postfoundational theology. Such are apt, inasmuch as the reconstructions of Newbigin's polarities—with the proposed responses—hold remarkable parallels to both van Huyssteen and Shults. Cf. J. Wentzel van Huyssteen, *Essays in Postfoundationalist Theology* (Grand Rapids: Eerdmans, 1997), and F. LeRon Shults, *The Postfoundationalist Task of Theology: Wolfhart Pannenberg and the New Theological Rationality* (Grand Rapids: Eerdmans, 1999).

[48]Newbigin, *The Other Side of 1984*, p. 55.

[49]Newbigin, *GPS*, p. 3; *Proper Confidence*, p. 93.

being pushed into the margins of the society feels it needs to be acknowledged, responding by catering to "values," while science, politics and the rest of the public arena take care of facts. Consequently, the church purports to influence choices in the private area alone and shies away from any attempt to present the gospel as any kind of "universal truth."[50] In modern theology this move away from the idea of the gospel as public truth to the catering of personal values was aided and guided by liberal theology, under the tutelage of Schleiermacher and others, which finally led to the "anthropologization" of theology.[51] When the statements of theology are noncognitive descriptions of religious "feelings" rather than "personal knowledge" with "universal intention"—to use Newbigin's key phrases borrowed from Polanyi—an attitude of "timidity" follows.[52]

Now, someone may ask why we are rehearsing this familiar Newbigin critique, the target of which is modernism rather than postmodernism, the topic under discussion. The reason is what we argued above, namely, that because in Newbigin's diagnosis postmodernism is but an offshoot from modernity, the church's response to postmodernism can only be reconstructed from the initial reaction to modernity.

Similar to the culture of modernity, we argue on behalf of Newbigin, the culture of postmodernity is willing to tolerate the church as long as it "behaves" according to the rules. As shown above, both cultures operate with the same distinction between values and facts. The difference is this: while the culture of modernity really believed that there are facts—and thus indubitable certainty—to be distinguished from personal, noncognitive values, postmodernism regards both "facts" and "values" as personal opinions.

The end result with regard to the church's mission, however, is the same: in this transitional period of time the church is tolerated only if it suffices to be "relevant" under the rules now of late modernity with its idea of "regimes of truths," none of which is better or worse off and none of which has any right whatsoever to consider other "truths" as less valuable or less "true." For the church now to succumb to the temptation of being silent about the gospel as public truth would, in Newbigin's opinion, just repeat the same old mistake of the church of modernity.

---

[50]Newbigin, *Foolishness to the Greeks*, p. 19; *GPS*, p. 2.

[51]Newbigin, *Foolishness to the Greeks*, pp. 40-41, 45.

[52]Newbigin, *Truth and Authority*, p. 81.

As an alternative—again following Newbigin's program for the church that wants to recover from the Babylonian captivity of modernity—there has to be a new initiative to question the basic beliefs of postmodern culture.[53] This means a shift from explaining the gospel in terms of the postmodern worldview with its denial of any kind of "universal truth" to explaining the postmodern worldview in terms of the gospel.[54] This bold initiative means nothing less than confronting the "revolution of expectations" in the postmodern world.[55] Similar to the call to the church facing the forces of modernity, Newbigin would call the church of this transitional period to the "conversion of the mind," not only of the "soul." The reason is simply that there is a radical discontinuity between the gospel and the beliefs of both modernity and late modernity.[56]

Interestingly enough, Newbigin compares his own view of the Bible and revelation to that of the liberation theologies. The basic purpose of liberationists is not to explain the text but rather to understand the world in light of the Bible. Liberationists resist the idea of the Bible student being a neutral, noncommitted outsider.[57] Newbigin's theological hero St. Augustine is also commended in this regard. Augustine was the first "postcritical" theologian and philosopher who subjected the prevailing culture, Greek rationalism—which was falling apart—to biblical critique. Rather than living in nostalgia, the Christian church should learn from Augustine a bold and unabashed approach to culture by taking the biblical message as an alternative worldview.[58] Only this kind of bold initiative would help the church balance the dual need to be relevant and to be faithful. How that may happen is the focus of the continuing discussion here.

Adopting fallibilistic epistemology while resisting the nihilism of postmodernism. A tempting way for the church to question late modernity's lack of confidence in knowledge would be simply to adopt an opposite standpoint of affirming the modernist program of indubitable certainty. However,

[53]Cf. Newbigin, *The Other Side of 1984*, p. 55 (which of course speaks of an initiative in relation to the culture of modernity).

[54]Cf. Newbigin, *Foolishness to the Greeks*, p. 22; *GPS*, p. 222 (which, again, speaks of the church in relation to modernity).

[55]Cf. Newbigin, *The Other Side of 1984*, p. 55.

[56]Cf. Newbigin, *GPS*, pp. 9-10.

[57]Ibid., pp. 97-99; Newbigin, *A Word in Season*, p. 111.

[58]Newbigin, *The Other Side of 1984*, p. 24.

this is not the way the bishop wants the church to perceive its role in this transitional period. Rather, in a surprising move he seems to be echoing some of the key concerns of postmodern epistemology by affirming a fallibilistic epistemology. Indeed, says the bishop: "We have to abandon the idea that there is available to us or any other human beings the sort of certitude that Descartes wanted to provide and that the scientific part of our culture has sometimes claimed to offer."[59] Here there is a link with postmodern orientations, and Newbigin is happy to acknowledge it:

> We accept the post-modernist position that all human reasoning is socially, culturally, historically embodied. We have left behind the illusion that there is available some kind of neutral stand-point from which one can judge the different stories and decide which is true. The "Age of Reason" supposed that there is available to human beings a kind of indubitable knowledge, capable of being grasped by all human beings which was more reliable than any alleged revelation, and which could therefore provide the criteria by which any alleged divine revelation could be assessed. This immensely powerful hang-over from the "modernist" position still haunts many discussions of religious pluralism. . . . But in a post-modernist context all this is swept away.[60]

Part of the situatedness of knowledge is to acknowledge—in the British bishop's case—its Eurocentric nature: "My proposal will, I know, be criticised as Euro-centric, but this must be rejected. We cannot disown our responsibility as Europeans within the whole evangelical fellowship. It is simply a fact that it is ideas and practices developed in Europe over the past three centuries which now dominate the world, for good and for ill."[61] That said, Newbigin of course also calls himself and other Europeans to take another look at how that legacy has been passed on with regard to other cultures; the acknowledgment of the situatedness of knowledge and preaching the gospel does not save Europeans from collaborating with their "brothers and sisters in the 'Third World' [in] the task of recovering the

[59]Newbigin, *GPS*, p. 35.

[60]Newbigin, "Religious Pluralism," p. 233.

[61]Lesslie Newbigin, "Gospel and Culture," audio recording of an address given to a conference organized by the Danish Missions Council and the Danish Churches Ecumenical Council in Denmark on November 3, 1995. Transcript available at www.newbigin.net/searches/detail.cfm?ID=1491, p. 8.

gospel in its integrity from its false entanglement with European culture, and so seek together to find the true path of inculturation."[62]

Because of the socially and locationally conditioned nature of human knowledge, Newbigin condemns any form of fundamentalism, a mistaken approach to revelation and the Bible in its search for an indubitable certainty by appealing to "evidence" to prove the Bible.[63]

If the Scylla of modernity is the illusion of indubitable certainty, the Charybdis of postmodernism is the lack of confidence in anything certain. As implied above, the way from the search of indubitable certainty to virtual epistemological nihilism goes via the way of doubt. The built-in self-contradiction of the Cartesian program is the necessity of doubt as the way to certainty. This "hermeneutics of suspicion," when taken to its logical end, of course leads to the doubting of everything—in other words, the dismantling of all certainty. At the end of this road, as explained above, there is the Nietzschean nihilism. This would close all doors to affirming the gospel as public truth.

Unlike both modernity and postmodernism, Newbigin—in keeping with Augustine's dictum *credo ut intelligam*—considers belief as the beginning of knowledge. Both Descartes and Nietzsche would disagree. Belief as the beginning of knowledge does not mean leaving behind critique and doubt. Rather, it means that doubt and critique are put in a perspective.[64] Even doubt entails some assumptions; the doubter begins with something else, a "tradition," an idea Newbigin borrows from Alasdair MacIntyre.[65] "But the questioning, if it is to be rational, has to rely on other fundamental assumptions which can in turn be questioned."[66] Briefly put, certainty unrelated to faith is simply an impossible and unwarranted goal.[67] Newbigin makes the

---

[62]Ibid.

[63]Newbigin finds many faults in fundamentalist Bible interpretation: (1) "It is difficult to maintain without a kind of split personality if one is going to live an active life in the modern world." (2) "Those who hold this position are themselves part of the modern world; consequently, when they say that the Bible is factually accurate, they are working with a whole context of meaning, within a concept of factuality that is foreign to the Bible." (3) In the final analysis, to "prove" the Bible, fundamentalists must appeal to experience, the experience of the church concerning the Bible; if so, then fundamentalists have succumbed to the same trap as liberalism, their archenemy. *Foolishness to the Greeks*, p. 46; cf. *GPS*, pp. 42-43, 49; *Proper Confidence*, pp. 85-86.

[64]Newbigin, *GPS*, p. 19.

[65]Ibid., p. 82.

[66]Newbigin, *Proper Confidence*, p. 50.

[67]Newbigin, *GPS*, p. 28; see also pp. 4-5.

delightful remark that both faith and doubt can be either honest or blind; it is not always the case that faith is blind while doubt is honest. One can also envision honest faith and blind doubt.[68]

While the Christian tradition represents confidence and "fullness of truth" promised by Jesus, the Christian concept of truth is not an "illusion" that "imagine[s] that there can be available to us a kind of certainty that does not involve . . . personal commitment," for the simple reason that the "supreme reality is a personal God." Thus, those who "claim infallible certainty about God in their own right on the strength of their rational powers" are mistaken. Bishop Newbigin reminds us that in interpersonal relationships we would never claim that![69]

As an alternative and cure for both the modernist illusion of indubitable certainty and the postmodern lapse into nihilism, Newbigin presents his own view of human knowledge as "personal knowledge." It is borrowed from Polanyi, who negotiated between Cartesian certainty and pure subjectivism. Personal knowledge

> is neither subjective nor objective. In so far as the personal submits to requirements acknowledged by itself as independent of itself, it is not subjective; but in so far as it is an action guided by individual passion, it is not objective either. It transcends the disjunction between subjective and objective.[70]

Polanyi's concept of personal knowledge serves Newbigin well in that it fits in with his view of reality as personal, as mentioned above. The "object" of Christian knowledge is not a "thing" but rather "who," a person, the incarnated Lord.[71] Being personal means that this kind of knowledge entails a risk, it is "risky business."[72] It is "subjective in that it is I who know, or seek to know, and that the enterprise of knowing is one which requires my personal commitment. . . . And it is subjective in that, in the end, I have to take personal responsibility for my beliefs."[73] Yet this kind of knowledge is not subjective because, again borrowing from Polanyi, it has a "universal in-

---

[68]Newbigin, *Proper Confidence*, p. 24; Newbigin, *Truth and Authority*, p. 7.
[69]Newbigin, *Proper Confidence*, p. 67.
[70]Michael Polanyi, *Personal Knowledge: Towards a Post-Critical Philosophy* (Chicago: University of Chicago Press, 1958), p. 300; see, e.g., Newbigin, *GPS*, pp. 51-52, 54-55.
[71]Newbigin, *Proper Confidence*, p. 67.
[72]Newbigin, *GPS*, p. 35.
[73]Ibid., p. 23.

tention." It is meant to be shared, critiqued, tested and perhaps even corrected. It engages and does not remain only my own insight. It is not only "true for me."[74] Thus, to repeat what was mentioned above, doubt and critique should not be abandoned; rather they should be put in perspective as secondary to faith.[75] Only this kind of epistemology might offer for a church that lives under the forces of modernity and postmodernism an opportunity to attain proper confidence.

Standing on a particular tradition while rejecting subjectivism. While half of contemporary Western culture still lives under the illusion of the possibility of indubitable certainty, the other half, the late-modern one, "has lapsed into subjectivism," which is the "tragic legacy of Descartes' proposal" and, even more ironically, the half into which theology usually falls.[76] Modernity, on the one hand, denies the whole concept of tradition in its alleged neutral standpoint. The Cartesian method mistakenly believes itself to be tradition-free. Postmodernism enthusiastically affirms traditions, "regimes of truth," happily existing side by side. No one tradition is better or worse, and no one tradition has the right to impose its own rationality on the others.[77] The implications for the church's mission are obvious. For the modern hearer of the gospel, any appeal to a particular tradition is an anathema and a step away from the alleged neutral, tradition-free search for certainty. For the postmodern hearer, the gospel is *a* good news but not *the* good news.

The way out of this dilemma for the bishop is to take a lesson from both Polanyi and the ethicist-philosopher Alasdair MacIntyre and speak robustly of the need to stand on a particular tradition.[78] The necessity of acknowledging the tradition-laden nature of all human knowledge is based on the shared postmodern conviction, nurtured by contemporary sociology of knowledge, according to which all knowledge is socially and thus contextually shaped. "There is no rationality except a socially embodied

[74]Ibid., p. 33.

[75]Newbigin, *Proper Confidence*, pp. 48, 105; Newbigin, *The Other Side of 1984*, p. 20; Newbigin, *GPS*, p. 20.

[76]Newbigin, *GPS*, p. 35.

[77]Newbigin, *A Word in Season*, p. 187.

[78]Newbigin also refers at times to the well-known philosopher of science Thomas Kuhn (*The Structure of Scientific Revolutions* [Chicago: University of Chicago Press, 1970]), who spoke of dramatic turning points in the development of science when new paradigms emerge and transform not only the methods and results but also the whole way of thinking scientifically; cf. *A Word in Season*, pp. 91-92.

rationality."[79] Any knowledge is rooted in and emerges out of a particular context, location, situation. The bishop boldly accepts that all truth is socially and historically embodied and thus aligns himself with a leading postmodern idea. Another ally here is, as mentioned, Alasdair MacIntyre:

> [The] idea that there can be a kind of reason that is supra-cultural and that would enable us to view all the culturally conditioned traditions of rationality from a standpoint above them all is one of the illusions of our contemporary culture. All rationality is socially embodied, developed in human tradition and using some human language. The fact that biblical thought shares this with all other forms of human thought in no way disqualifies it from providing the needed center.[80]

The situational nature of human knowledge means that knowing can only happen from within tradition. This state of affairs, however, does not mean that therefore no one can claim to speak truth. Indeed, to "pretend to *possess* the truth in its fullness is arrogance," whereas the "claim to have been given the decisive clue for the human search after truth is not arrogant; it is the exercise of our responsibility as part of the human family."[81] This seeking after the truth happens first and foremost in the Christian community. Whereas modernity focuses on the individual person's knowledge, Christian rationality—in this regard, aligning with the ethos of postmodernism—believes in a communally received knowledge, even when the act of knowing is personal, as explained above. "It would contradict the whole message of the Bible itself if one were to speak of the book apart from the church, the community shaped by the story that the book tells."[82]

For Newbigin, the church is a truth-seeking community that seeks to understand reality from its own vantage point. Relying on Polanyi, Newbigin claims that there is a certain kind of correspondence between the Christian and scientific community as both build on "tradition" and "authority." Even new investigations happen on the basis of and in critical dialogue with accumulated tradition, represented by scholars who are regarded

---

[79]Newbigin, *GPS*, p. 87.

[80]Newbigin, "Religious Pluralism and the Uniqueness of Jesus Christ," p. 50; cf. p. 52; the reference is to Alasdair MacIntyre, *Whose Justice, What Rationality?* (London: Duckworth, 1988).

[81]Newbigin, "Religious Pluralism and the Uniqueness of Jesus Christ," p. 54.

[82]Newbigin, *Proper Confidence*, p. 53.

as authoritative. For the Christian church this tradition is the narrative story of the gospel confessed by all Christians:

> The Christian community, the universal Church, embracing more and more fully all the cultural traditions of humankind, is called to be that community in which tradition of rational discourse is developed which leads to a true understanding of reality; because it takes as its starting point and as its permanent criterion of truth the self-revelation of God in Jesus Christ. It is necessarily a particular community, among all the human communities. . . . But it has a universal mission, for it is the community chosen and sent by God for this purpose. This particularity, however scandalous it may seem to a certain kind of cosmopolitan mind, is inescapable.[83]

There is always the danger of domestication of the tradition or, as in postmodernism, its reduction into *a* story among other equal stories—that, in Newbigin's mind, would lead to pluralism and denial of the particularity of the gospel. The gospel can be protected from this kind of domestication, he believes. "The truth is that the gospel escapes domestication, retains its proper strangeness, its power to question us, only when we are faithful to its universal, supranational, supracultural nature."[84] By making universal truth claims, Christian faith coexists with other traditions and their claims to truth.[85] Out of the framework of the gospel narrative, Christian tradition, the church seeks to understand reality—rather than vice versa.[86]

As mentioned before, rather than explaining the gospel through the lens of postmodern culture—or modern culture for that matter—this missional ecclesiology seeks to explain the world through the lens of the gospel. Here there is of course a link with the thinking of George Lindbeck and postliberal thought. Dissatisfied with both the fundamentalistic "Propositional Model" of revelation and the liberal "Experiential Model," Lindbeck suggests an alternative that he calls the "Cultural Linguistic Model." That model sees Christian claims and doctrines as "rules" that govern our way of speaking not only of faith but also of the world. While sympathetic to postliberalism's

---

[83]Newbigin, *GPS*, pp. 87-88.

[84]Lesslie Newbigin, "The Enduring Validity of Cross-Cultural Mission," *International Bulletin of Missionary Research* 12 (1988): 50.

[85]Newbigin, *GPS*, p. 64; Newbigin, *Truth and Authority*, p. 52.

[86]Newbigin, *GPS*, p. 53.

insight,[87] Newbigin still considers Christian doctrines, based as they are on the dynamic narrative of the Bible, as historically factual and thus in some sense "propositional." For Newbigin, the crux of the matter is to raise the question "Which is the *real* story?"[88]

The insistence on the factual basis, not only the "linguistic," of the Christian narrative is essential to Newbigin as he willingly admits the "confessional" nature of his starting point. This confessional standpoint, however, in his opinion is no affirmation of fideism or subjectivism, AKA postmodernism:

> I am, of course, aware that this position will be challenged. It will be seen as arbitrary and irrational. It may be dismissed as "fideism," or as a blind "leap of faith." But these charges have to be thrown back at those who make them. Every claim to show grounds for believing the gospel which lie outside the gospel itself can be shown to rest ultimately on faith-commitments which can be questioned. There is, indeed, a very proper exercise of reason in showing the coherence which is found in the whole of human experience when it is illuminated by the gospel, but this is to be distinguished from the supposition that there are grounds for ultimate confidence more reliable than those furnished in God's revelation of himself in Jesus Christ, grounds on which, therefore, one may affirm the reliability of Christian belief. The final authority for the Christian faith is the self-revelation of God in Jesus Christ.[89]

This clinging to the historical event of Jesus Christ takes us to the heart of his desire to defend the gospel as public truth.

Holding on to the gospel as public truth while critiquing the "timeless statements" of modernity. The church in this transitional period finds itself faced with a twofold challenge in regard to its mission: on the one hand, there is the modernist search for indubitable certainty and on the other hand, the nihilism of postmodernism. At least this is the way Newbigin paints the picture.

In order to continue reconstructing the proper response to such a transitional era, a brief summary of our findings so far is in order. First, while the church seeks to be relevant, it has to resist the temptation to accommodate itself to the strictures of the existing culture. Second, this can be

---

[87]E.g., Newbigin, *GPS*, pp. 24-25; Newbigin, *A Word in Season*, pp. 83-84.

[88]Newbigin, *A Word in Season*, p. 85 (emphasis added). Shults has elucidated, among other things, the crypto-foundationalism of Lindbeck. Shults, *Postfoundationalist Task of Theology*, pp. 52-55.

[89]Newbigin, "Religious Pluralism," p. 236.

done best on the basis of committed, personal knowledge, which avoids the trap of the nihilism of postmodernism and the illusion of modernity. It is knowledge with the aim to be shared with the rest of creation. Third, this kind of committed, "proper confidence" can only be had from within a particular tradition. This tradition-driven knowledge is an alternative to the alleged neutral standpoint of modernity and the subjective, noncommitted, "regimes of truth"–driven view of postmodernism. Christian tradition avoids the dangers of domestication because it is a tradition shared and tested by an international community, and it is based on a universally oriented "true" story of the gospel. Now, this all leads to the affirmation of the gospel as public truth while resisting any notion of the timeless truths of modernity.

Where modernity fails is that it does not acknowledge the social nature of its knowledge. Where postmodernism fails is in its one-sided focus on the socially embodied nature of human knowledge to the point where there is no overarching Story, framework, criterion. All stories exist side by side and everyone is free to choose.

The affirmation of the gospel as public truth is based on the foundation of the unique authority of Christian tradition based on God's self-revelation. That self-revelation happens in secular history,[90] and Christ is the clue.[91] The peculiar nature of the Christian story with regard to its truth claims is the "total fact of Christ."[92] The *factum* nature (from Latin *factum est*, "it's done") of Christian claims to truth in Christ has to do with history.[93] While the Christ-event is part of salvific history, it is also an event in universal history. Therefore, the subjectivist interpretation of existentialism, according to which the events of salvation history such as the resurrection only "happened to me," is a totally mistaken view. The Christian gospel is story, narrative, but is more than that: "Christian doctrine is a form of rational discourse."[94] Having occurred in history, its claims are subject to historical scrutiny. The historicity of the Christian story,

[90]Chapter eight in *GPS* is titled "The Bible as Universal History." This view of course resonates with Wolfhart Pannenberg's view of revelation as history. For some reason, Newbigin does not engage this Lutheran theologian's ideas, even though many of them, including the historicity of the resurrection and the importance of eschatology, are obvious common points.

[91]Chapter nine in *GPS* is titled "Christ, the Clue to History."

[92]Newbigin, *GPS*, p. 5.

[93]Lesslie Newbigin, *The Open Secret: An Introduction to the Theology of Mission*, rev. ed. (Grand Rapids: Eerdmans, 1995 [orig. 1978]), pp. 50-52.

[94]Newbigin, *Truth and Authority*, p. 52.

then, is the reason why "its starting point [is] is not any alleged self-evident truth. Its starting point is events in which God made himself known to men and women in particular circumstances." In a sense, the argument is thus circular: the church interprets God's actions in history as God's actions yet regards them as happening in history. But, says the bishop, the same principle applies to science too, which is, in this sense, circular in its reasoning.[95]

If the historical nature of the Christian tradition is the safeguard against the charge of the modernist self-evidence of truth, the historical and thus factual nature also marks it off from the postmodern view with no interest in the historical basis. Christian rationality necessarily has to raise the question of its "objective" basis:

> The central question is not "How shall I be saved?" but "How shall I glorify God by understanding, loving, and doing God's will—here and now in this earthly life?" To answer that question I must insistently ask: "How and where is God's purpose for the whole of creation and the human family made visible and credible?" That is the question about the truth—objective truth—which is true whether or not it coincides with my "values." And I know of no place in the public history of the world where the dark mystery of human life is illuminated, and the dark power of all that denies human well-being is met and measured and mastered, except in those events that have their focus in what happened "under Pontius Pilate."[96]

In other words, with all his insistence on the socially embodied nature of human knowledge and its tradition-driven nature, Newbigin is not willing to succumb to the postmodern temptation of leaving behind the "facts." True, against the modernists Newbigin claims the risky, "personal" nature of human knowledge, but at the same time, against postmodernists he sets forth the argument for the historical and factual nature of key Christian claims. This is no easy middle way but rather a radical middle!

Affirming "committed pluralism" while condemning "agnostic pluralism." In light of the fact that for Newbigin *pluralism* is a virtual synonym for late modernity, as observed above, it is surprising that he is not willing to abandon the concept altogether. Rather, to paraphrase MacIntyre, he is raising the all-important question, Whose pluralism? Which pluralism? The bishop is against

---

[95]Newbigin, *GPS*, p. 63.

[96]Newbigin, "Religious Pluralism and the Uniqueness of Jesus Christ," p. 54.

that kind of pluralistic ethos of contemporary Western society in which no truth can be considered truth, an ideology of parallel and equal "regimes of truth" without any criteria or parameters. In his opinion, this kind of pluralism is based on the fatal distinction between facts and values. Whereas in the area of values no criteria exist, in the domain of facts, mutually assumed criteria can still be applied quite similarly to the ethos of modernity. In other words, while, say, a scientist as a private person may have no right to argue for the supremacy of his personal values, as a *scientist*, however, she is supposed to stick with the rules of the game. In medicine, physics and chemistry there is no "wild west" of pluralism; some claims and results are considered to be true, while others false. "No society is totally pluralist."[97] As mentioned above, this "heretical imperative" is highly selective.

A significant contribution to the discussion comes from Newbigin's distinction between two kinds of pluralism, one desired, the other one to be rejected, namely, "committed pluralism" and "agnostic pluralism." He defines agnostic—sometimes also called anarchic—pluralism in this way:

> [I]t is assumed that ultimate truth is unknowable and that there are therefore no criteria by which different beliefs and different patterns of behavior may be judged. In this situation one belief is as good as another and one lifestyle is as good as another. No judgments are to be made, for there are no given criteria, no truth by which error could be recognized. There is to be no discrimination between better and worse.[98]

In other words, this is the pluralism stemming from the failure of the modernist program in delivering its main product, indubitable certainty. The latter type of pluralism, committed pluralism, is an alternative to the former. The best way to illustrate its nature is again to refer to the way the scientific community functions. That community is "pluralist in the sense that is it not controlled or directed from one center. Scientists are free to pursue their own investigations and to develop their own lines of research." This type of pluralism is committed to the search of the truth following mutually established guidelines and operating "from within the tradition." It takes into consideration the authority of tradition while maintaining the freedom to

---

[97]Newbigin, *A Word in Season*, p. 158.
[98]Ibid., p. 168.

pursue new ways of understanding the reality and truth.[99] In order for the church to come to such a place, it has to appreciate its tradition in a way similar to the scientific community.[100]

In a pluralist society of late modernity, says the bishop, "There are only stories, and the Christian story is one among them."[101] The attitude of committed pluralism drives the church to dialogue with other traditions and modes of rationalities. If the church believes it is a witness to—if not the possessor of—the gospel as public truth, the "logic of mission"[102] pushes the church out of its comfort zone to share the gospel. While the gospel truth does not arise out of the dialogue, it calls for a dialogue with a specific goal in mind, namely to present the gospel faithfully and authentically:

> [T]he message of Christianity is essentially a story, report of things which have happened. At its heart is the statement that "the word was made flesh." This is a statement of a fact of history which the original evangelists are careful to locate exactly within the continuum of recorded human history. A fact of history does not arise out of a dialogue; it has to be unilaterally reported by those who, as witnesses, can truly report of things which have happened. Of course there will then be dialogue about the way in which what has happened is to be understood, how it is to be related to other things which we know, or think that we know. The story itself does not arise out of dialogue; it simply has to be told.[103]

This Christian view of dialogue thus differs radically from the understanding of dialogue under the influence of agnostic pluralism. For that mindset, "Dialogue is seen not as a means of coming nearer to the truth but as a way of life in which different truth-claims no longer conflict with one another but seek friendly co-existence." That kind of model of dialogue bluntly rejects any kind of "instrumental" view of dialogue as a means to try to persuade. It only speaks of "the dialogue of cultures and of dialogue as a celebration of the rich variety of human life. Religious communities are not regarded as bearers of truth-claims. There is no talk about evangelization and conversion."[104]

---

[99]Ibid., pp. 168-69.
[100]Ibid., p. 170.
[101]Newbigin, "Religious Pluralism," p. 233.
[102]"Logic of Mission" is the title of chapter ten in *GPS*.
[103]Newbigin, "Religious Pluralism," p. 233.
[104]Ibid., p. 240.

Since for the Christian, church dialogue is not an alternative to evangelization, one has to think carefully of how the attempt to persuade with the power of the gospel may best happen in late modernity.

Trusting the power of persuasion while abandoning any notion of the will to power. In late modernity, any hint of the old Christendom way of resorting to political power as a means of furthering a religious cause is a red flag. Bishop Newbigin was the first one to condemn any such attempt on the church's part: "I have argued that a claim that the Christian faith must be affirmed as a public truth does not mean a demand for a return to 'Christendom' or to some kind of theocracy. It does not mean that the coercive power of the state and its institutions should be at the service of the Church."[105]

The suspicion of the will to power in late modernity, however, is deeper and more subtle than the fear of the church's political power. The postmodern suspicion has to do with the church's desire to confront epistemology that has lost all criteria in negotiating between true and false. Therefore, postmodernists argue, "There is to be no discrimination between better and worse. All beliefs and lifestyles are to be equally respected. To make judgments is, on this view, *an exercise of power* and is therefore oppressive and demeaning to human dignity. The 'normal' replaces the 'normative.'"[106] It is here where the church, rather than succumbing to the mindset of agnostic pluralism, should confront the people of late modernity with the offer of the gospel as public truth. While there is no way for the church faithful to its mission to avoid this confrontation, the church should also do everything in its power to cast off any sign of the will to power.

In Newbigin's vision, the church is a pilgrim people, on the way, and thus does not claim the fullness of truth on this side of the eschaton, it only testifies to it and seeks to understand it more appropriately.[107] Even the

---

[105]Newbigin, *A Word in Season*, p. 170. Newbigin notes in another context how ironic it is that the introduction by the West of ideas, science, technology and such products of "development" were for the most part not considered as the "will to power" in the Third World. Rather, they were welcomed and embraced. Ibid., pp. 122-23.

[106]Ibid., p. 168.

[107]Newbigin at times calls the witnesses "seekers of the truth" and commends the apophatic tradition of Christian theology for its acknowledgment that "no human image or concept can grasp the reality of God." *GPS*, p. 12.

Christian witness waits for the final eschatological verification of the truth of the gospel.[108] Such a witness does not resort to any earthly power, rather he or she only trusts the power of the persuasion of the truth.

Consequently, time after time, the bishop recommends to the church an attitude of humility and respect for others. While witnesses, Christians are also "learners."[109] The church does not possess the truth but rather testifies to it, carries it on as a truth-seeking community and tradition.[110]

The refusal of the will to power goes even deeper than that of the cultivation of a humble and respectful attitude toward others. It grows from the center of the gospel truth as it is based on the cross of the Savior:

> What is unique in the Christian story is that the cross and resurrection of Jesus are at its heart. Taken together (as they must always be) they are the public affirmation of the fact that God rules, but that his rule is (in this age) hidden; that the ultimate union of truth with power lies beyond history, but can yet be declared and portrayed within history. The fact that the crucifixion of the Incarnate Lord stands at the centre of the Christian story ought to have made it forever impossible that the Christian story should have been made into a validation of imperial power. Any exposition of a missionary approach to religious pluralism must include the penitent acknowledgement that the Church has been guilty of contradicting its own gospel by using it as an instrument of imperial power.[111]

In other words, any attempt to usurp power means nothing less than a perversion of the message of the gospel.

In Lieu of Conclusion: Seedthought for Further Reflections

It seems to us it is in keeping with Lesslie Newbigin's evolving and dynamic way of thinking that no "closing chapter" be offered to the reflections on the mission and life of the church in the transitional era between modernity and postmodernism. More helpful is to reflect on some tasks and questions for the future and map out some remaining areas of interest.

---

[108]Ibid., pp. 53-54.

[109]Ibid., pp. 34-35.

[110]Ibid., p. 12.

[111]Newbigin, "Religious Pluralism," p. 234.

We first return to our methodological musings in the beginning of the essay. Again, in this context we are not concerned about methodology primarily for the sake of academic competence; rather, our interest in it has everything to do with the material presentation of Newbigin's missional ecclesiology and epistemology. We argued that rather than tabulating references to postmodernism in Newbigin's writings, nor even looking primarily at those passages that may have a more or less direct reference to postmodernism, a more helpful way of proceeding would be to take lessons from his response to modernity, particularly with regard to the transitional period when the church lives under two modes of rationalities. This kind of methodology seemed to be viable in light of Newbigin's conviction that postmodernism is parasitic on modernity. If our methodology is appropriate and does justice to Newbigin's own approach, then it means that his writings on missional ecclesiology and cultural critique continue to have their relevance even if the shift to postmodernism will intensify in the future.[112]

If our hunch is correct, then a main task for the church of the West at this period of time is to pay attention to the nature of the transition. We do not believe that we live in a culture in which modernity has given way to postmodernism. Rather, we regard Newbigin's insight that what makes the end of the twentieth and the beginning of the twenty-first century unique culturally is the process of transition. Modernity is alive and well not only in the West but also in the global South. At the same time, as a result of the massive critique of and disappointment with it, there is an intensifying desire to cast off the reins of modernity. However, that distancing from the Enlightenment heritage does not mean leaving behind its influence; rather, it is a continual reassessment of modernity as we continue living under its massive influence. To repeat: it is the transition that makes our time unique. To that dynamic Bishop Newbigin's thinking speaks loud and clear.

We have mentioned in our discussion several movements of thought and thinkers to which Newbigin either gives a direct reference, such as Lindbeck and postliberalism, or clearly has some affinity, such as Reformed episte-

[112]Our own growing conviction is that, similarly to modernity, postmodernity has such built-in contradistinctions in its texture that it may not survive for a long time. Its contribution has been mainly deconstructive: it has helped the culture of the West to wake up from the modernist slumber. What becomes "post" this, we are not yet sure.

mology or, say, Stanley Hauerwas. It would be a worthwhile exercise to reflect on similarities and differences between the Reformed epistemology of Alvin Plantinga and others who maintain that Christian faith should unabashedly adopt God as the "foundation" rather than trying to look somewhere else.[113] Similarly the Hauerwasian connection with its idea of the church as a unique "colony" and thus unique way of understanding reality would make a helpful contribution to our thinking of missional ecclesiology. When it comes to postliberalism, it seems to us that Newbigin's sympathies—even with some critical notes—might have been a bit misplaced. We have a hard time in imagining a *postliberal* advocate of the gospel as public truth!

We are not mentioning these tasks for further study primarily to advance academic inquiry but rather out of our desire to better understand the scope and location of Newbigin's missional ecclesiology in the larger matrix of contemporary thinking. Is it the case that Newbigin's missional ecclesiology and epistemology represent a movement sui generis, or is it rather that—like any creative and constructive thinker—he has listened carefully to a number of contemporary voices and echoes their motifs in a fresh way?

---

[113]Keskitalo (*Kristillinen usko*, pp. 167-72) offers an insightful excursus on the topic; unfortunately, it is not accessible for English readers.

5

Holistic Theological Method and Theological Epistemology

Performing Newbigin's Plurality of Sources in the Pluralist Context

Steven B. Sherman

There is good reason for using the term *holistic* as a descriptor for Lesslie Newbigin's theological method and theological epistemology—the bishop's work and life personifies such. This chapter focuses on these two central aspects of Newbigin's theological commitments: methodology and epistemology. We begin with consideration of Newbigin's characteristically holistic approach to theology, and then examine several features of Newbigin's broad-ranging theological epistemology. Finally, we present briefly some potential ways forward in "performing his play" in the pluralist context.[1]

Newbigin's Theological Method

Newbigin uses multiple sources and authorities that provide warrant for his convictions. While a full analysis of his theological method is beyond the scope of this chapter, we will sketch its contours along three trajectories: faith seeking understanding; missional, confessional and contextual; and trinitarianism and christocentrism.

[1]Some of the material in the first part of this chapter has been adapted from my book, *Revitalizing Theological Epistemology: Holistic Evangelical Approaches to the Knowledge of God* (Eugene, OR: Pickwick Publications, 2008).

Faith seeking understanding. Any assessment of Lesslie Newbigin's theological method ought to begin with the bishop's own joyful admission that he is first and foremost a pastor.[2] This self-understanding underscores his whole body of work, providing a consistent lens through which to appreciate and assess Newbigin's approach to theology, epistemology, ecclesiology, culture, and so on. It also explains his enduring theological praxis concerns—or, better, faithful theology performances—backed by generally well-informed and substantive theological reflection.[3] Moreover, the exceptional breadth of kingdom service—encompassing multiple occupations, disciplines and contexts—richly contours Newbigin's theological method, which might best be viewed as a robust and holistic *fides quaerens intellectum* approach. For Newbigin, the starting place for theology matters—the locus of confidence being *not* in our own competence in knowing but rather in "the faithfulness and reliability in the one who is known."[4]

Newbigin's missionary years in southern India awakened him to competing philosophical and theological systems that powerfully contested the predominant Eurocentric viewpoint. Alternative worldviews, rather than being "barbaric," were highly systematic and pragmatically viable for particular cultures, which his Enlightenment heritage had inadequately prepared him to effectively engage. He therefore sought an apologetical methodology that would seriously consider different cultural worldviews while preserving an irenic—yet also vigorously evangelical—Christian theology and faith. The way forward encompassed old and new strategies: a return to the ancient Augustinian *credo ut intellegam,* plus a fresh appropriation of Michael Polanyi's "personal participation" philosophy.[5] Together, these approaches provide a legitimate and

---

[2]This claim was reiterated by various Newbigin scholars and other presenters at a recent missiology conference focused on considering Newbigin's *The Gospel in a Pluralist Society* (Grand Rapids: Eerdmans, 1989) twenty-five years after its original publication (Missiology Lectures 2014, "Still Pluralist? Lesslie Newbigin in the 21st Century" [School of Intercultural Studies, Fuller Theological Seminary, Pasadena, California, November 13–15, 2014]).

[3]Among others, Augustine, Karl Barth, Dietrich Bonhoeffer and Hendrik Kraemer appear regularly as highly regarded theological interlocutors throughout the Newbigin corpus.

[4]Lesslie Newbigin, *Proper Confidence: Faith, Doubt, and Certainty in Christian Discipleship* (Grand Rapids: Eerdmans, 1995), pp. 66-67.

[5]Polanyi began his career in the scientific arena but became a philosopher and epistemologist whose writings have influenced multiple disciplines. See his most well-known book, *Personal Knowledge* (Chicago: University of Chicago Press, 1958). I am indebted to Geoffrey Wainwright for his numerous insights into Polanyi's method and influence. Moreover, I will be making use of Wainwright's text throughout this chapter, and it should be understood that when citing or quoting Newbigin from

substantive response to both the resolute empirical scientific method and reason-driven fundamentalism with Gnostic-like tendencies.

Missional, contextual and confessional. Newbigin's integrative theological method infuses key elements of his own life and work, *mission* serving as one center point, grounded most centrally in Christ and within a trinitarian framework. The church has been given a mission of reconciliation, and this is the highest priority. Even theological reflection must be done through the lens of mission, as well as concrete experience. Nevertheless, as Newbigin would clarify on multiple occasions, the church first must be *reconciled to itself*; otherwise, the call of others to reconciliation with God in Christ will go largely unheeded. The household of God must actively seek reconciliation and reunification.[6] Mission, theology, apologetics, ecclesiology, religious dialogue, worship, teaching and preaching are all part of the same larger picture: the Creator's desire for his creatures to know and glorify him as universal Lord, experiencing and growing in reconciliation and wholeness by means of the redemptive work of Jesus Christ on their behalf.

The settings in which Newbigin lived, worked and thought varied significantly—each tangible milieu informing his theological reflection while not calling into question the objective reality of God and the transcendent work of Christ. This variegated situatedness highlights Newbigin's insistence that history and culture affect theological and epistemological views. Thus, theologians bear a divine mandate for authentic living and thinking *within their specific environments.* Perhaps one of Newbigin's most formative contextual-awareness moments came when he stepped back onto British soil after having been away for nearly forty years. Immediately, he felt the culture-shift effects underway in the West. The Enlightenment project had failed to provide the backbone, the values or the utopia anticipated by so many who had trusted in its supposedly objective and "foolproof" system. Consequently, forms of Enlightenment-entangled Christianity were being met with increased intolerance. Questioning all truth and authority claims progressively came to characterize the final decades of

---

Wainwright, much of the material exists in unpublished works or in personal conversations between Wainwright and Newbigin. See his *Lesslie Newbigin: A Theological Life* (Oxford: Oxford University Press, 2000).

[6]Newbigin's years in India provide a rich backdrop and framework for what later would become his classic works in ecclesiology and apologetics.

twentieth-century Britain, as well as most (if not all) of Western Europe. Here was a new era with a new philosophy. How would—or *could*—the gospel be heard again in the new context? Newbigin would become substantially preoccupied with this question throughout his mature years, which deeply informed his theological reflection.

Newbigin's cultural engagement from multiple arenas and ministries makes his already incisive—sometimes even prophetic—observations particularly compelling. Speaking and writing ahead of his time, Newbigin sagaciously comprehends cultural vicissitudes and their outcomes, sometimes years before his contemporaries. He keeps pace with many vital occurrences through a broad compass and quality of reading, demonstrating a widely informed and cross-disciplinary methodology. Numerous authors from various fields and disciplines influence Newbigin's theological outlook.[7] His eagerness to engage diverse philosophies—prompted by a Reformed allegiance to "all truth is God's truth"—ameliorates possible fundamentalist-like concerns over discovering other "truths" undermining the Scriptures. Thus, while maintaining that truth has not been constrained by God to *solely* biblical or theological domains, Newbigin's strong confessional stance remains in agreement with historic Christian dogma. His theological method and theological epistemology reveal deep commitments to both fixed core doctrines of the unchanging gospel *and* a program that authentically (re)presents that gospel in ever-changing contexts.

While no single theological system defines Newbigin's theology, as a Presbyterian he would firmly favor Reformed over Arminian or Anabaptist claims on most matters. Nevertheless, the bishop's far-reaching ecumenical experiences open him to occasionally accepting perspectives not espoused—sometimes rejected—by his denominational tradition.[8] Ultimately, Newbigin's broad experience and deep reading and reflection—including beyond his particular denominational and confessional borderlines—lead him to

[7]For instance, Newbigin fully integrates the thinking of scientist-turned-philosopher Michael Polanyi, which will be discussed shortly.

[8]One example of this involves Newbigin affirming the theological validity of certain charismatic movements. Even as early as 1952 in *The Household of God* (London: SCM Press, 1953), Newbigin shows remarkable openness to Pentecostalism, dedicating a chapter to Pentecostals. Additionally, his involvement with Holy Trinity Brompton in the 1990s helps place Newbigin in greater touch with charismatics.

acquire ways of considering God's character and works different from those generally reflective of his own theological tradition.[9]

Trinitarian and christocentric. Newbigin's forthright commitment to essential, historic Christian doctrines is well documented. The starting point for Newbigin is God's personal revelation in the history of Israel and, finally, in Jesus Christ: *God spoke and acted.* Consequently, his approach comprises a systematic trinitarianism that is both robustly christocentric and—among Reformed-minded theologians—exceptionally open to the work of the Spirit.[10]

Quintessential to Newbigin's theological method is embodying a christomorphic life, theology and epistemology. Rather than unavoidably involving a precritical naiveté, this way calls for a *christocentric* interpretive paradigm—grounded in a robust *trinitarian* framework. Where one stands on this core worldview, Newbigin might say, determines the focal point for theological knowledge—whether reason or faith and revelation. Such opposing outlooks necessitate radically incompatible methodological outcomes for Christian thinkers, setting the agenda for theological epistemology. With this in mind, Newbigin contends that ultimately it is inappropriate for those who have embraced the gospel to rely on other "collateral sources of information" in attempting to know the truth since "the truth surely is not that we come to know God by reasoning from our unredeemed experience but that what God has done for us in Christ gives us the eyes through which we can begin to truly understand our experience in the world."[11]

In sum, Newbigin's approach to theology unites *credo ut intellegam*, missional, contextual, confessional, christocentric and trinitarian elements in providing a robust, holistic theological method.

Theological Epistemology

Not surprisingly, Lesslie Newbigin's theological epistemology follows a pattern similar to his theological method, particularly in terms of being *highly integrative*—in a way that defies precisely defined boundaries and categories. Nonetheless, for reflection and assessment purposes, we will par-

[9]For instance, concerning one's normative spiritual journey and salvation, Newbigin attributes priority to the Christian community rather than to the individual (as will be seen later in this study).

[10]Newbigin was even willing to grant the so-called Toronto Blessing as a work of God's Spirit.

[11]Newbigin, *Proper Confidence*, p. 97.

tition his theological knowledge approach into several major categories, while remaining cognizant of the bishop's characteristically holistic schema.

Postfoundational and holistic. The major methodological shift in the Middle Ages—owing to the rediscovery of Aristotelian thought and its subsequent influence on Christian theology, especially through Aquinas—unfortunately prepared the way for reception of René Descartes's views. Descartes would construct an entirely alternative knowledge foundation—the self—commencing from a standpoint of *doubt* rather than faith, and seeking indubitable certainty over against a growing discord among Christian traditions (*opinio*). His highly influential method essentially reversed Augustine's maxim; the course to knowledge would now begin with doubt rather than faith, dominating practically all of Western thought for three hundred years. However, since the mid-twentieth century, this *scientio*-focused quest has encountered insurmountable problems and is effectively self-destructing.

Seeing the scientific method's fallacy and failure to impart incontrovertible objective knowledge and truth, Newbigin commends a *post*foundationalist approach, viewing all knowing as interconnected with believing and a priori commitments. One must begin with Augustine rather than Aquinas—by *credo ut intelligam*—although without strictly dividing what may be realized by faith and revelation on the one hand, and by reason on the other.[12]

Against the prevailing modernist method that regards reason or experience as singularly authoritative sources for the knowledge of God, Newbigin espouses a *whole-life* outlook, with the interconnectivity of Scripture, tradition and proclamation being essential. Reason and experience are neither disconnected nor uninvolved sources for theological knowledge, but rather *part of the whole* Christian faith and life. Our story and the gospel story must interconnect; through that connecting—by way of Scripture, the community, experiences within the community, the use of reason and apologetics within the community, and the Holy Spirit's work within the community—people come to know God intimately.

Historical, cultural and contextual. Newbigin champions the *particularity of all knowledge* perspective—knowledge as historically, culturally and contextually grounded. This outlook unequivocally challenges the Enlightenment

[12]See Lesslie Newbigin, *Truth and Authority in Modernity* (Valley Forge, PA: Trinity Press International, 1996), pp. 3-4.

idea of a pure objectivity of knowing being potential or actual for human beings, yet without particularity diminishing the gospel's objectivity and universally intended metanarrative. Newbigin consistently eschews *a*historical, *a*contextual, *a*cultural theologies, questioning whether these are theologies at all. Purporting to be "above and beyond" historical-cultural frameworks, pretended "God's eye" points of view are most likely what human minds conceive when utterly reliant on reason, subversively shaping thinkers being molded by their contexts. Thus, Newbigin—in the strongest of terms—rejects Enlightenment rationalism and the scientific method as ostensibly definitive for theological knowledge. He also emphatically denies natural theology, deeming it closer to idolatry than to delivering partial theological knowledge.[13] For Newbigin, extraordinary thinkers like Augustine and Polanyi ought to be effectively used to counter faulty Enlightenment assumptions in a post-Christendom, postmodern world, challenging reductionistic ways of knowing, especially in terms of sources for theological knowledge.

Newbigin's thought also displays a strongly *contextual* emphasis, aware of the indispensable interplay between theological thinking and principled praxis in concrete conditions. Moreover, the bishop understands competing views, seeing their problems and potential remedies, while showing an ability to "'out-narrate' the stories told by those whose ultimate commitments lie elsewhere—for the achievement of the Father's purpose, and so to the glory of the Triune God."[14]

Newbigin's proficiency in effectively engaging in theological reflection and praxis *within diverse communities and contexts* reveals wisdom to be gleaned by contemporary Christian thinkers, which I hope to reflect in part by means of considering his identified sources for theological knowledge.

Revelational and metanarratival. Some of Newbigin's earliest theological writings demonstrate his nascent theological epistemology—perhaps seen most clearly in a paper written during his studies at Cambridge in 1935–1936. Therein, the young scholar understands God's self-revelation as necessary for human knowledge of God, with faith being the reception of revelation; to know God through divine self-disclosure requires a sensitive and trustful response to God's revelation. But in regards to our knowledge being true,

---

[13]See ibid., pp. 18-19.

[14]Wainwright, *Lesslie Newbigin*, p. 230.

Newbigin's focus involves both "inward understanding and valuing" and "a reality external to our minds." Furthermore, inasmuch as that revelation is passed down through historic community, *the church is the location of, and the Bible is an instrument for, reception of the divine self-disclosure.*[15]

Newbigin's claim for the primacy of divine initiative in the process of human knowledge of God suggests an ontological basis: "If the reality that we seek to explore, and of which we are a part, is the work of a personal Creator, then authority resides in this One who is the Author." This is owing to knowledge of a *person* being incumbent on that person's willingness to self-disclose—a view rejected by the Enlightenment concerning God's own authority. And "because personal being can be known only insofar as the person chooses to reveal himself or herself, and cannot be known by methods that are appropriate to the investigation of impersonal matters and processes, then authority, in this view, must rest on divine revelation."[16]

Newbigin sees this divine authority as powerfully evident in the teaching and healing work of Jesus as he "embodied final authority," unlike the scribes who bound themselves to the authority of the Torah. Thus, ultimate authority does not rest with Enlightenment rejection of appeals to revelation and tradition as sources of authority, but rather directly with the revelation-based authority of the personally disclosed Creator—most clearly and finally witnessed in Jesus Christ.[17] Throughout each stage of Newbigin's developing theological epistemology, *Jesus remains central and definitive*. In the Scriptures, the object of faith is sought: Christ and his work, in trinitarian terms.[18] Scripture is where, through the testimony of his first followers, Christ is encountered in his person, words and works: they bear witness to "God's redeeming act once for all at a point in history."[19] With this move, Newbigin opts to follow Barth in disallowing all allegedly authoritative arbitrators of truth set to judge the confessed authority of God's self-revelation. Contributing to this perspective is his general belief in the fiduciary character of all knowledge.

---

[15]Ibid., p. 34.

[16]Newbigin, *Truth and Authority*, pp. 1-2.

[17]Ibid., pp. 2-3.

[18]From Lesslie Newbigin, *The Reunion of the Church*, 2nd rev. ed. (London: SCM Press, 1960), as quoted in Wainwright, *Lesslie Newbigin*, p. 89.

[19]Ibid.

Central to Newbigin's perspective on revelation is commitment to the *gospel metanarrative as ultimate story* concerning the knowledge of God and reality. This narrative orientation contrasts with more proposition-oriented approaches to the biblical text, without denying or downplaying explicit didactic assertions about truth and knowledge within the biblical story and its diverse genres. Moreover, the biblical context as a whole is fundamental in safeguarding against erroneously disconnecting Jesus from the story and in effect rendering him a mythical figure, or construing the whole story apart from the living and authoritative word of God, Jesus.

Newbigin centers on the narrative preeminence encompassing the biblical writings—essentially a story that claims to be *the* story, and which includes the cosmos and human life within it.[20] Against the Cartesian-Newtonian pursuit of "timeless realities governed by eternal laws," which aim for "a total knowledge that leaves no room for either faith or doubt," he works to ground his case for theological knowledge in *the* story—its proclamation and believers' immersion within it.[21] This instrumental use of Scripture involves a looking *through* rather than *at* biblical texts, which calls us "to *indwell* the story, as we indwell the language we use and the culture of which we are a part."[22] Living in the story of the Bible, in company with our own contextual story, compels us to construct "an internal dialogue as the precondition for true interpersonal dialogue."[23] Thereby, we continue growing in theological knowledge, together with relevant reflection and praiseworthy praxis, exercising humble fidelity to the gospel metanarrative while participating in the story in real time. In addition, the story-oriented approach is also highly relevant for the present cultural context.[24]

Personal trust and obedience. Arguably no contemporary thinker has shaped Newbigin's epistemological views more than Michael Polanyi, especially via his monumental tome, *Personal Knowledge*. Polanyi's discernments concerning knowledge within the scientific sphere—with particular applica-

[20]See Newbigin, *Truth and Authority*, pp. 38-39.

[21]Ibid., pp. 80-81.

[22]Ibid., p. 42.

[23]Ibid., pp. 42-43.

[24]It seems evident that most cultures of the world, regardless of the historical context, are story-oriented, and that the primarily Western Enlightenment approach to knowledge more likely represents an anomaly in time than a universal given.

bility to religious and theological realms—has markedly affected the bishop's own understanding. One celebrated Polanyi thesis maintains that all human knowledge is of a fiduciary character, whether the discipline encompasses natural science, psychology or theology. Accordingly, Newbigin recognizes that if all knowledge is of a personal and fiduciary character, then trust is inherent to the process of knowing.[25] At the outset there is the given, comprising the data and the knowing tradition, which contains its language and conceptual method. Knowing encompasses being exposed, mind and senses, to "the great reality which is around us and sustains us." Thus, "in order to be informed, we have to make acts of trust in the traditions we have inherited and in the evidence of our senses."[26]

Therefore, in emphasizing personal commitment, Newbigin merges Polanyi's argument for the fiduciary character of knowing with an effort to recapture the premodern impulse toward trust as central to theological knowledge. This insightful amalgam rejects the impersonal Enlightenment and self-centered authoritative norm for a biblical relatedness orientation, wherein God is central and human personal mutuality (i.e., serving one another) is the rule.[27] Claims of indubitable certainty (*pace* Descartes) altogether fail because knowledge does not reside in the mind of the knower, but rather in the *personal incarnation*. This demonstrates "ultimate reality to be personal in nature, which means that it can only be known by self-revelation on the part of the Creator and by an answering response on the part of the human knower. Such knowledge comes by way of an inseparable trust and obedience toward the call of Christ."[28] As a result, Christian confidence rests squarely in the One who is known and on his trustworthiness, rather than in the competence of one's own knowing; moreover, the knower does not possess perfect knowledge of final truth, but merely is on the path leading toward eschatological luminescence that awaits humanity. Again, trust remains the fundamental element. Neutrality exists solely as a fallacious myth.[29]

---

[25]See Polanyi, *Personal Knowledge*, pp. 266-67, 280-86.

[26]From Newbigin, *Proper Confidence*, pp. 25, 49, 96, as quoted in Wainwright, *Lesslie Newbigin*, p. 49. Unfortunately, none of the pages Wainwright references contains the exact quotation.

[27]Wainwright, *Lesslie Newbigin*, p. 257.

[28]Ibid., p. 50.

[29]For example, see Polanyi, *Personal Knowledge*, pp. 266-67.

Newbigin reflects on the diverse types of knowledge recognized outside modernity's limited ideal that reduce all knowledge to "mathematical formulae" and that undervalue the personal realm while overvaluing impersonal rationalism. For instance, he asserts the Bible presents the central meaning of "to know" in relation to knowing another person, in a trust-centered journey with the other who "discloses his own mind and heart to me."[30]

Ecclesial and communal. Newbigin's church-oriented focus existed decades before certain contemporary evangelical scholars contended for a more ecclesial-centered theology (i.e., theology *for* the church) in place of a prevailing academy-oriented tone. His theological epistemology is intimately linked with the body of Christ as Newbigin is convinced God was made known explicitly *in* Jesus Christ and *to* the church. Moreover, his efforts in uniting the Church in South India have shaped and maintained his church-centric theological reflection. Furthermore, it is the local congregation that Newbigin sees as the dominant location for which "the reality of the new creation is present, known, and experienced," and primarily for the sake of mission.[31]

Throughout the premodern church, disciples of Jesus lived out *immersed participation* in the faith community; knowledge of God via such communities is vital today as well. Thus, the sociology of knowledge model has come to the fore. As previously noted, Newbigin pictures the church as a crucial source for theological knowledge. Applying Polanyi's judgment of knowledge/discoveries located in the sciences, Newbigin stresses that knowledge of God, like all knowing, is permanently part of a tradition—occurring as individuals become learners in an apprenticeship within the Christian heritage, indwelling its language, concepts, models, images and assumptions.[32]

---

[30]Wainwright, *Lesslie Newbigin*, pp. 66-67. Unfortunately, the Newbigin source is not cited.

[31]Newbigin, *GPS*, pp. 232-33.

[32]Newbigin, *Proper Confidence*, p. 46. One important exception to the communitarian-apprenticeship model would be the evident faith commitment made by one of the two thieves on the cross; another would be the numerous testimonies of individuals claiming to have come to saving faith in God through Christ outside of any known Christian communities or influences. Presenting a more nuanced account of the church community/Christian tradition view would likely have alleviated concerns over seemingly unavailable means of grace outside of the normally normative apprenticeship way into theological knowledge.

Drawing on Polanyi again (particularly from *Personal Knowledge*), Newbigin

> shows that all knowledge is a "skill" that has to be learned; that all knowledge is "an activity of persons in community," involving mutual trust and accountability to certain standards; that all knowledge entails at least a provisional commitment to an existing framework of thought and knowledge, but that advances in knowledge occur only when the risk is taken that one may be proved wrong.[33]

Consequently, an individual's vocation as articulated in God's revelation is that of *learner* or *apprentice*—learning how to learn and know. This spirit of apprenticeship calls for connectedness to another or others who know the way: particularly the path to the knowledge of God. In this, Newbigin designates to the faith community (or tradition) a principal and reciprocal role in helping shape the knowledge and worldview of its adherents.[34]

Therefore, as it relates to theological knowledge, the question becomes, who is to be trusted as to knowledge of God claims? In *The Gospel in a Pluralist Society,* Newbigin points to the broad Christian heritage:

> Tradition is not a separate source of revelation from Scripture; it is the continuing activity of the Church through the ages in seeking to grasp and express under new conditions that which is given in Scripture. The study of Scripture takes place within the continuing tradition of interpretation.[35]

In addition, there is a three-way shared relationship between individuals, the written Word and the lived tradition: "it is only by 'indwelling' the Scripture that one remains faithful to the tradition."[36] Devotion of authentic worshipers to the story's Creator is the intended ultimate goal, and immersion in the expressions of worship within the tradition entails genuine learning in community—growing in the grace and knowledge of God, part of the "activity of persons in community" invested in the tradition's worldview. This includes *theologizing in worshipful contexts.* Newbigin sees

---

[33]Wainwright, *Lesslie Newbigin*, pp. 348-49. Internal Newbigin quotations are from Lesslie Newbigin, *Honest Religion for Secular Man* (London: SCM Press, 1966).

[34]See Newbigin, *Truth and Authority*, pp. 12-13.

[35]Newbigin, *GPS*, p. 53.

[36]Newbigin, *Truth and Authority*, p. 49.

worship as the central work of the ecclesia, with everything else in its life having meaning and value only as it focuses on worship.[37]

Moreover, supremely authoritative church practices (i.e., the sacraments of baptism and Communion) are vehicles for theological knowledge where these point *to* Jesus and *through* Jesus to the Trinity. In consequence, obedient faith-community praxis demonstrates human knowledge of God. Concurrently, Newbigin affirms the gospel calls *individuals* to salvific knowledge of God in Christ, while maintaining that growing in the knowledge of God occurs above all as learners within the Christian community context. Both personal and corporate commitment to responsibility and witness are crucial, with the resident congregation functioning as "the local presence of the one holy catholic and apostolic Church that we acknowledge in the creeds."[38] Clearly, theological reflection and praxis must hang together.

Doing justice and mercy, being inclusive and dialogical. Newbigin also declares—from a mission-focused context that included critique of liberation theology (and later, capitalism)—that "to know the Lord" involves performing justice and mercy in concrete situations. He asserts that those who "claim to know the Lord and do evil are deceived." They are far from God since there is "no knowledge of God apart from the love of God, and there is no love of God apart from love of the neighbor."[39] Only the biblical story and the authority of Jesus Christ can rightly determine what are true justice and mercy, not an unchallenged "proletariat praxis," which characterizes the Marxist coercion of much liberation theology. So even while liberation theology may be assessed as closer to the biblical models of salvation and liberation than Enlightenment-driven theology that separates theory from praxis, for those who appear to imply that action itself is the truth, the biblical text functions "as a source of judgment upon the praxis of those who have the Scriptures in their hands."[40] Therefore, the "supreme moral value" is in fact "obedience to the personal calling of Jesus Christ in

---

[37]See Wainwright, *Lesslie Newbigin*, pp. 151, 153. The source of this claim concerning Newbigin's view is not cited, but apparently is the Constitution of the Church of South India (CSI). See also Lesslie Newbigin, *Unfinished Agenda* (Edinburgh: Saint Andrews Press, 1993), pp. 85-87.

[38]From Lesslie Newbigin, *Truth to Tell: The Gospel as Public Truth* (Grand Rapids: Eerdmans, 1991), p. 28, as quoted in Wainwright, *Lesslie Newbigin*, pp. 74-75.

[39]Lesslie Newbigin, *The Open Secret: Sketches for a Missionary Theology* (Grand Rapids: Eerdmans, 1978), p. 109; see also Jer 22:16 and 1 Jn 4:20.

[40]From Newbigin, *Open Secret*, pp. 127-34, as quoted in Wainwright, *Lesslie Newbigin*, p. 188.

and through his community. The ultimate model, in terms of which I am to understand what is the case and what is to be done, is furnished by the biblical story."[41] Newbigin observes the gospel has always inspired acts of justice and mercy (e.g., healing the sick, feeding the hungry, and serving the poor and destitute). The believing community accomplishes God's purposes through these deeds and consequently manifests the knowledge of God in seeking to make visible the prayer, "Thy will be done."[42]

For Newbigin, the pursuit of justice and mercy proceeds dialogically. While the gospel presupposes a bold proclamation of Jesus as the way, the truth and the life, Newbigin charges us to avoid the two extremes of either pessimistic exclusivism or fanciful pluralism, instead embracing *biblical realism*[43]—one of several elucidations within the inclusivist category found in many of his works.[44] This *wideness* perspective envisions knowledge of God extending beyond Christianity's perimeter (as a religion); since Christ is Lord of all, knowledge of God ought to be expected in multiple contexts. Rather than soliciting persons to embrace a religion, the gospel calls to all people, offering God's grace through faith in a person, Jesus Christ.

Thus, while Newbigin emphasizes the importance of Christian (particularly evangelical) engagement in interreligious dialogue, these discussions must commence and conclude with commitment to the gospel—not detached reason—as ultimately authoritative, including the dialogical purpose for Christians involving a witness for Christ in various ways.[45]

Experience and reason. Before my study of Newbigin's theological method and theological epistemology concludes with a modest constructive section focused on performing his play (i.e., practicing his program), I will first venture a brief retrieval and advance of his basic perspective on the role of experience and reason—two primary sources of authority in Enlightenment-oriented epistemology.

Newbigin remains rather unconvinced with regard to experience serving

---

[41]From Newbigin, *Open Secret*, pp. 123-34, as quoted in Wainwright, *Lesslie Newbigin*, pp. 187-89.

[42]From Newbigin, *Open Secret*, pp. 102-3, as quoted in Wainwright, *Lesslie Newbigin*, p. 186.

[43]This designation is widely attributed to Hendrik Kraemer.

[44]See, for instance, two chapters, "No Other Name" and "The Gospel and Other Religions," in *Gospel in a Pluralist Society*.

[45]Newbigin considers this the normative approach since Jesus is the source by which all other religions, and the totality of experience, are understood (see Wainwright, *Lesslie Newbigin*, pp. 226-27).

as an authoritative source for theological knowledge. He notes that the way in which the term operates in recent vernacular does not exist before the early nineteenth century; only then does it come to fruition in the thought of F. D. E. Schleiermacher, who sought an apologetic for Christianity for the "cultured despisers" of his era, concentrating attention on an imagined universal "feeling of absolute dependence" on God.[46] Thus, Newbigin disapproves the idea of a stand-alone (or separate source of) authoritative experientialism. Instead, he rightly claims that experience more appropriately belongs *within a particular conceptual and interpretive framework*. "All experience is interpreted experience," the bishop avers;[47] treating it as a "distinct source of authority for Christian believing" would be misleading inasmuch as "the character of our experience is a function of the faith we hold."[48]

Viewing all experiences, conceptual and interpretive frameworks, and claims to truth as contestable plausibility structures does not mean Newbigin presumes or promotes a resultant radical relativism. On the contrary, while fully functioning within both Christian and alternative plausibility structures and leaving the "ultimate outcome" to the "one who alone is judge," he proclaims the trinitarian faith brings together both the whole story (corporate) and each life story (personal) in a deeply harmonious and experiential way. Connecting these stories means that "there is thus no dichotomy between the inward experiences of the heart and the outward history of which each of us is a part. . . . Through the work of the Spirit we are led into an even fuller understanding of it [God's revelation in Jesus] as the Spirit takes of the things of Jesus and shows them to us through the experiences of our place and time."[49]

And what about reason? Should it be considered a separate source of theological knowledge, extricated from tradition and culture? Such autonomy for reason is rejected entirely by Newbigin. Instead, reason serves to facilitate individuals and communities in making sense of particular elements composing their experiences. In contrast to an Enlightenment trust in ahistorical and acultural rationalism, Newbigin asserts that "all rationality is socially and culturally embodied":

---

[46]See F. D. E. Schleiermacher, *The Christian Faith* (New York: T & T Clark, 1928).
[47]Newbigin, *GPS*, p. 58.
[48]Newbigin, *Truth and Authority*, p. 61.
[49]Newbigin, *GPS*, p. 164.

> Reason operates within a specific tradition of rational discourse, a tradition that is carried by a specific human community. There is no supracultural "reason" that can stand in judgment over all particular human traditions of rationality. All reason operates within a total worldview that is embodied in the language, the concepts, and the models that are the means by which those who share them can reason together.[50]

But if this particularity of reason is valid, how can a Christian worldview possibly elude the perceived relativism? The question of *adequacy* is key—testing Christianity's account of reality against all other accounts. "The fact that it is thus rooted in one strand of the whole human story in no way invalidates its claim to universal relevance."[51] Newbigin proclaims the Christian vision

> will convince people of its superior rationality in proportion to the intellectual vigor and practical courage with which those who inhabit the new plausibility structure demonstrate its adequacy to the realities of human existence. This will call for the most vigorous and exacting use of reason . . . [and] I suspect that one of the main functions of the church in the twenty-first century will be to defend rationality against the hydra-headed *Volksgeist*.[52]

Such committed employment of reason does not mean working toward a Cartesian indubitable certainty for Christian knowledge and truth (reserved solely for the eschaton). Instead, Christians are called presently to *trust and follow* the One having reconciled us through the cross, who says not "follow reason," but "follow me."

Newbigin also develops the idea of *interpersonal*—rather than impersonal and autonomous—reason: a matter of the role reason is given to play. Autonomous reason is under my full control as I determine and ask the questions, make the claims, force answers and exploit reason to service my own sovereign will. Yet in interpersonal relations with others—for our purposes, *the* Other—I must surrender control, listen, reveal and question myself, and allow reason to be "a listening and trusting openness, instead of being the servant of a masterful autonomy."[53] Reason is not abandoned;

---

[50]Newbigin, *Truth and Authority*, p. 52.
[51]Ibid.
[52]Ibid., pp. 53-54.
[53]Ibid., pp. 55-56.

its role is changed. And as Nietzschean interpretations have become fashionable among current elites claiming knowledge as merely disguised assertions of power,[54] such circumstances present the church with opportunities to utilize reason in service to the Master. It is the nature of the gospel to speak into the diverse collapses of the "plausibility structures" throughout the world—and to do so thanks to the resurrection, which is "the beginning of a new creation, the work of that same power by which creation itself exists" and therefore "the starting point for a new way of understanding and dealing with the world."[55]

In sum, Newbigin's approach to theological knowledge unites postfoundational, historical, cultural, contextual, revelational, metanarratival, christocentric, personal, trustful, participatory, ecclesial, apprenticeship, justice, mercy, inclusivist, dialogical, experiential and interpersonally reasoned elements in providing a robust holistic theological epistemology.

Performing Newbigin's Plurality of Sources in the Pluralist Context

Three overarching questions underlie my modest constructive proposal for enacting Lesslie Newbigin's play amid our own *Sitz im Leben*: What warrants Newbigin's method serving archetypally? What are plausible ways of performing his routine? And what outcomes might be anticipated from such a performance?

Newbigin's theological method and theological epistemology provide abundant treasures that the church and the Christian academy would do well to retrieve constructively in this ever-evolving twenty-first-century context. Enacting Newbigin's approach involves what I am calling "performing his play"—in other words, critically adopting and adapting the holistic theological and epistemological performance that has come to characterize the bishop's life and work. The following three "acts" suggest important parts of the bishop's play that call for faithful and effective performance today.

---

[54]Wainwright writes that "deconstruction" is viewed by Newbigin as an "ultimate absurdity" with its premise that "all claims to speak of truth may appear untenable" (Wainwright, *Lesslie Newbigin*, p. 73).

[55]From Newbigin, *Truth to Tell*, p. 28, as quoted in Wainwright, *Lesslie Newbigin*, p. 73.

Faithful reflection and cross-disciplinary praxis. Performing Newbigin's play will involve emulating his lifelong commitment to faithful and holistic theological reflection and practice *for the sake of the gospel, the church, and the other.* Spanning decades of experience in multiple cultures and contexts, the bishop conscientiously developed and engaged in understanding, clarifying and utilizing a biblically based, Christ-centered, trinitarian-framed theological approach—to God's glory and the church's benefit. Likewise, his broad experience with diverse worldviews, cultures, historical periods, churches, traditions and denominations fosters a certain reliability and esteem. Equally commendable is Newbigin's panoramic viewpoint, crossing boundaries of East and West, privileged and oppressed, intellectual and experiential, modern and postmodern, Christendom and post-Christian cultures.

Consequently, following this act of Newbigin's play will require many Christian and evangelical intellectuals to move beyond familiar territory marked out by modernity: traditionalism, modernist-fundamentalist categories, foundationalism, ahistoricism, aculturalism, acontextualism, propositionalism, triumphalism, objectivism, ethnocentrism, certainty, hubris and more. In its place, a model must arise incorporating biblical perspectives and insights from multiple Christian traditions, along with critically evaluated post-Enlightenment theology and epistemology: a holistic approach by faithful scholars enacting Newbigin's script—representing both tradition-conserving reformist and conservative tradition-reforming perspectives. This new paradigm will involve commitment to critically analyze and learn from myriad disciplines and interests. Newbigin's example bodes well for scholars willing to transcend specialization and preference for generous cross-disciplinary conversations; the bishop's résumé demonstrates a breadth of subjects and cultural mastery that rarely appears in this era of ever-narrowing expertise. Therefore, a prerequisite will be listening to *other voices*—beyond conservative Christian and evangelical communities—for valuable contributions to the current theological knowledge discussion. Perhaps this will involve taking up virtue epistemology, as some evangelical academicians have done. It might evoke judicious reading and critique of French and other postmodern philosophers whose epistemological views have radically altered both intellectual and popular scenes throughout the (mainly Western) world.

Research and developments in sociology, linguistics, philosophy, hermeneutics and other disciplines related to theology call for a concerted interpretive and assessment effort among Christian intellectuals, perhaps most helpfully by way of communal, conference and inquiry contexts (such as sponsored endowments and grant programs) on global, national and regional/local levels. This multidisciplinary attitude will increase sensitivity levels relating to diverse theological and epistemological approaches while synonymously adhering to Newbigin's *irenic yet full confession of faith* model, which takes seriously the dictum "All truth is God's truth," agreeing with Kuyper's declaration, "There is not one square inch of the entire creation about which Jesus Christ does not cry out, 'This is Mine! This belongs to me!'"[56]

Respectful, analogical and generous. Newbigin's assimilation of Michael Polanyi's thought transformed the bishop's understanding as to the personal nature of knowledge, including knowledge of God. Performing this particular act of the Newbigin play will involve deepening our appreciation for the predominantly narratival and relational character of the Bible and, relatedly, a theological focus on the gospel metanarrative in both its particularity and universal intent. This paradigm performs well since only by grace did God choose self-disclosure to human creatures, most manifestly in Christ Jesus. It is past time for rejecting, as regulatory for knowing, the modern scientific method and its hard evidentialism saturated with fact/value and related faulty dualisms. Properly attending to a *personal* orientation for theological knowledge ought to ensure remaining centered on Jesus Christ: God-with-us. The New Testament instrumentally endorses this by pointing out truth and knowledge of God being *constituted* and *incarnated* in Messiah Jesus. Furthermore, this (re)direction better aligns with the more relational (than rational) emphasis of both the biblical drama and post-Enlightenment sensibilities.

Following Newbigin's performance in this act also means rejecting hubris and exclusivist tendencies detrimental to the cause of the gospel and its gaining a hearing among alternative views of reality. Instead, a more gracious and inclusivist approach is called for, while simultaneously disavowing unmitigated open-endedness and salvific theological pluralism. Moreover,

---

[56]From a university lecture presented in Amsterdam, as quoted in Richard J. Mouw, *Uncommon Decency: Christian Civility in an Uncivil World* (Downers Grove, IL: InterVarsity Press, 1992), p. 147.

in the post-Enlightenment condition, reason need not be discarded, but rather recast as one among other useful, divinely provided tools—a tool to be employed faithfully and imaginatively within a Christian belief mosaic in the quest for theological insight and wisdom, centered on the Object of faith and knowledge. Newbigin's "middle way" calls us to remain true to the gospel while open to the mercy of God by means of grace beyond human understanding.

Enacting Newbigin's play also entails embracing contextual and epistemic particularity—though with universal intent—over the notion of universality in how and what individuals and cultures reflect and know. This move correctly understands that although an Archimedean point is not available presently to human beings, a non-reductive and faith-seeking-understanding historicism is sufficient and presupposes the reality of knowledge and truth constituted in God and the will of God.[57] Here we ought to follow Newbigin (vis-à-vis Aquinas) in understanding that the quantitative difference between divine and human limits our speaking of God to an *analogical* sense, and thus in using the language of creatures to speak of God, we cannot *fully*—yet we may *adequately*—reflect or comprehend God and God's will. Performing this act in Newbigin's play entails moving the unchanging gospel forward in the ever-changing garb of new historical and cultural contexts. Thus, our theological and epistemological approaches must successfully bridge the two worlds—biblical and contemporary, the communicated word and the receiving world.

Performing Newbigin's play also involves joining with him in trusting the "presence of the Spirit of God in power"[58] to draw people to the particular Savior Jesus, leading the church "into ever fuller understanding of the truth" as the church "lives in the power of the Spirit," learning what it is to share "in the suffering and rejection of Jesus."[59] At the same time, enacting this performance likewise means maintaining a more open stance toward accepting a certain level of theological truth and knowledge within other world religions and spiritualities, keeping in mind the necessary distinctions and nuances to be made concerning the salvific value of such knowledge

[57]As theologians Stanley Grenz and Wolfhart Pannenberg have argued in many of their published works, a rejection of *ontological* realism is not a necessary consequence of denying *epistemological* objectivity.

[58]Newbigin, *GPS*, p. 119.

[59]Ibid., p. 123.

and truth. This shift toward greater openness to the Spirit's role in the knowledge of God ought to be both enthusiastically and critically welcomed.

Performing Newbigin's play also calls for reviving other ways of knowing—such as *opinio*—that have too often been considered merely tertiary support for things known autonomously. While carefully guarding against elevating *opinio* to an idolatrous level, retrieving it will allow for more open dialogue with various Christian and non-Christian traditions, increasing the room for Scripture, wisdom, experience, practices, community, and mystery in theological and epistemological matters. This also implies willingness to incorporate critically into our theological method more of the "great tradition of belief,"[60] including insights provided by the larger tradition of the church, embracing that which has been believed by nearly all Christians at nearly all times and nearly everywhere. Such acts will include intercommunity dialogue—Christian scholars involved in constructive discussion and debate on questions concerning theology and culture, including the bi-directional impact. Further, this dialogue encourages opening cherished theological systems to greater scrutiny, especially to the scriptural priorities, focusing attention on fidelity to the gospel metanarrative in present historical and cultural contexts. Emulating Newbigin in this will demand painstaking patience, effort, sacrifice, time and a genuinely open attitude.[61]

For Christian theology and epistemology, this move ought to encourage an apologetic commending a more biblically derived functional/relational emphasis on God's revelation to humanity.[62] Such an effort might best be carried out within a broadly evangelical (or still wider) Christian context, involving judiciously tested claims about knowledge of God made by believers, particularly for understanding and evaluating these assertions in light of Scripture, tradition, virtue, Christian maturity and the like. Intercommunity dialogue among diverse Christian and evangelical academics on certain theological subjects (e.g., "knowing/doing God's will") is difficult and induces disagreements. Nevertheless, we ought to follow Newbigin's lead in

---

[60]See Roger E. Olson, *The Mosaic of Christian Belief: Twenty Centuries of Unity and Diversity* (Downers Grove, IL: IVP Academic, 2002), pp. 32-39, 46-47.

[61]Conferences, colloquia, and theology and culture projects offer vital opportunities for such communication environments.

[62]This is the central thesis of John Courtney Murray, *The Problem of God: Yesterday and Today* (New Haven, CT: Yale University Press, 1964).

pressing toward constructive engagement on these and other issues and their biblical criteria, and in a spirit of peace and tolerance; ecumenical and dialogical attitudes will shape the potential interaction and fruitful advancement of twenty-first-century theological and epistemological apologetics.

Participatory and eschatological. Performing Newbigin's play also calls for (re)turning theological method and theological knowledge to their "home base" orientation: immersed participation in the ecclesial community. Worshiping together and partaking in the sacraments—in a "community of praise"—provide a focal point for gratitude and growth in the grace and knowledge of the Lord "that can spill over into care for the neighbor."[63] This additionally means forging better connections between the Christian academy and the *ecclesia*, both locally and globally. One reasonable bridge-building tactic includes offering advanced theological education in local churches, making such opportunities available for parishioners unable to attend seminary or university—while not diminishing Christian higher education institutions. This new emphasis could involve theologically based training and dialogue among congregations: seekers and Christ-followers otherwise unlikely to experience systematic theological learning beyond church walls. Christian university and seminary "satellite campuses" should be welcomed into Christ-honoring local church communities as one way of guiding people to love God with all their minds, while remembering to be careful in presenting material "so that the non-specialist reader will not be misled. It is an exercise in communication, which is sadly not always the scholar's greatest aptitude."[64]

Finally, since theology and human knowledge are never complete or absolute until the eschaton, we ought to perform Newbigin's play by adopting an eschatological realist orientation,[65] being mindful that while we presently share in the cultural mandate as God's image-bearers (i.e., filling the earth and constructing the world), only in the future—with God as subject and the purposes of God realized—will the knowledge of God be expressed

---

[63]See Newbigin, *GPS*, p. 227.

[64]From R. T. France, "Evangelical Disagreements About the Bible," *Churchman* 96 (1982): 238, as quoted in Mark A. Noll, *Between Faith and Criticism: Evangelicals, Scholarship and the Bible in America* (New York: HarperCollins, 1987), p. 170.

[65]Stanley Grenz claims that "Christian theology is inherently eschatological, because it is the teaching about the promising God, who is bringing creation to an eternal *telos*"; see Grenz, *Renewing the Center: Evangelical Theology in a Post-theological Era* (Grand Rapids: Baker Academic, 2000), pp. 216-17.

and experienced with certainty. Faith and hope will be swallowed up in that which never fails: love. Therefore, performing this act today involves allowing space for the work of the Spirit within all cultures, contexts and even religions, remembering the future fulfillment of God's purpose will bring about the eschatological community of God. Without assuming salvific efficacy, knowledge of God may be characterized in various ways that connote the truth of the Spirit's omnipresence, and thus the triune God's universal accessibility throughout the world.

6

Honoring True Otherness in a Still-Antipluralist Culture

Esther L. Meek

It is a most valuable exercise in which we are cooperating—to reconsider, twenty-five years out, the message and impact of a great thinker's work. We may from this vantage point identify dimensions and implications of the work that at the time of publication were sensed as unspecifiable intimations. Lesslie Newbigin's *The Gospel in a Pluralist Society*, like any profound truth, continues to live and surprise us.[1] As you will see in this essay, I think that this project therefore honors the signature of reality and of what it means to know.

I came to Newbigin's work already formed as a Polanyian epistemologist, and also already embarked on the mission to which Newbigin the missiologist was calling his readers in the West. I heard his summons as follows: something is stopping the ears of people in the West, such that they do not even hear the gospel. That something is defective epistemology. Newbigin has drunk deeply at the well of Michael Polanyi to identify that defective epistemology and to offer Polanyi's fresh, positive alternative—not the patching together of warring opposites. Polanyi himself did not set about to address matters of church and mission, but rather of science and, secondarily, of the broader culture. In my own work as a Christian believer I was tapping his insights for reasons deeply similar to Newbigin's: to justify my Christian belief to myself, and to help people considering Christianity who

[1]Lesslie Newbigin, *The Gospel in a Pluralist Society* (Grand Rapids: Eerdmans, 1989).

have questions about knowing—thus, for preevangelism. Newbigin's work has lent vision, encouragement and resources as I have gone on to develop my own proposals in covenant epistemology.

From my vantage point, Newbigin's major contributions are as follows. First, he channeled and popularized the valuable work of Michael Polanyi. Polanyi's insights are profoundly sophisticated and cross-disciplinary. They are also deeply liberating. His legacy has been thwarted by people who misunderstand him or oversimplify him, as well as by people so liberated by his ideas that they subsequently attributed their fresh insights to themselves rather than to this humble innovator.[2] Unlike many, Newbigin succeeded with respect to all three of these, keeping alive and significantly disseminating the Polanyian message.

Second, and faithful to a Polanyian vision, Newbigin maintains, quite distinctively, that epistemology is the key to mission in the West.[3] Third, and this is obviously a personal value, not at all widespread: Newbigin's work shapes my own covenant epistemology, as will become evident. And fourth, foremost and most obvious to all, Newbigin has offered Christian believers in the West a fresh, movement-starting vision of what it means to be the Christian church in mission.

I have worked especially with Newbigin's *Proper Confidence.*[4] My agenda has continued to be entirely epistemological, since it fascinates me. I earnestly believe that in the West most ordinary Christian believers and churches still languish in a damaging, defective epistemology. I call it the defective epistemic default, or the knowledge-as-information mindset.[5] It continues to domesticate the gospel, as Newbigin and David Kettle, and Old Testament

---

[2]Scholars whose work is widely known, such as Alasdair MacIntyre, Charles Taylor and T. S. Kuhn, drew on Polanyi's work—and that is not widely known. With respect to Kuhn, Polanyi himself registered a bit of conflict with regard to encouraging his work or criticizing it. Later, he was concerned that Kuhn had both plagiarized his work and misrepresented it. An entire recent issue of the Polanyi Society Journal, *Tradition and Discovery* 33, no. 2 (2006–2007), is devoted to this matter.

[3]Newbiginian David Kettle does as well; David J. Kettle, *Western Culture in Gospel Context: Towards the Conversion of the West; Theological Bearings for Mission and Spirituality* (Euguene, OR: Cascade, 2011).

[4]Lesslie Newbigin, *Proper Confidence: Faith, Doubt and Certainty in Christian Discipleship* (Grand Rapids: Eerdmans, 1995).

[5]"Defective epistemic default": Esther Lightcap Meek, *Loving to Know: Introducing Covenant Epistemology* (Eugene, OR: Cascade, 2011), chap. 1; "knowledge-as-information mindset": Esther Lightcap Meek, *A Little Manual for Knowing* (Eugene, OR: Cascade, 2014).

scholar Walter Brueggemann, put it.[6] It continues also to hamper science and business and engineering and artistry and everything else. It continues to depersonalize and render the world two dimensional, leaving us bored and clueless as well as disconnected from, and distrustful of, reality. Brueggemann pronounces that this epistemology prohibits the proclamation of the resurrection of Christ.[7] On the other hand, our defective epistemic default feeds our ambition to amass, control and commodify. Epistemological therapy is my mission. When a person's understanding of how to know is reoriented, this both restores humanness and bears witness to the Lord.[8] It also makes us better at knowing ventures, no matter the field.[9]

In this essay I will argue that the West is not, and perhaps never was, pluralist. It is characterized, rather, by homogeneity, since it remains caught in the debilitating dynamic of the ancient Greek problem of the one and the many. The one-many dynamic is perpetuated in the West's deeply entrenched defective epistemology. Thus, if Michael Polanyi's epistemology offers epistemic corrective, we in the West need to have it traced over again and again for our healing reorientation to occur. Newbigin accurately represents Polanyian epistemology as he adapts it so powerfully to his breathtaking vision of the church and mission. Twenty-five years ago, and perhaps still today, however, Christian readers of *The Gospel in a Pluralist Society* can hear the accent placed, with respect to Polanyi's subjective and objective poles of knowing, very much on the subjective pole. I believe that it is important now to shift the accent to the objective pole.

This has been my own trajectory as well: twenty-five years ago I very much needed the message regarding the subjective pole of knowing. I needed to hear that from Polanyi. But thanks to apprenticeship in Polanyian epistemology for decades now, I have grown to be enamored of the real, and to trust the real in confidence. It is the "repersonalization of the real" that I would like to commend to you in this essay.

To that end, I will trace over Polanyian epistemology in *The Gospel in a Pluralist Society*. I will acquaint you with its augmentation in my own cov-

[6]Walter Brueggemann, *The Prophetic Imagination*, 2nd ed. (Minneapolis: Augsburg Fortress, 2001).
[7]Walter Brueggemann, *Truthtelling as Subversive Obedience* (Eugene, OR: Cascade, 2011), pp. 50-51.
[8]Meek, *Loving to Know*.
[9]Meek, *Little Manual*.

enant epistemology, an augmentation that underscores the objective pole of Polanyian knowing. Covenant epistemology reorients us to a fresh epistemic vision of knowing as transformative encounter, in which the real is personlike, and knowing is interpersonally relational. Perichoresis, dancing around, is the healthy dynamic of interpersonhood, which holds only in a universe that has at its heart the dynamic mutual relatedness of persons in love.[10] Since perichoresis is the dynamic of covenant epistemology, shifting our epistemic orientation is also shifting to a dynamic of perichoresis. This holds concrete, healthy implications for mission.

HOMOGENEITY: "THE SPECTER AT THE BANQUET OF MODERNITY"

First I want to address the matter of whether this culture is—in the words of the conference title where this chapter was first presented—still pluralist. I suggest the answer is no, and that in some sense perhaps it never has been. Modern Western culture is still trapped in the damaging dynamic of the ancient problem of the one and the many. The great old pre-Socratic question is about reality: Is reality ultimately one—a monism? Or is reality ultimately many—a pluralism?

The *problem* of the problem of the one and the many is that the very question thrusts you into an unstable tension of opposites that is always tending toward imbalance and mutual absorption. If you overemphasize one, it eats up the other. It also turns into the other. In our own day we can see this: we emphasize the many so much that we passionately say that everybody is unique. But effectively, then, everybody is unique just like everybody else. Strangely, you feel pressure to be unique.[11] That is the dynamic of the problem of the one and the many at work. The one-many dynamic is intrinsically debilitating and unhealthy. It depersonalizes—in fact, it never was personal—and it eclipses and prevents true particularity. The dynamic is one of power and control—or loss thereof.

The opposing tension of these opposites characterizes the entire Western

[10]The specific sense of *perichoresis* that I employ here follows the rendering given it by Colin Gunton in *The One, the Three, and the Many: God, Creation, and the Culture of Modernity* (Cambridge: Cambridge University Press, 1993).

[11]This fall I visited Austin, Texas. Widely offered for sale are T-shirts, mugs and so on enjoining people to "Keep Austin weird." This exemplifies the pressure to be the same in being unique.

tradition of ideas.[12] Plato's form of the Good, or Aristotle's Unmoved Mover, is the one. Individual, concrete things are the many. Greek philosophy privileges the one over the many—general, essential characteristics, seen as immaterial, eternal, ideal and abstract. There always remains ambivalence about particulars: they are not interesting for their particularity but only for the things they have in common. In fact, maybe they aren't real in their particularity at all. After all, they are changing, transient, material.

You can see particular and general as both necessary in any statement we make. If someone says, "Esther is a philosopher," the speaker is choosing a particular item, and the predicate affirms something general of the item. You can infer that you need to work with both to have not just communication but, more fundamentally, knowledge. Additionally, the Greek tradition tends to emphasize the general as the locus of knowledge and reality. The one, the general, gets privileged over the particular. And the particular can fall by the wayside.

Here, in part, I follow the argument of trinitarian theologian Colin Gunton in his 1993 book *The One, the Three, and the Many.*[13] Gunton is concerned that humans' relationship to non-human culture is deeply broken and is damaging both it and us. It manifests itself in the way we treat the environment, the paradoxical busyness of our lives, the continuing challenges of totalitarianism alongside notions of utter freedom, the triumph of skepticism, and the loss of meaning in a culture committed to certainty and truth. What we need desperately, Gunton urges, is a philosophy of engagement—a way of understanding ourselves as deeply connected with the world.[14] Without it, he says, we are doomed.

Modernity as forged by Rene Descartes's *Cogito, ergo sum* is one in which the solitary self is *disengaged* from the world.[15] In the modern world, God has been effectively displaced. How did this come to be? Gunton proposes that Christendom's defective understanding of the Holy Trinity, especially with respect to the three divine persons' involvement with creation, led it, in premodernity, to succumb to the deep dynamic of the ancient philo-

[12]See D. C. Schindler, "Surprised by Truth: The Drama of Reason in Fundamental Theology," in his book *The Catholicity of Reason* (Grand Rapids: Eerdmans, 2013).

[13]I devote chap. 12 of *Loving to Know* to Gunton's thought.

[14]Gunton, *The One, the Three, and the Many*, p. 15.

[15]Ibid., p. 13.

sophical problem of the one and the many.[16] In ancient Christianity, God came to be identified with the one, and immanent reality with the many. This defective Christian theology, then augmented in the 1300s by William of Ockham's exaltation of the will, came, untreated, into modernity. The modern era begins, we might say, around 1600 with Francis Bacon's still popular "Knowledge is power." Bacon claimed that humans should pursue what is properly theirs: supreme mastery over nature. Descartes followed Ockham in eschewing final causes, purposes, in nature. All that is interesting about nature is mechanistic causality. Humans, then—actually, disembodied minds—are "little mortal absolutes," set up to wrest what they will from nature. There remains no place for God in such a scheme. He is the transcendent one whom we must unseat in order for human reason to reign. The Enlightenment was that cultural exaltation of reason. Human reason becomes the immanent one.

Despite the pretentiousness of it, the philosopher G. W. F. Hegel was correct in diagnosing in this Western milieu a historical dialectic of idea driven by alienation, in which thesis generates its own antithesis. Hegel's dialectic epitomizes the intrinsically flawed and degenerating dynamism of the problem of the one and the many. The only hope is for synthesis to come from the struggle. But that synthesis would never be shalom, for it would be a fresh thesis, generating through alienation its own antithesis.

Friedrich Nietzsche rightly sensed the disease and decadence endemic to Western culture's exaltation of reason—and the Christian coopting of it that makes God the immaterial, unchanging, incurably abstract One. He was the first to name its abuse of power. Recent generations, thankfully, are way more attuned to the connection between power and what is taken to be truth. The times in which Newbigin wrote *The Gospel in a Pluralist Society* witnessed the onset of a rebellious and vocal exaltation of particulars, an effort to cast off all power-infected generality. This was and is our pluralist society.

But the problem with Nietzsche and also with our generation is that his and our best proposals fail to escape the deadly dynamism of the problem of the one and the many. If truth is perspective, if you exalt the individuals,

[16]Ibid., chap. 1.

individuality collapses into its own monism. The French philosophers known as postmodern (Jean-François Lyotard, Jacques Derrida and Michel Foucault) have bequeathed us amazing studies of very concrete particularities rightly sensitive to how things like power shape truth. They open our eyes to intriguing and important detail that we perhaps have never even noticed. But similar to Nietzsche, they do not ultimately escape the one-many dynamic itself. The result assassinates the one but thereby neither redeems the many nor ultimately escapes the one to attain true particularity, true otherness, true freedom.

Modernity thus involves an immanent monism, according to Gunton. He cites Stanley Jaki's evocative and memorable claim "The specter at the whole banquet of modernity is homogeneity."[17] Homogeneity in modernity continues to issue in control (or lack of it), power (or its abuse), quantification, commodifation, expansion, totalization. It continues to foster depersonalization and loneliness of persons, and misappropriation of the nonhuman world.

The exaltation of pluralism in Newbigin's and our day is only the current form of opposition to the oppressive rule of the immanent One. Homogeneity—inappropriate pressure that inhibits others from being their true selves in abiding otherness—and not pluralism is the problem.[18]

My sense of our times is that now we are past postmodernism and are back to modernism.[19] We are as modern as we ever were, if not more so. Postmodernism was a desperate attempt to challenge homogeneity with pluralism, but it did not win the day because it itself remains caught in the one-many dynamic. What we have now is what I call a "perforated modernism." We have brought our postmodern suspicion with us to perforate the metanarrative; that is how we keep homogenous power at manageable levels.

Protestant Christians, in our marriage to modernism, are often the ones most powerfully infected with the epistemic default. Newbigin's work is to

---

[17]Gunton, *The One, the Three, and the Many*, p. 44. Original reference: Stanley Jaki, *God and the Cosmologists* (Edinburgh: Scottish Academic Press, 1989), p. 37.

[18]"Abiding otherness" is D. C. Schindler's phrase in *Catholicity of Reason*, p. 45. I regret that space does not permit me to weave Schindler's work into this essay.

[19]Alternatively, we may say that postmodernism fell short of dislodging modernism. Either way, we recognize the tension of the faulty one-many dynamic.

challenge Christians' modernist epistemology, which domesticates the gospel.[20] It is thus not only the public, atheistic sphere that remains haunted by the specter of homogeneity, caught in the debilitating one-many dynamic. Christians are caught as well. And we are clueless about the one-many problem.

PERICHORESIS

Gunton proposes that we recover a strong doctrine of the Trinity, specifically with respect to the three persons' ongoing involvement in creation.[21] He commends the work of Irenaeus over that of Augustine. And he proposes that the key to true resolution of the problem is to replace the deadly one-many dynamic with one that is entirely different: *perichoresis. Perichoresis* means dancing around and through. The Cappadocian fathers introduced this motif as a great way to picture the dynamic interaction of the persons of the Trinity. In perichoresis you have nothing abstract or general at all. You have a mutually feeding relationality (or relatedness) and particularity (or individuality or otherness).

Dancing is an all-encompassing mutual relationship that actually enhances each dancer's distinctive particularity. Each becomes more him- or herself in the relationality of the dance. At the same time, each dancer becoming more themselves actually makes the whole dance better. Thus, relationality feeds and accentuates particularity; particularity feeds and accentuates relationality. Each is for the other—as opposed to the tense and unstable opposition that the one-many dynamic affords. The result is dynamic communion that deepens over time.

The persons of the blessed Trinity do nothing but give themselves in love to one another. Each becomes more himself in that self-giving love. The resulting overflowing exuberance actually is, I believe, what creation is, and what we are. Perichoresis just is the definitive dynamic of interpersonal love. Love is at the core of all things.

Great relationships enact perichoresis—what psychologists term *differentiation*.[22] Defective relationships involve emotional fusion; they devolve

---

[20]Kettle, *Western Culture*, continues this work, heightening its intensity.

[21]Gunton, *The One, the Three, and the Many*, pp. 53-54.

[22]David Schnarch, *Passionate Marriage: Keeping Love and Intimacy Alive in Committed Relationships* (New York: Henry Holt, 1997), chap. 2. Chapter 11 of *Loving to Know* is my engagement of Schnarch and differentiation.

into something like the one-many dynamic. When things get clicking along well in a relationship, business, church or government, that organization is approaching perichoresis. When things aren't going well, it can be seen as playing out the one and the many. Perichoresis alone establishes true particularity. The perichoretic relationship (alone) contributes true liberty, and in that dynamic, enriching, hospitable space, the individuals in that relationship flourish to become truly themselves.

As I imagine it, when a dynamic state of perichoresis is attained, in a relationship of any sort or size, it's as if a beautiful form comes into focus—a phenomenon that stands out from its backdrop in splendor.[23] A design team may say, we've got a good thing going! A football team may win the championship. A church may say, the Holy Spirit is present. And a mission may result in the fruit of mutually redemptive, mutually enhancing communion, rather than in the effacing perpetuation of a religious and social power inequity.

Gunton says that "redemption means the redirection of the particular to its own end and not a re-creation."[24] The purpose of all human action is the sacrifice of praise to the creator that, when directed toward the world, is action directed to allowing the world to be truly itself before God. Perichoresis is what Gunton proposes as the philosophy of engagement that alone will bring healing to humans' relatedness to the world. But in these lines we may also properly hear a perichoresis of mission. This is the heart of what I am commending in this essay.

Gunton is critical of most cultural artifacts and ventures with respect to this matter—since so many are imbued with the damaging one-many dynamic. He cites very few with approbation, but one is the epistemology of Michael Polanyi. Subsidiary-focal integration (SFI) is intrinsically perichoretic.

I will explain SFI presently and show how it embodies perichoresis. But first let me summarize my claim thus far: I believe that the one-many dynamic plays out in Western culture as the historic Greek balancing of the general and particular. General and particular exhibit a mutually antagonistic and unstable opposition. The one-many dynamic offers no space to true plu-

[23]Schindler's proposals in *Catholicity of Reason* lead me to suggest this. Additionally and tellingly, this aptly describes the coherent focal pattern that merges subsidiaries in Polanyi's epistemology.
[24]Gunton, *The One, the Three, and the Many*, p. 230.

ralism, true otherness, for it has within it no possibility of persons in relation. Perichoresis, by contrast, is the health-giving, shalom-evolving dynamism in which the pair is not many and one, particular and abstract. The proper dynamic is not particularity and generality, but rather particularity and relatedness. Each partner gives to the other in encounter and interpersonhood. Perichoresis alone fosters true particularity—true pluralism.

Tracing over the Polanyian Lines in Newbigin

Now let us note Polanyian lines of argument employed by Newbigin. *The Gospel in a Pluralist Society* displays that Newbigin taps not just one but many dimensions of Polanyi's thought. As I list them here, I also want to group them roughly in connection with what Polanyi himself calls the subjective pole and the objective pole of knowing. Polanyi himself placed greater emphasis on the subjective pole as he composed *Personal Knowledge* around 1950 for the Gifford Lectures.[25] Subtitled *Towards a Post-Critical Epistemology*, his magnum opus defended the personal, responsible, faith-like commitment that is justifiable and necessary for all knowing. Polanyi argued that it is legitimate to hold a belief responsibly and with conviction even if it might prove to be false. But in later years Polanyi said, in retrospect, that his most original insight in *Personal Knowledge* had been his subsidiary-focal integration; and in later essays, he tells us, he emphasizes it over the faith-commitment dynamic.[26]

Newbigin's *The Gospel in a Pluralist Society* evidences an emphasis similar to Polanyi's earlier work. The following themes emphasize the subjective pole of knowing. Newbigin repeats in full Polanyi's Critique of Doubt.[27] *The Gospel in a Pluralist Society* exposes the faith commitments that undergird the widespread claim opposing public facts to private values, calling us to confident affirmation in this intellectual climate.[28] Newbigin follows Polanyi in affirming that all knowing begins with faith;[29] it is, in Newbigin's own

[25]Michael Polanyi, *Personal Knowledge: Towards a Post-Critical Philosophy* (Chicago: University of Chicago Press, 1958; corrected ed., 1969).

[26]Michael Polanyi, *The Tacit Dimension* (Chicago: University of Chicago Press, 2009), p. xviii.

[27]Newbigin, *GPS*, p. 19.

[28]Ibid., p. 7.

[29]Ibid., pp. 19, 33.

words, "on the way," and there are "no insurance policies."[30] Newbigin adopts Polanyi's concept of indwelling; he calls Christian believers to indwell tradition, to indwell the Christian story as lenses, to indwell God's ongoing action.[31] He calls for acceptance of the Christian vision as a personal act.[32] He emphasizes patience and learning as part of such indwelling.[33] Newbigin pairs tradition, plausibility structure and hermeneutic with indwelling. He employs the wonderfully provocative Polanyian word *clue* to designate Christ, the clue to the larger pattern of God's purposes in history.[34] Indwelling, in fact, can be said to be *The Gospel in a Pluralist Society*'s major takeaway. The church is to be the hermeneutic of the gospel as it indwells the Christian story.

These more subjective Polanyian themes offered Newbigin critical aid in his critique of the complexities of modernity. In a way, he helped evangelicals be okay with subjectivity by rendering all knowing appropriately subjective. In subsequent years many have appropriated the notion of story and narrative—a motif in Newbigin but never in Polanyi—as that which we indwell. Newbigin did it well and helped the Christian church be more Christian in a pluralist society.

But Newbigin does Polanyi well—not just the subjective but the objective pole in Polanyian knowing. The following are Polanyian motifs of the more objective sort that can be glimpsed in Newbigin's *The Gospel in a Pluralist Society*. Newbigin obviously applies the motifs explicitly to Jesus Christ and his gospel. They take breathtaking form in Newbigin's central "new fact" of Christ.[35] In Christ, "something radically new is given," claiming to be the truth.[36] Newbigin calls this the starting point for a new way of understanding. It "opens a world of infinite possibilities that beckons us into ever fresh regions of joy."[37] Newbigin repeatedly notes Polanyi's distinctive claim that knowing has both subjective and objective poles: personal commitment with universal intent.[38] He notes how this asymmetric duality "opens the way for

[30]Ibid., p. 12.
[31]Ibid., pp. 38, 46, 51.
[32]Ibid., p. 47.
[33]Ibid., p. 126.
[34]Ibid., chap. 9.
[35]Ibid., p. 5.
[36]Ibid., p. 6.
[37]Ibid., p. 12.
[38]Ibid., pp. 23, 35.

new and often unexpected discovery."[39] He speaks of grasping reality fumblingly—reality that will reveal its truth through further discoveries as we continue to seek.[40] The committed discoverer claims to be in contact with a reality beyond him- or herself.[41] Newbigin notes, with Polanyi, orderliness in reality, hidden and waiting to be discovered.[42]

What is more, present in Newbigin is an important emphasis that goes beyond what Polanyi himself registered, into the range of covenant epistemology's themes, and into the range of the claims I am commending in this essay. Newbigin explicitly affirms *the real* as personal.[43] We should in our engaging it be listening, trusting—rather than acting as if we are entitled to masterful exploration. Reality as personal addresses us.[44] Newbigin explicitly states a key thesis of this essay: reality at root is relationship; he contrasts this with the dynamic of the one and the many.[45] For Newbigin the reality that comes is the reign of God: a present reality among us the church, a reality whose presence is veiled but which creates crisis, calling for our patient cooperation.[46] Finally—and this comment of Newbigin's suggests the final outcome of my work in this essay—Newbigin calls us to welcome all the signs of the grace of God at work in the lives of those who do not know Jesus as Lord. "In our contact with people who do not acknowledge Jesus as Lord, our first business, our first privilege, is to seek out and to welcome all the reflections of that one true light in the lives of those we meet."[47] In this we reflect Jesus Christ and the welcome that lies at the heart of God and the gospel.

Thus, Newbigin is true to Polanyi in both subjective and objective themes, and also in stipulating their interconnectedness. Newbigin deeply understands the crucial implications of the entirety of Polanyian epistemology to redraw the epistemic playing field therapeutically—and the critical importance of this for the West's apprehension of the gospel. But I

[39]Ibid., p. 35.
[40]Ibid., p. 23.
[41]Ibid., p. 192.
[42]Ibid., p. 44.
[43]Ibid., p. 61.
[44]Ibid., p. 169.
[45]Ibid., p. 172. My thesis in this essay offers no addition to Newbigin's understanding.
[46]Ibid., pp. 105-6, 132-33, 181-82.
[47]Ibid., p. 180.

wonder whether his readers may have come away with the subjective emphases, and not so much with the objective ones. My problem is this: subjectivity by itself, even when it is well done, fails to challenge the debilitating one-many dynamic and cultivate true particularity. We need to hear Newbigin afresh, and hear Polanyi as well. Further, we need to augment Polanyian epistemology, such as my own covenant epistemology does, to deepen and enrich the objective as personal. Without this emphasis, it is possible for us to accept our subjectivity but still fail to honor true particularity, in ourselves and others. We need this clarification now, twenty-five years out from *The Gospel in a Pluralist Society*'s first publication, even more than we did then.

SFI and IFMs: Polanyian Epistemology and Its Respect for the Other

Thus far I have given a somewhat unfair portrayal of both Newbigin and Polanyi. Now as I explicate Polanyi, this portrayal will be reoriented in a way that makes my case. What I have described up to this point is a misrepresentation in this very critical respect: even though "subjective pole" and "objective pole" is Polanyi's own language, using the terms in an unqualified manner is simply false to the Polanyian vision. The fact is that Polanyian subsidiary-focal integration ties these together integrally and transformatively. Apart from a full grasp of subsidiary-focal integration, the reader of either scholar has entirely misunderstood Polanyian epistemology. With subsidiary-focal integration, you no longer have either subjective or objective in the common sense.[48]

All knowing has a two-level structure: we rely on and attend from clues we subsidiarily indwell to pursue, integratively shape and focus on a coherent pattern, which we then submit to as a token of reality.[49] To expound this briefly, think about learning to read a new language—let's say, Chinese.

[48]Recall that I earlier repeated Polanyi's remark that this was his most original insight, and the one that moved him beyond the more subjective-sounding themes of his earlier *Personal Knowledge*. See also Marjorie Grene, "Tacit Knowing: Grounds for a Revolution in Philosophy," *Journal of the British Society for Phenomenology* 8 (1977): 164-71. Many readers miss this and misunderstand Polanyi.

[49]I develop subsidiary-focal integration throughout *Loving to Know*, chap. 4, and in chap. 4 of *Little Manual*.

At first you focus on the page, on the shapes of the characters. You entrust yourself to an authoritative guide and painstakingly follow his or her direction to associate the characters as directed. Eventually there must come a kind of shift from attending to the *characters and sounds* to attending to their *meaning*—attending *from* them, relying on them *subsidiarily*, to attending *to*, *focusing* on the coherent pattern that is the sense of their meaning. And that shift is not linear or deductive. It is a creative *integration*, often an aha moment of insight. Integration transforms disparate particulars, first, anticipatively, into clues, and then, in the breakthrough of insight, into meaningful aspects of the coherent pattern. All knowing sustains this two-level structure in which subsidiary is connected to focal in a logically creative, integrative relation. Pattern makes sense of clues; it is fraught with the signature character of the clues.

In an act of knowing, that which is subsidiary cannot be articulated; it is logically unspecifiable. This doesn't mean that you can't ever articulate subsidiaries; it means that you can't articulate them while you are relying on them subsidiarily. You rely on them acritically. This is what it means to indwell clues subsidiarily. In any knowing event, your body as felt—your felt body sense—comprises one of the three sectors of clues melded into an integrative feat. (The other two are the situation you are making sense of and the directions that guide you.[50]) But, Polanyi says, this bodily indwelling just is your feeling your body to be your own. In sustaining the performance of bike riding, for example, you know your body in the balance it keeps subsidiarily as part of the performance. All other clues you indwell subsidiarily—tools, language, directions, theoretical frameworks, even the bodies of others to whom you are listening—effectively expand your body in its subsidiary bearing on the focus.

In *Personal Knowledge*, Polanyi spoke of faith as "our manner of disposing ourselves" toward that to which we attend. I find this immensely helpful: it renders subjective-sounding faith in bodied key. Pittsburgh Pirates outfielder Andrew McCutcheon disposes himself toward catching the line drive. I dispose myself toward my bike as I ride it: I rely on it, trust it—you can throw religious-sounding words at the very palpable but inarticulable phe-

[50]Meek, *Loving to Know*, part 3.

nomenon that we all know well. Balance keeping is *not* subjective. It's palpable, developable and absolutely critical to riding a bike.

Subsidiary never occurs without focal and vice versa. They cannot be broken apart—just like part and whole can't be broken apart. At the same time, neither is reduceable to or determined by the other. You can have the inbreaking focal pattern without having its subsidiaries exactly right. You can have the "necessary" components and remain forever blind to that pattern. They are integrationally, transformatively related. They are *perichoretically* related as well—a dynamic, mutually enhancing duality.

Polanyian indwelling just is subsidiarily relying on clues as we integratively shape and focus on a pattern. Creatively scrabbling to indwell clues—to indwell the thing that we are trying to understand—actually prompts the logical leap of integration to discovery or understanding. In Polanyi, indwelling actually can't be either subjective or objective in the old sense; indwelling is intrinsically both—or, better yet, neither. Our entire epistemic orientation to the world is from-to, proximal-distal, subsidiary-focal.

All knowing is skilled knowing. And every act of coming to know what we do not yet know must involve that shift from creative, responsible, active shaping of clues into a pattern, which we then submit to as a token of reality. In the trajectory of learning or discovery, or the creative act, our groping and imaginative struggle to make sense of puzzling clues is guided by a "sense of increasing proximity to an as-yet unspecified solution."[51] The moment of insight brings that struggled-for but never determinable shift in which reality breaks in. That integration transforms the knowers, and the world we have therein apprehended, changing us and it and leading us in ever deepening understanding and communion with the real.

Newbigin's *The Gospel in a Pluralist Society* is faithful to Polanyi in this, although he does not emphasize that it is critical to understand subsidiary-focal integration to get Polanyian epistemology. But Western readers are marked deeply by the defective one-many dynamic and its attending implications, including a defective epistemology that divorces subjectivity from ob-

[51]Marjorie Grene, ed., *Knowing and Being: Essays by Michael Polanyi* (Chicago: University of Chicago Press, 1969), p. 171. Polanyi also refers to this as a "gradient of deepening coherence": *Personal Knowledge*, pp. 124-25; "The Creative Imagination," *Chemical and Engineering News* 44 (1966): 88.

jectivity. Such readers who also possess only a passing exposure to Polanyi can have their "indwelling" fall apart: their sense of it can revert to the subjectivity or to an objectivity that is totalizing and repressive—or both. We can hear Newbigin as condoning subjectivity. We fail to hear Newbigin revamping what we take to be objective, and we haven't connected the two integrally.

That is Polanyi's subsidiary-focal integration: let's call it SFI. Proceeding on with Polanyi: in that moment of inbreaking insight, "we know that we have made contact with reality when we anticipate an indeterminate range of as yet unknown (and perhaps yet inconceivable) true implications."[52] This is what I came to designate as IFMs: a sense of indeterminate future manifestations. When I heard this sentence of Polanyi's, it fell on my modernity-parched ears as an oasis might fall on the vision of a desert traveler. Reality might be there!

Knowing intrinsically reaches beyond itself. It must—or it fails. It involves risky commitment to what you do not yet know. In the moment of deep insight when you espy the focal pattern, as well as leading up to it and, later on, from it, you anticipate and trust those tantalizing IFMs in their witness to the profundity of your insight.

Inbreaking reality doesn't so much answer our questions as dispel them. It comes on its own terms, not on ours. We know we have grasped the real just when the real surprises—*not* when it confirms. It can break in graciously when we simply don't have all our subsidiary ducks in line. We may even have a defective epistemic default—perish the thought!—and yet still be blessed with its coming. Reality is far bigger than we have hitherto imagined, and far more dynamic. As a Christian believer, I connect this with the gracious descent of God and with the motif of reality as gift.

The twin theses of SFI (subsidiary-focal integration) and IFM (indeterminate future manifestations attending contact with reality) are key to Polanyian epistemology and Polanyian realism. Readers of Newbigin's *The Gospel in a Pluralist Society* might not have understood them fully. But now let us tie in Gunton's insights: subsidiary-focal integration is intrinsically *perichoretic*. The focal pattern transforms the clues. The subsidiaries imbue the pattern with their signature particularity. With respect to pattern, the

[52]Polanyi, *Personal Knowledge*, p. viii.

subsidiaries can be changing, just as my body sustains a rich dynamism of efforts as I balance on my bike. Indeed, since our bodies as felt comprise one of the three sectors of clues, your apprehension of a sunset and mine will be fraught with a distinct array of felt body responses as we co-celebrate the sunset. Likewise, the focal pattern itself develops. Our sense of it unfolds and deepens as we apprehend and yet are surprised by those IFMs. This underscores what both Newbigin and Kettle, as well as others, claim: that epistemology is key to redemptive gospel flourishing. Epistemology is key to enacting perichoresis.

Covenant Epistemology

Polanyi's two theses, SFI and IFM, are what led me to develop covenant epistemology. It seemed to me that if what Polanyi is describing is true—and I had come to trust him in this—that the whole thing had about it "hints of interpersonal reciprocity." Over the years of indwelling Polanyian epistemology, intrigued especially as I am with its connection to reality, I came to be struck by the person-like response of reality to the knower. Discovery of the real doesn't explain so much as redraw my questions. Reality has a profoundly deeper objectivity, with the capacity ever to surprise. Reality appears to be in the driver's seat. It walks in, sometimes, and takes over, changing me. Reality somehow behaves like a person. This, in turn, suggested to me that best epistemic practices should involve treating reality as we would a person. I should see knowing as *inviting the real.*

Newbigin's work played a key role in this insight for me. In *Proper Confidence,* he talks of Polanyi's promise of IFMs. He draws out of it an implication that Polanyi himself had never named: that reality is like that because it is God's, and because it is personal.[53] I had also seen both that biblical covenant, according to theologian Mike Williams, was itself relationship, and that Annie Dillard, in "stalking muskrats" as she calls it, exhibited covenantal behavior.[54] She effectively binds herself to live life on the terms of the yet-to-be-known, in order to invite it. Add to these that Newbigin, and also education guru

---

[53]Newbigin, *Proper Confidence*, p. 62.

[54]Meek, *Loving to Know*, chap. 7 and chap. 2; see also Annie Dillard, *Pilgrim at Tinker Creek* (New York: HarperCollins, 1974), chap. 11; and Michael D. Williams, *Far as the Curse Is Found: The Biblical Drama of Redemption* (Phillipsburg, NJ: P & R, 2005).

Parker Palmer, argue that reality is personal, and I set about to craft and defend the covenant epistemology thesis. Covenant epistemology commends, as the paradigm of all knowing, the interpersonal, covenantally constituted relationship. Specifically, that paradigm is the redemptive encounter in which we are redemptively and transformatively known by Christ. Covenant epistemology seeks to provide what all of these thinkers have enjoined.[55]

Intrinsically, perichoretic SFI remains a sine qua non of covenant epistemology. But interpersonhood, as I call it, augments it. I work with insights from John Macmurray, Martin Buber, James Loder, Colin Gunton and others to make the case for the real as personal and for knowing as mutually transformative encounter.[56] The real graciously self-discloses through and within our loving pledge to live life on its terms and follow where it may lead. I offer an extensive "epistemological etiquette"—surprising best practices for inviting the real. Knowing isn't information so much as it is transformation. Paraphrasing Abraham Joshua Heschel, we should learn not in order to comprehend but, rather, in order to be apprehended.[57] We invite the real by loving in order to know, pledging ourselves to "love, honor and obey" the yet-to-be-known that we seek to know.[58] We invite the real in our readiness to know—that is, in maturing into great lovers who give the gift of the self.[59] We invite it in a posture of humility, respect and patience. We strategically locate ourselves in the place where reality is likely to break in. We practice hospitality and welcome. We listen actively, taking the risk to move beyond our preconceived categories, to be changed ourselves, to be the ones needing to hear. Such listening is no longer a passive registering of information but invites the self-disclosure of the real. Our epistemic goal is no longer comprehensive information or total, homogenizing sameness. Our goal is communion. The goal itself invites the real. Communion is friendship; it is perichoresis, in which I and the other become more ourselves in true particularity and otherness. I came to see that the knower and yet-to-be-known relationship should be perichoretic—overture and response, welcome and

[55]Meek, *Loving to Know*, chap. 2.
[56]Ibid., part 4.
[57]I have borrowed this paraphrase from my colleague, Robert M. Frazier.
[58]Ibid., chap. 15.
[59]John Paul II, *Man and Woman He Created Them: A Theology of the Body*, trans. Michael Waldstein (Boston: Pauline, 2006).

consent. These are highly personal, illocutionary acts. Knowing is knowing and being known in perichoresis.

In *A Little Manual for Knowing*, released last year, I summarize covenant epistemology in a "how to" for knowing ventures in any field. I cast the knowing venture as pilgrimage graciously met with gift. Pilgrimage involves love and pledge, invitation and indwelling. Reality's self-disclosure may come in gracious response, which leads to mutually transformative encounter. The relationship of knower and known continues in dancing communion toward shalom.[60]

So covenant epistemology takes subsidiary-focal integration's intrinsic openness to a surprising reality and, as it were, props the door open permanently by putting a person in it. More objective than objectivity, Parker Palmer would say, is the objectivity of a person who, in their trustworthy character, nevertheless surprises, a person whose gracious overtures of love invite our response of love. Knowing can no longer be the same.

Knowing as per covenant epistemology has as its heart dynamic perichoresis—the very dynamic that alone successfully redraws the one-many conflict that continues to deface Western culture. Perichoretic relationship is healthy interpersonal relationship characterized by face-to-face, mutually indwelling, mutually transformative encounter in which each may be truly other, truly themselves. No wonder my decades of being a Polanyian have gently transmuted my suspicion of reality into trust! No wonder reality seems now to me to be intoxicatingly beautiful, fraught with the presence of God. Healing epistemology *is* key to the conversion of the West. This is a posture, a welcome, into which the welcoming God may come.

Implications for Church and Mission

I am proposing that this healing epistemology is also key to mission in and beyond the West. The impact of Newbigin's work is massive and important, without doubt. But if what has generally been heard is its subjective insights,

---

[60]The example that comes most readily to my mind is my relationship with my own garden. My garden presents me with itself. I respond to its need, and to my vision of it, by cultivating, watering, pruning, mowing, making new beds, mulching and so on. I make overtures every early spring. It responds throughout the summer. I have planted and replanted my deciduous azalea three times. Finally I have gotten it into a bed that receives ample sunshine. Finally it is responding with a full complement of buds. This is perichoresis, ongoing communion, to the end of shalom.

even its great injunction to indwelling is perhaps being grasped only in defective form. It may fall short of the robust perichoresis of SFI and IFM. It may thus fail to redraw the damaging, unstable dynamic of the one-many, fraught as it is with power, control and commodification. It may fail to reinstate the very dynamic that, I would argue, is the heart of reality, and the heart of the gospel.

In the West we have moved beyond postmodernity to something I call "perforated modernism." Western culture is as modern as ever, but we tap our postmodern suspicion: we keep homogenizing power at manageable levels by poking holes in it. Hacking is a great example of this. This situation continues to display the one-many dynamic.

The Christian church in the West continues to embrace the defective epistemology of modernism, a knowledge-as-information mindset, and it continues to bear the mark of the one-many dynamic. It may mistakenly assume the problem is that we are pluralist. We continue to be plagued with a kind of evangelical imperialism. The one-many dynamic lends an imperialist tinge to our "kingdom" work. We see mission as spread of Christ's kingdom, and rightly so; but we subtly infect the notion of kingdom with a dynamic of power. We implicitly imagine that we have something to bring to the other, who, without us, is clueless and with us, will become like us. Or, in fear of wielding inappropriate power, we seek to qualify or limit mission. In saying this, I am not suggesting that we do not bear witness to the objective truth of the gospel of the Lord Jesus Christ. But do we, whether we are aware of it or not, still bear the entrenched patterns of the one-many dynamic, such that our vision and our efforts retain the feel of it to others? Or does the gospel to which we witness bear the telltale marks of our wonder at its mystery—our wonder at it being greater than what we might package and dole out, fundamentally different from items we might amass?

Where reality is impersonal, we may amass and commodify with little sense of the presence and abiding otherness of the other. We may be pursuing mission in a way that actually dishonors the real, personal, other—God and his creatures, both nonhuman and human. This is inconsistent with the heart of the gospel, and with the heart of reality. And we may be persisting in this in an era that more than ever needs to be delivered of the depersonalizing one-many struggle.

What I am calling for is a repersonalization of the real. We want to see the face of God everywhere before us—in the world and in the person or persons it is our mission to reach for Christ. What if we treated reality—that is, God and his stuff, both humans and nonhuman culture—as persons or person-like, in which we as persons anticipate perichoretic relatedness? Would we not see ourselves as seeking the true redemptive particularity, the abiding otherness of the other? Would we not simultaneously see ourselves as seeking to be apprehended by Christ in a relationship with the other that proves mutually transformative?

What if we remembered that there is no corner of the world where and no person to whom the Lord that cannot help but be his gracious, personed, self-revealing self?[61] What if, further, we treated the Lord in his proper otherness by entering a new place and a new interchange with another with the delighted anticipation of finding that the Lord is already there and at work, that he himself is reaching through that other to woo us? What if our missional strategy was one of inviting the real—inviting God and inviting the other to God-redeemed flourishing particularity?

Newbigin himself, as I noted earlier, enjoins us to welcome all signs of the grace of God at work in the lives of those who do not know Jesus as Lord. Expectancy and welcome—all reflections of the one true light. "In our contact with people who do not acknowledge Jesus as Lord, our first business, our first privilege, is to seek out and to welcome all the reflections of that one true light in the lives of those we meet." In this we reflect Jesus Christ and the welcome that lies at the heart of God and the gospel.

The Christian church must reorient to a perichoretic involvement with a reality as with a personal other. But reorienting epistemically to embrace a perichoretic dynamic of knower and known restores knowing to love- and pledge-borne perichoretic invitation to the real. And when it is invited and welcomed, reality may bless both with its gracious self-disclosure and its restoration to a dynamic, personal other. We welcome the personal other; we expect with delight to be surprised by truth.

---

[61]Parker Palmer quotes the German poet Rainier Marie Rilke: "There is no place at all that isn't looking at you—you must change your life"; Palmer, *To Know as We Are Known: Education as a Spiritual Journey* (San Francisco: HarperSanFrancisco, 1966), p. 16.

What might missional perichoresis look like? It would be loving, seeing and seeking the face and person of God in the world and in the other. It would be recognizing the Lord and his action already at work before us—in both senses. We would listen for what the Spirit is already at work doing. We would invite him and his transformative self-disclosure in the persons we seek to reach for Christ and, through them, to ourselves. We would listen and confer dignity and welcome, honoring the otherness of the other. We would anticipate mutual transformation—we need them to have God. We would preserve the otherness of these persons as persons, anticipating with delight that we will be surprised by truth. We may anticipate, in this his world, the descent of God.

Conclusion

I have argued, first, that the debilitating dynamic of the ancient problem of the one and the many continues to characterize our modern world. This dynamic adversely impacts the West in our engagement of the world. The Christian church is not immune to it. The one-many dynamic is of a piece with the West's defective epistemology, the knowledge-as-information mindset. A healthy epistemology is, as Newbigin, Kettle and others have argued, key to unleashing the true Christian gospel, church and mission in the West. Newbigin espouses Polanyian epistemology. Covenant epistemology augments Polanyian epistemology to underscore its implicit perichoresis, the healing dynamism of reality, by placing the accent on the objective (understood in a Polanyian sense) pole of knowing—on the real—as personal and self-transcending, overflowing with its signature indeterminate future manifestations. This emphasis is consistent with Newbigin's vision and helps us be even better at carrying it forward.

Most fundamentally, perichoresis must be the dynamic of mission. Love and pledge, invitation and indwelling, pilgrimage in search of gift. Then—surprise! Encounter! Transformation—*our* transformation! Dancing communion toward shalom.[62] This is the true trajectory of all knowing ventures in a repersonalized world belonging to the Lord, and accords deeply with the shape and tenor of Newbigin's majestic vision.

---

[62]These are the motifs I employ in *Little Manual* to describe any knowing venture.

7

Pluralism, Secularism and Pentecost

Newbigin-ings for *Missio Trinitatis* in a New Century

Amos Yong

The bold thesis of this chapter is that a greater expansion of pneumatological themes will extend the legacy of Lesslie Newbigin, particularly in terms of the Christian missiological engagement with Western culture.[1] More specifically, there are ontological, epistemological and ecclesiological aspects of pneumatology that are underdeveloped, even in Newbigin's trinitarian theology, and these have the potential to further underwrite and empower his missional apologia vis-à-vis the progress of science in the modern world. The two parts that follow, first, unfold a more robust pneumatological missiology from out of select resources latent in Newbigin's mission theology and, second, explore how such can revitalize Christian life and witness in a twenty-first-century world dominated by scientific achievements that see no prospect of diminishment.

The Spirit and Mission Theology: Expanding Newbigin's Reach

This first section is primarily descriptive, albeit with a hermeneutical twist. Chiefly, I read Newbigin as a trinitarian missiologist and epistemologist,

[1]Note that the focus of George R. Hunsberger, *Bearing the Witness of the Spirit: Lesslie Newbigin's Theology of Cultural Plurality* (Grand Rapids: Eerdmans, 1998), is on what is in the subtitle rather than the pneumatology suggested in the main title; to my knowledge, to date Newbigin scholarship has focused on his trinitarian theology, but not specifically on his pneumatology—hence this chapter also aspires to fill a gap in the existing literature.

though from a Pentecostal perspective.[2] I will then retrieve and foreground the pneumatological threads in his writings largely as they pertain to these themes but also show how they can and ought to be filled out in ways and for reasons consistent with his overall project.

Newbigin as trinitarian missiologist: A Pentecostal and pneumatological perspective. If a theologian like Karl Barth was almost single-handedly responsible for revitalizing the doctrine of the Trinity for Christian theology in the twentieth century, it is not too far-fetched to think that Lesslie Newbigin (1909–1998) played an essential role in retrieving trinitarian theology for theology of mission and mission theology in the wake of Barth's attainments. Newbigin's 1963 book, *Trinitarian Faith and Today's Mission*,[3] can now, in retrospect, be viewed as a manifesto that opened up conversations between ecumenists, theologians and missiologists across a chasm that had separated those working in the dogmatic disciplines from those laboring in what was considered the more practical fields of ministry and mission. The brilliance of Newbigin's trinitarian theology of mission derives at least in part from how he understood the historicity of Christian faith in its pentecostal and especially incarnational events as foundational for Christian witness to the gospel in the modern world.[4] Thus the proclamation of the gospel revolved around Jesus, "the one who announces the coming of the reign of God, the one who is acknowledged as the Son of God and is anointed by the Spirit of God."[5] As such, then, Christian mission can be understood no more or less than "as proclaiming the kingdom of the Father, as sharing the life of the Son, and as bearing the witness of the Spirit."[6] Such is manifest as Christian faith, love and hope in action: testifying to the gospel, embodying the gospel in love of

[2]I use *Pentecostal* in this chapter in a twofold sense: first as related to the Day of Pentecost account in Acts 2, always capitalized, although those occasions when this is used adjectivally in this Lukan sense will be uncapitalized; and second as related to the modern Pentecostal movement, my own ecclesial tradition, of which various cognates are always capitalized.

[3]Lesslie Newbigin, *Trinitarian Faith and Today's Mission*, study pamphlets, World Council of Churches Commission on World Mission and Evangelism 2 (Richmond, VA: John Knox Press, 1963), reprinted as *Trinitarian Doctrine for Today's Mission* (Carlisle, UK: Paternoster, 1998); cf. also the section "Trinitarian Mission" in *Lesslie Newbigin, Missionary Theologian: A Reader*, ed. Paul Weston (Grand Rapids: Eerdmans, 2006), pp. 81-92.

[4]Adam Dodds, "Newbigin's Trinitarian Missiology: The Doctrine of the Trinity as Good News for Western Culture," *International Review of Mission* 99, no. 1 (2010): 69-85.

[5]Lesslie Newbigin, *The Open Secret: An Introduction to the Theology of Mission*, rev. ed. (1978; Grand Rapids: Eerdmans, 1995), p. 21.

[6]Ibid., p. 29.

neighbor, and living out the gospel in transformative and hopeful action that makes a difference in the world.[7]

Now while it is more often than not the case that trinitarian theologies are more accurately called binitarian (in terms of their neglect of pneumatology),[8] this criticism fortunately applies less to Newbigin. To be sure, Newbigin's christocentrism is palpable throughout much of his theological output so that one might be tempted to judge that his pneumatology is just as anemic as those found in other putatively trinitarian theological visions.[9] Yet this is done only by overlooking the efforts he expended to probe specifically pneumatological matters at significant points over decades of work.[10] For our purposes, we can summarize such pneumatological considerations along at least the following three lines.[11] First, Newbigin's pneumatology was part and parcel of his doctrine of God and of God's redemptive activity. Thus Christians can only bear witness to the gospel in and through the power of the sovereign Holy Spirit. The mission of God for and through the church, including the church's election, was inaugurated with the Pentecost event, so that the *missio Dei* is no more or no less than the *missio Spiritus*.[12] Further, and second, that the church participates in the mission of the Spirit indicates that the church does so from a position of weakness (in effect), certainly reliant not on their own efforts

---

[7]These are the fourth through sixth chapters of *The Open Secret*, which flesh out at least some of the details of Newbigin's trinitarian missiology.

[8]This applies even to Barth, as argued by Robert W. Jenson, "You Wonder Where the Spirit Went," *Pro Ecclesia* 2, no. 3 (1993): 296-304.

[9]Newbigin's Christology is pervasive throughout his published work, so it is difficult to point specifically to what might be called his christocentric trinitarianism. Yet two windows into the centrality of Christ for Newbigin's missiology are his article "Christ and the Cultures," *Scottish Journal of Theology* 31, no. 1 (1978): 1-22, and chap. 9, "Christ, the Clue to History," in his *The Gospel in a Pluralist Society* (1989; repr., Geneva: WCC Publications, 1997), pp. 103-15. See also John Reilly, "Evangelism and Ecumenism in the Writings of Lesslie Newbigin and Their Basis in His Christology" (PhD diss., Gregorian University, Rome, 1978), and Joe M. Thomas, *Christ and the World of Religions: Lesslie Newbigin's Theology* (Carrollton, TX: Ekklesia Society Publications, 2011).

[10]E.g., from 1960, Lesslie Newbigin, "Missions and the Work of the Holy Spirit," which is included as chap. 3 of Newbigin's *A Word in Season: Perspectives on Christian World Missions* (Grand Rapids: Eerdmans, 1994), pp. 21-32, to 1990, Newbigin, *Come Holy Spirit: Renew the Whole Creation*, Occasional Paper 6, Selly Oak Colleges (Birmingham, UK: Selly Oak Colleges, 1990).

[11]Here I draw particularly from Newbigin, *The Open Secret*, chap. 6, "Bearing the Witness of the Spirit: Mission as Hope in Action."

[12]Newbigin first learned this important theological, missiological and, indeed, pneumatological truth from his years of service in India; see Newbigin, "Missions and the Work of the Holy Spirit," esp. p. 32, and *The Holy Spirit and the Church* (Madras: Christian Literature Society, 1972), chap. 1.

but on the power of God. Such a posture of vulnerability hence also characterizes the transformative process that emerges out of where the church meets others—those in other faiths, cultural others, and so on—and interacts with them under the leading of the Spirit.[13] Last but not least, then, the work of the Spirit is oriented toward the eschatological promise of the gospel. The Spirit carries the church forward in hope, enabling human witness and mission that heralds and anticipates the coming reign of God. As Newbigin writes,

> It will be the work of the Holy Spirit to lead this little community [the church], limited as it now is within the narrow confines of a single time and place and culture, into "the truth as a whole" and specifically into an understanding of "the things that are to come"—the world history that is still to be enacted.[14]

I would like to think that the reason for the relative richness of Newbigin's pneumatology within his overarching trinitarian missiology could be traced at least in part to his attentiveness early on to a burgeoning Pentecostal movement. Even at mid-century, Pentecostalism was registered as "the community of the Holy Spirit" and a "third stream of Christian tradition" (besides the Roman Catholic/Orthodox and Protestant traditions).[15] Perhaps it was this Pentecostal insight that matured over time so that Newbigin would come to see the gift of the Spirit as the divine response to believers awaiting the full and final redemption of God. The eschatological gospel poured out through the Spirit at Pentecost neutralized, if not removed, finally what was begun with the election of Abraham—the curse of Babel—and made accessible to all the nations of the world the good news in their own languages.[16] As he indicates elsewhere, "Pentecost is the biblical warrant for saying that God accepts languages."[17]

While space constraints limit what else we might want to say about Newbigin's pneumatology, it would still be accurate to identify his more as a christological rather than pneumatological trinitarianism. This is not a

[13]Newbigin's example here is the encounter between Peter and Cornelius (see *Open Secret*, p. 59); I return to this point about vulnerability later.

[14]Newbigin, *Open Secret*, p. 179; also, *The Holy Spirit and the Church*, chap. 3.

[15]See chap. 4 of Lesslie Newbigin, *The Household of God: Lectures on the Nature of the Church* (1953; repr., New York: Friendship Press, 1954), quotations from p. 94.

[16]Newbigin, *Open Secret*, p. 58; cf. Hunsberger, *Bearing the Witness of the Spirit*, pp. 251-55.

[17]Newbigin, *GPS*, p. 185.

criticism of the resulting theology of mission but simply recognition that in the development of trinitarian theological discourse, the bulk of the work accomplished in the twentieth century lay across the christological rather than pneumatological register.[18] Against this backdrop, Newbigin can be credited not only with carrying more than his fair share of the trinitarian load during the decades of his writing but even to have been slightly ahead of his contemporaries in recognizing that any fully trinitarian theology or missiology must be robustly pneumatological as well. However, having acknowledged Newbigin's contributions along these lines, one should still hesitate to overstate the magnitude of his pneumatological theology. Developments in this arena since the last years of the preceding century have certainly pushed the discussion forward in ways only dimly anticipated even in the work of this insightfully constructive and ecumenical theologian.[19]

Perhaps not surprisingly, one of the streams of pneumatological inquiry that has opened up to a torrent since the last days of Newbigin's career belongs to the Pentecostal movement that he had long ago urged to watch, observe and learn from. To be sure, as late as a festschrift published not too many years before his death, Walter Hollenweger, a leading scholar of Pentecostalism, noted, in the spirit of Newbigin's reflections on the movement, that Pentecostals still had not developed the needed theology of creator Spirit to empower Christian witness in a pluralistic world.[20] Hollenweger himself was after, with the help of pneumatological considerations honed from close study of Pentecostal spirituality, what he called a more theologically responsible syncretism that could account for faithful contextualization or indigenization of the gospel in a world of many languages, cultures and religions.[21] Although going beyond Newbigin's own proposals in some significant respects, it is possible to read Hollenweger's proposal

---

[18]Even in 1984, it was still lamented that the Spirit was the "shy" or "hidden" member of the Trinity; see Frederick Dale Bruner and William Hordern, *Holy Spirit: Shy Member of the Trinity* (Minneapolis: Augsburg Fortress, 1984).

[19]For more on the development of pneumatology over the last generation, see Veli-Matti Kärkkäinen, *Pneumatology: The Holy Spirit in Ecumenical, International, and Contextual Perspective* (Grand Rapids: Baker Academic, 2002).

[20]See Walter J. Hollenweger, "Toward a Pentecostal Missiology," in *Many Voices in Christian Mission: Essays in Honour of J. E. Lesslie Newbigin,* ed. T. Dayanandan Francis and Israel Selvanayagam (Madras: Christian Literature Society, 1994), pp. 59-79.

[21]For explication, see Hollenweger's *Pentecostalism: Origins and Developments Worldwide* (Peabody, MA: Hendrickson, 1997), pp. 132-41.

within the emerging field of a world or global Christianity as consistent with that of Newbigin's efforts to forge an authentic Christian witness in the pluralistic Western public square. It has been in the last two decades, then, that Pentecostal theologians have begun to appear and, inspired by Hollenweger among others, energetically advance the discussion in Pentecostal theology, pneumatology and pneumatological theology.[22]

There is no space within the scope of this chapter to do justice to these undertakings. I venture, however, cursory remarks on three lines of development that are relevant to the ontological, the epistemological and the teleological dimensions of Newbigin's theology of mission. In my reading of Newbigin, he only rarely connects these themes specifically to pneumatology. How might a pentecostal and pneumatological perspective further secure the trinitarian credentials of Newbigin's missiological theology?

The Spirit in a pluralist society: Newbigin-ings for* missio Trinitatis *in the present discussion? I begin with epistemology since arguably this was the starting point for much of Newbigin's missional apologetic.[23] In the throes of advances in science and technology since the Enlightenment, Newbigin discerned that twentieth-century humanity had bought into the modernist bifurcation between public facts (scientific and secular) and private values (religious or moral) and this had effectively removed religion from broader cultural and political influence. In response, Newbigin drew from the personalist and post-critical epistemology of scientist-philosopher Michael Polanyi (1891–1976),[24] in particular from the latter's argument that all knowing involves personal judgments and commit-

---

[22]For an overview of the development of Pentecostal theology, see my article "Pentecostalism and the Theological Academy," *Theology Today* 64, no. 2 (2007): 244-50; cf. also my essay "Pentecostal and Charismatic Theology," in *The Routledge Companion to Modern Christian Thought*, ed. Chad Meister and James Beilby (New York: Routledge, 2013), pp. 636-46.

[23]The first five chapters of *GPS* were basically epistemological; other places where epistemology features substantially in Newbigin's writings include *Foolishness to the Greeks: The Gospel and Western Culture* (Grand Rapids: Eerdmans, 1986), chap 4; *Truth to Tell: The Gospel as Public Truth* (Grand Rapids: Eerdmans, 1991), chap. 1; and *Truth and Authority in Modernity* (Valley Forge, PA: Trinity Press International, 1996), esp. chaps. 1-2.

[24]Polanyi's notion of personal knowing ought to be distinguished from the personalism of earlier French and North American philosophers like Emmanuel Mounier and Borden Parker Bowne, but his can also be understood as a species of personalist thinking honed especially in dialogue with the epistemology of science; see, e.g., Joan Crewdson, *Christian Doctrine in the Light of Michael Polanyi's Theory of Personal Knowledge: A Personalist Theology* (Lewiston, NY: Edwin Mellen Press, 1994).

ments, and that even scientists are situated amid and in relationship to, rather than apart from, their so-called objects of inquiry; hence, scientific advances accrue through intersubjective adjudication wherein researchers subject their interpretations of data to critical assessment and participate in, or indwell, the task of exploration within communities of inquiry.[25] So if scientific knowing depends on traditions of cultural practices (called scientific research) in which fiduciary presuppositions and tacit assumptions are continuously negotiated and even contested by researchers, is such accumulated knowledge qualitatively different from religious knowledge?

Newbigin urged that Christian doctrine and theology also emerges as those in the Christian community live into, even indwell, the claims of the gospel bequeathed by the apostolic followers of Jesus and try the veracity of such claims in the places and times of succeeding generations.[26] The difference is that whereas much of scientific work is focused in circumscribed areas, arenas or locales of investigation, the testing of the gospel unfolds across the full scope of ecclesial and human history, surely concretely manifest in the incarnational and pentecostal events of the first century but with subsequent, ongoing and anticipated implications and applications by and for the church in relating missionally to the world.[27] For this reason, Newbigin urged consideration of Christian congregations as "hermeneutic of the gospel"[28] in the sense that the meaning and significance of the *euangelion* as good news could only be accessed by the world insofar as particular communities of faith embodied its relevance and coherence. Even Christian believers come to know the gospel as public truth not only or even at all because they have studied its teachings objectively but inasmuch as they

---

[25]See Harry Prosch, *Michael Polanyi: A Critical Exposition* (Albany: State University of New York Press, 1986), chap. 5; cf. John C. Puddefoot, "Indwelling: Formal and Non-formal Elements in Faith and Life," in *Belief in Science and Christian Life: The Relevance of Michael Polanyi's Thought for Christian Faith and Life*, ed. Thomas F. Torrance (Edinburgh: Hansel Press, 1980), pp. 28-48.

[26]See Paul Weston, "Michael Polanyi and the Writings of Lesslie Newbigin," in *Critical Conversations: Michael Polanyi and Christian Theology*, ed. Murray Rae (Eugene, OR: Pickwick, 2012), pp. 157-79.

[27]Thus Newbigin's *GPS* begins with analysis and applications of Polanyi's epistemology in the first few chapters and then turns to the arena of history in chaps. 6-9. For excellent expositions of this logic of Newbigin's epistemology, see Hunsberger, *Bearing the Witness of the Spirit*, esp. chap. 4, and Hunsberger, "Faith and Pluralism: A Response to Richard Gelwick," *Tradition & Discovery (The Polanyi Society Journal)* 27, no. 3 (2000–2001): 19-29.

[28]Newbigin, *GPS*, chap. 18.

indwell its message as members of the body of Christ (and the fellowship of the Holy Spirit, I would add).

Although Newbigin did observe the scriptural traditions linking human knowing to the work of the Spirit, he brought pneumatological themes to bear not on his appropriation of Polanyian epistemological insights but on how the church comes to know the gospel as the people of God in history.[29] Pentecostal thinkers more recently, however, have begun to ask questions about epistemology from a specifically pneumatological perspective.[30] It is not just that the Spirit leads the church into all truth, but that the Spirit who is poured out on all flesh according to the Pentecost narrative (Acts 2:17) mediates the truth through the materiality, historicity and sociality of human constitutedness. In that case, knowledge of God is surely given through Scripture as well as tradition, reason and experience, as Newbigin argued, but this mediation is actually accomplished by the Spirit.[31] Such pneumatological knowing also emerges from indwelling, by the Spirit, of the church and also history itself. In that respect, human knowers are not only culturally conditioned but also culturally informed, and hence they are uniquely situated to negotiate the claims of the gospel with that of culture as they inhabit both ecclesial and cultural spaces, oftentimes simultaneously. In this way, the Day of Pentecost narrative points to both God's acceptance of the multiplicity of human languages, as Newbigin averred, and to the redemptive power of the gospel vis-à-vis the many cultures that are linguistically intertwined. Put another way, if the many tongues of Pentecost are indissoluble from the many cultures and even religious traditions of the world, then the redemption of many languages signaled at the Pentecost event foreshadows also, however dimly, God's salvation-

---

[29]The Spirit's role is prominent in six of the seven summary statements on how we come to know revelation in history; see Newbigin, *GPS*, p. 78.

[30]Beginning with James K. A. Smith, *Thinking in Tongues: Pentecostal Contributions to Christian Philosophy* (Grand Rapids: Eerdmans, 2010).

[31]For Newbigin's account of divine authority coming through these four elements of Scripture, tradition, reason and experience (the so-called Wesleyan quadrilateral, although he did not use this nomenclature), see *Truth and Authority*, chap. 2; for a Pentecostal and pneumatological version of such, see my *Spirit-Word-Community: Theological Hermeneutics in Trinitarian Perspective*, New Critical Thinking in Religion, Theology and Biblical Studies Series (2002; repr., Eugene, OR: Wipf & Stock, 2006).

historical project of salvaging and deploying cultural and even religious plurality for divine purposes.[32] We will return to expand on the ontological implications of such momentarily.

Intrinsic to such a pentecostal epistemology, however, is the teleological dimension of pneumatology and pneumatological theology. As already mentioned, Newbigin clearly diagnosed the modern predicament as involving, among other bifurcations, the divorce of purpose and design from analysis and explanation. He thus argued tirelessly that the salvific power of the gospel lay in its capacity to orient human life toward that which was supremely meaningful and hence that only such a teleological focus related to divinely elected purposes could provide the overarching vantage point for understanding Christian faith and motivate embodying and living out its commitments. In that respect, Christianity could be finally assessed only teleologically, and its publicness and truthfulness could only be determined in the eschatological long run.

This establishes Christian life in an eschatological framework, related to the ultimate purposes of the divine reign instated in the life, death and resurrection of Jesus, and initially made available to those in Christ by the Holy Spirit. Newbigin clearly recognized that the Spirit "is the presence in foretaste of the kingdom."[33] However, he did not quite, from this perspective, connect the teleological character of Christian knowing and doing with this pneumatological eschatology (or eschatological pneumatology, so it could be argued). So even if the giving of the Spirit at Pentecost heralded the coming reign of God and empowers Christian mission toward that end,[34] Newbigin did not close the loop between such a pneumatologically configured eschatology and the teleological rationality that he otherwise sought to develop in his epistemological considerations.

---

[32]For an introduction to these aspects of pentecostal and pneumatological thinking, see my *The Spirit Poured Out on All Flesh: Pentecostalism and the Possibility of Global Theology* (Grand Rapids: Baker Academic, 2005), esp. chap. 4.

[33]Newbigin, *GPS*, p. 137; this pneumatological aspect of the "foretaste of the kingdom" is repeated numerous times in the preceding pages and chapters of this volume, following the Pauline reference to the Spirit as the down payment or pledge of the coming divine reign (cf. Eph 1:13-14).

[34]Jürgen Schuster, *Christian Mission in Eschatological Perspective: Lesslie Newbigin's Contribution*, Edition AFEM, Mission Academics 29 (Nürnberg, Germany: VTR Publications; Bonn: VKW, 2009), pp. 159-61, discusses the Spirit as an aspect of Newbigin's eschatological missiology rather than provides what I am suggesting here: a pneumatological *and* eschatological missiology.

In this respect the proposal of Thomas Foust to consider Newbigin's as an eschatological epistemology can be understood pneumatologically.[35] Such a pneumatological reframing achieves two important gains. First, Newbigin's teleological rationality is situated more securely in the divine purposes unfolded in the eschatological events of incarnation and Pentecost; in this case, the purposes related to the how, why and what of knowing is not just philosophically developed but also theologically articulated in relationship to the trinitarian mission of God. Second, such a teleological-eschatological-pneumatological connection ensures a theological, even trinitarian, grounding for epistemological considerations against the allegedly but overreaching neutral standpoint sought for by the Enlightenment quests for knowledge and certainty. The full scope of such a pneumatological approach to epistemological concerns will need to be fleshed out elsewhere, but the point to be made is that the intercommunicative intersubjectivity opened up by the Pentecost event invites a reconsideration of epistemic indwelling made possible by the outpouring of the Spirit on all flesh.

Pentecostal theologians have charted both of these trajectories. My own work features the discernment of what I have called a "pneumatological imagination" that reconsiders the challenges and opportunities for the contemporary epistemological discussion in terms of the pluralistic, intersubjective and eschatological communicative event that is the Day of Pentecost narrative.[36] Within this context, the eschatological work of the Spirit bequeaths a fundamentally teleological dynamic that opens up the triune revelation to practical habituation and performative confirmation as members of the body of Christ and the fellowship of the Spirit live into the promises of the gospel and certify its effectiveness, relevance and truth. Knowing in the Spirit is thereby fundamentally eschatological and teleological as the Spirit's gift empowers thinking, feeling and acting according to the purposes of the age that has already arrived in part, but is also clearly not yet.[37]

[35]Thomas F. Foust, "Lesslie Newbigin's Epistemology: A Dual Discourse?," in *A Scandalous Prophet: The Way of Mission After Newbigin*, ed. Thomas F. Foust, George R. Hunsberger, J. Andrew Kirk and Werner Ustorf (Grand Rapids: Eerdmans, 2002), pp. 153-62, esp. p. 162.

[36]For an overview of the pneumatological imagination as I have developed it, see the concluding chapter to my book *The Dialogical Spirit: Christian Reason and Theological Method for the Third Millennium* (Eugene, OR: Cascade, 2014).

[37]For more on such a pneumatological and teleological imagination, see my *The Spirit of Creation: Modern Science and Divine Action in the Pentecostal-Charismatic Imagination*, Pentecostal

If epistemology follows ontology, as is arguably the case,[38] then any pneumato-eschatological epistemology will presume ontological commitments of one sort or other. Ontologically speaking, then, I want to connect more tightly the link between Newbigin's understanding of plurality and contemporary pneumatological discourse. It is clear that he thought deeply and at length about plurality, first during his almost thirty years in India and then in the last few decades of his life back in Britain, where he observed through ever increasing patterns of migration the transformation of the nation into a multiethnic, multicultural and multireligious society. He distinguished the historical and cultural fact of plurality from the ideology of *pluralism* that celebrated such to the point of insisting that differences are due to perceptions and are not matters of truth or falsehood, and dedicated much of his writing during the last quarter of the twentieth century to exploring how to proclaim the gospel in this context.

Yet for all of his renown as apologist against the ideology of pluralism, religious and otherwise, it needs to be highlighted that Newbigin was convinced that Christians could not only learn from but also be transformed in their encounters with others in the pluralistic public square. Without denying his admonishment that any engagement with religious otherness ought to proceed from a firm christocentrism, Newbigin nevertheless insisted that:

- "Each religion must be understood on its own terms and along the line of its own central axis."[39]
- "[Christians] will expect to learn as well as to teach, to receive as well as to give, in this common human enterprise of living and building up a common life."[40]
- "We are prepared to receive judgment and correction, to find that our Christianity hides within its appearance of obedience the reality of dis-

---

Manifestos 4 (Grand Rapids: Eerdmans, 2011); the whole of my systematic theological project is thoroughly pneumatological, trinitarian and eschatological at its core—see Amos Yong, *Renewing Christian Theology: Systematics for a Global Christianity*, images and commentary by Jonathan A. Anderson (Waco, TX: Baylor University Press, 2014).

[38]Here I follow physicist-theologian John Polkinghorne; see "From Quantum Mechanics to the Eucharistic Meal: John Polkinghorne's 'Bottom-up' Vision of Science and Theology," in Yong, *The Dialogical Spirit*, chap. 7.

[39]Newbigin, *Open Secret*, p. 171.

[40]Ibid., p. 175.

obedience. . . . We are [hence] eager to receive from our partners what God has given them, to hear what God has shown them."[41]

- "[This] means that we are vulnerable. We are exposed to temptation. We have no defenses of our own. . . . Much so-called 'Christianity' may have to be left behind in this meeting. . . . The Christian partner in the dialogue of the religions will certainly put his or her 'Christianity' at risk . . . [and] must recognize that the result of the dialogue may be a profound change in himself or herself."[42]

The point is not to diminish the import of Christian conviction in approaching the interfaith encounter, but to highlight that such commitments do not immunize Christ-followers from being transformed in their interactions with religious others.

As Newbigin, however, I am concerned to ground the possibility of such mutual transformation theologically. My more pneumatological approach thus complements his christological angle, with the intention of furbishing a more vigorous trinitarian theology for missional engagement with the pluralistic public square. To be sure, Newbigin himself understood the alethic character of trinitarian faith in a pluralistic world,[43] but there is some question about the coherence of such trinitarianism, especially in terms of how to understand the relationship between the Spirit and the Son.[44] My suggestion is to emphasize how trinitarian faith has implications for thinking about creational plurality, in which case, the renewal that is Pentecost redeems, restores and reorients such creational diversity toward divine purposes.

If in fact Newbigin devoted much of his writing career to developing a viable Christian response to the pluralism endemic to Western culture in the second half of the twentieth century, Pentecostal theology has come of

---

[41]Ibid., pp. 182-83.

[42]Ibid., pp. 184-86.

[43]See Newbigin's "Trinity as Public Truth," in *The Trinity in a Pluralistic Age: Theological Essays on Culture and Religion*, ed. Kevin J. Vanhoozer (Grand Rapids: Eerdmans, 1997), pp. 1-8.

[44]For instance, Dale W. Little, "The Significance of Theology of the Holy Spirit for Theology of Religion and for Theology of Mission in the Writings of Lesslie Newbigin and Clark Pinnock" (PhD diss., Trinity Evangelical Divinity School, 2000), p. 261, suggests that "the Spirit's work is linked to the Son in Newbigin's theology of mission but is freed from the Son in his theology of religion." My response hopefully clarifies that a solution lies in understanding the pneumatological connections between epistemology and ontology, something that Newbigin did not probe.

age and arguably matured precisely from grappling with pluralism not only outside of its ranks but as inherent to Pentecostal spirituality, ecclesiality and reality as a whole. For this task, Pentecostal theologians have thought not only missionally about pneumatology but also ontologically about how to understand the Spirit in relationship to the human experience of plurality. The Day of Pentecost narrative has served, in this capacity, to fuel ontological, theological and trinitarian reflection about diversity and manyness, albeit with missional implications, to be sure.[45]

Pentecost and Modern Science/Technology: Toward a Pneumatological Missiology

What would it be like, then, to develop Newbigin's thinking about mission in a pluralistic, scientistic and modernistic world especially in the light of the pentecostal and pneumatological gestures already present in his work? In the rest of this chapter, I want to reconsider Newbigin's trinitarian theology of mission within the modern scientific and technological context, but do so in a way that redefines pluralism and secularism according to the ontological, epistemological and teleological pneumatology developed above. In particular, a pneumatological approach to the theology and science conversation can situate the many disciplines within a larger narrative of eschatological (rather than modernistic) progress, and a pentecostal understanding of technology might also suggest alternative possibilities for indwelling, and thereby redeeming, the promise of modernity. This dual redirection, I suggest, provides Newbigin-ings for Christian belief and practice for the twenty-first century that are consistent with the missional thrusts promoted by our protagonist.

Modern science: toward a pentecostal-eschatological understanding. Much of the modern period has seen what A. D. White long ago called a "warfare" between science and theology, as one-sided as this account is.[46] To the degree that the chemical and physical sciences claimed to discover natural laws that constrained, produced and even dictated what happened, even within the human realm, thus undermining, at least on the surface, the perceived supernaturalism of the biblical accounts; to the degree that the

[45] I sketch the rudiments for a pneumatological ontology in my *Spirit-Word-Community*, part 1.

[46] See A. D. White's classic, *A History of the Warfare of Science with Theology in Christendom*, 2 vols. (New York: Dover Publications, 1896–1900).

geological and paleontological sciences suggested the earth was a lot older than what the biblical genealogies added up to; to the degree that the biological sciences indicated that human creatures had evolved from earlier non-human life forms rather than specially created; to the degree that the astronomical and cosmological sciences eviscerated the heavens from angels, demons and other spiritual beings, and predicted a final universal and cosmic conflagration or heat death, and so on—to that same degree many believed that science and religion were incompatible. Hence naturalists and materialists felt that modern science had eliminated the need for religious faith in a transcendent reality even as biblicists rejected science as godless and believed its claims would be eventually proven untrue, even according to its own methods. The latter also repudiated attempts to blend theistic faith with the modern scientific consensus since such was considered more often than not to have accommodated too much to science rather than remained faithful to the perceived supernaturalism of the Bible.

Part of the problem was that scientific advances proceeded at least in part because of modern science's capacity to identify material and efficient causes that enabled a range of technological advances. While we will return to pick up on this discussion in a moment, the point is that modern science's ability to identify causation gradually removed the need for God or other supernatural causes prevalent in the premodern mind. Yet the gains made in this direction were at the expense of understanding or even allowing for final causes. Newbigin himself emphasized that the bifurcation of teleology from scientific inquiry contributed to the overall sense of naturalistic and materialistic purposelessness.[47]

Still, unlike some biblicists, Newbigin's apologetic response was not dismissive of science. Instead, as already indicated, he drew from Polanyi's personalistic and participatory epistemology to equalize the playing field, so to speak, between science and Christian faith. Science itself proceeded from assumptions that the world was both rational and contingent, and these were indispensable to scientific inquiry. If that were the case, then "the whole work of modern science rests on faith-commitments which cannot themselves be demonstrated by the methods of science."[48] Further, from a close analysis of the scientific method of observation, hypothesis-formation

[47]Newbigin, *Foolishness to the Greeks*, chap. 4.
[48]Newbigin, *GPS*, p. 20.

and experimentation, the roles of imagination, intuition, insight, inference, abduction, and trial and error all suggest that there "is no knowing without believing, and believing is the way to knowing," and that science, "like every human activity, is a socially embodied exercise."[49] Hence for Newbigin, the alleged distinction between scientific knowledge and religious faith is just that: purported and asserted rather than based in fact or reality. Epistemologically, as we have already noted above, religious knowledge and faith are structurally similar to scientific knowledge and its presuppositions.

Newbigin's further response as a missionary to Western culture, rightly in my estimation, was to emphasize how Christian faith provided the broader cosmic *telos* that complemented the knowledge of the present material and physical world. Christian beliefs and practices thus gave ultimate meaning and significance to human lives beyond what science, with its limited foci, could provide. While correct insofar as this goes, such a response of "putting science in its place"[50] still appears a bit too defensive and may not go quite far enough in reorienting and even redeeming science itself toward a teleological vista. There are at least two aspects to this reorientation that I believe are implicit in Newbigin's views regarding science, but which could benefit from being more clearly registered. First, it has repeatedly been shown that scientific inquiry cannot altogether bracket final causality in its work.[51] Try as they might, for instance, biologists cannot separate questions about design and purpose from evolutionary science. The issue here is how to factor such aspects into research on biological evolution without undermining the path of inquiry. Relatedly, and second, research itself is driven by purpose, as Polanyi accentuated. Even scientists who work at their craft for no more than research's sake still are motivated to make a contribution and to advance the existing pool of knowledge. Hence, there is a teleological dimension to the scientific vocation and if so, then such may connect at a deeper level to Christian commitments.

I suggest that the scientific enterprise itself can be boosted with such teleological reorientation. If the origins of modern science derived from

---

[49]Ibid., pp. 33 and 214.

[50]This is how Newbigin is read by Tim Stafford, "God's Missionary to Us," *Christianity Today*, December 9, 1996, pp. 24-33, quote from p. 26.

[51]E.g., Richard F. Hassing, "Modern Natural Science and the Intelligibility of Human Experience," in *Final Causality in Nature and Human Affairs*, ed. Richard F. Hassing (Washington, DC: Catholic University of America Press, 1997), pp. 211-56.

Christian convictions—for instance about the rationality and contingency of the created order—then is it too much to expect that Christian faith might, even in the present climate, renew and revitalize the scientific undertaking by recapturing a more overarching *telos*? Having learned from Polanyi, Newbigin urges that believers "have to *indwell* the [biblical] story, as we indwell the language we use and the culture of which we are a part."[52] I suggest that the present Christian contribution to science may emerge from out of believers indwelling not only the scriptural narrative but also their own scientific cultural praxis. Is it not the case that the tacit and personal knowledge shaped by such mutual indwelling allows for skillful and seamless habitation and navigation in both domains? This is not to inappropriately synthesize or syncretize the research lab and the congregation. It is to suggest that only those who are deeply and appropriately formed by the beliefs and practices of both locales are able to translate, discursively and practically, the convictions from one arena to the other, and able to simultaneously discern how best to proceed on the Christian path with scientific knowledge and how best to push forward in the scientific sphere with Christian vision.

I further suggest that such discernment emerges most naturally from out of a Christian self-understanding that includes an explicit delineation of what might be understood as the redemptive possibilities for modern science. Here I draw also from the Day of Pentecost narrative that invites consideration of how the preservation of the many languages provides a window into the Spirit's redeeming the cultural domain. If languages are essentially and profoundly related to cultures, then the miracle of Pentecost involves not only the cross-linguistic communicative comprehensibility but also the cross-cultural and intercultural constitution of the new people of God. This is not to now baptize every aspect of any and all cultures even as it does not automatically sanctify every element of any and all human languages. It is only to point to the potency of the Spirit's pentecostal outpouring: that in principle, no cultural-linguistic group is beyond the pale of the gospel's renewing and redeeming work, and that part of the task of Christian witness is translation of the *euangelion* into

[52]Newbigin, *Truth and Authority*, p. 42; italics in original.

any and all other cultural-linguistic idioms that Christ-followers might come into contact with.[53]

When considering the modern scientific enterprise, however, I suggest a further extension of this pentecostal principle. Scientific disciplines can be considered, analogously, to be distinctive cultural-linguistic traditions. There is not only a plurality of sciences—from the physical to the bio-environmental, from the natural to the human, from the material to the technological—but expertise in each of these requires an intentional, intensive and prolonged form of socialization wherein one goes through a process of indwelling a certain scope of theoretical assumptions, of gaining facility with a certain modality of experimental practices, and of inhabiting or inculturating over years a certain set of institutional, academic and organizational arrangements.[54] Conversations across disciplines are not easily achieved, and sometimes there is outright disagreement separating one group of researchers from others. The point is this: there are many scientific disciplines, each of which opens up windows into the nature of the world and, in their own way, are capable of "speaking about God's deeds of power" (Acts 2:11), understood from the standpoint of faith. There is no reason why the power of the pentecostal outpouring of the Spirit on all flesh to renew, retrieve, reappropriate and, ultimately, redeem the many cultural-linguistic traditions of the world ought not also to be applicable to the range of sciences and their discursive cultural practices.[55]

This does not mean that any and all aspects of the many scientific disciplines are amenable to such renewal and even redemption. It only provides a theological and eschatological horizon for a Christian and pentecostal understanding of the sciences and invites believers to not have to shed their

[53]See here Lamin O. Sanneh's classic, *Translating the Message: The Missionary Impact on Culture*, 2nd ed. (Maryknoll, NY: Orbis, 2009); for my pentecostal and pneumatological appropriation, see Yong, *Spirit of Love: A Trinitarian Theology of Grace* (Waco, TX: Baylor University Press, 2012).

[54]See, e.g., Frederick Grinnell, *Everyday Practice of Science: Where Intuition and Passion Meet Objectivity and Logic* (Oxford: Oxford University Press, 2009), esp. part 1.

[55]Whether or not Donald Le Roy Stults, *Grasping Truth and Reality: Lesslie Newbigin's Theology of Mission to the Western World* (Eugene, OR: Wipf & Stock, 2008), is correct to say that Newbigin's was an overly generalized negative portrait of the Enlightenment, he is on the right track to diagnose that a more one-sided appropriation of Polanyian epistemology inhibits appreciation of science as a dialogue partner for the sake of the gospel (pp. 261-63); in that regard, this chapter suggests a pneumatological way forward for such a trinitarian and redemptive missiology vis-à-vis the modern scientific endeavor.

faith commitments in their scientific undertakings. Such a pneumatological theology of the sciences, then, opens up to embrace scientific multidisciplinarity (the fact of disciplinary plurality), inter-disciplinarity (wherein on many questions, multiple disciplinary perspectives are required for more adequate comprehension) and even trans-disciplinarity (which highlights the dynamic character of scientific development that is able to appreciate the distinctive contributions of various disciplines while also recognizing their fluid and expansive character morphing as the state of knowledge advances).[56] In this framework, the scientific task can be understood as one avenue for the outworking of the Christian scholarly vocation, one that receives scientific inquiry as a divine gift and that anticipates that the work of science will continue to illuminate the nature of creation in anticipation of the coming reign of God.

If Newbigin's strategy for Christian mission in a pluralistic and secular Western culture involved telling a story that is larger and more encompassing than that told by the modern world,[57] my point is to resituate modern science within the gospel account so that Christ-followers can inhabit that scientific space as part of, rather than separate from, their spiritual vocation. If the many tongues of Pentecost include the many scientific disciplines, then there is theological, not just pragmatic, rationale for Christians to reconsider their teleological character and to commit to working in the sciences as part of their missional vocation. In this case, then, there are Newbigin-ings for a Christian apologetics in relation to modern culture that, rather than merely evening out the playing field between the plurality of scientific disciplines and the Christian faith, actually resituate scientific pluralism amid the eschatological hope of the Day of Pentecost's redemptive trajectory.

Modern technology: toward a pneumato-missiological engagement. Yet modern science includes not just its disciplinary plurality but also its capacity to discipline, if not deform, a Christian way of life. This happens with the

---

[56]For more on such a pentecostal theology of multi-, inter- and trans-disciplinarity, see my *Spirit of Creation*, chap. 2; cf. also Yong, "The Spirit and Creation: Possibilities and Challenges for a Dialogue Between Pentecostal Theology and the Sciences," in *Journal of the European Pentecostal Theological Association* 25 (2005): 82-110, esp. part II.

[57]This strategic approach is unfolded in Newbigin's *Truth and Authority*, chap. 3.

technologies that modern science has produced.[58] The pervasiveness of technology in shaping Christian sociality is more subversive than the disciplinary experimentation that affects only those initiated into the scientific quest since the former envelops and engulfs all of us.[59] In other words, modern technology is even more potent in informing, as well as undermining, Christian commitments since it works on us subtly in the background of our daily lives rather than more overtly (as in a scientific laboratory). Herein lies a disguised pluralism, one that habituates our indwelling into at best a nominal theism and at worst a practical atheism,[60] and hence has subversive power against which any postsecular apologetic may be otherwise impotent. Although ours is a postmodern, post-Enlightenment, postsecular age in many respects, it would be a mistake to think that the advances of science and technology are going to disappear, and that secularity itself will thereby gradually wither away. If instead the secular will be perpetuated at least technologically, then the Christian mission to Western culture will also need to be recalibrated in late-modern terms, precisely part of the goal of this essay.[61]

The way forward is to render more visible—naming and identifying—the invisible pluralism of modern technology.[62] Isn't it the case that the undermining of Christian identity in the modern world derives precisely from tech-

---

[58]While there is a clear distinction between science as an empirical process of discovery and technology as the entire human world of artifacts, systems and constructions, for the purposes of this chapter, I am interested primarily in scientifically informed technological developments. Even here, the literature is too vast and the issues too complex to treat adequately. For a helpful introductory discussion to these matters, see Dennis W. Cheek, "Is There Room for the Spirit in a World Dominated by Technology? Pentecostals and the Technological World," in *Science and the Spirit: A Pentecostal Engagement with the Sciences*, ed. James K. A. Smith and Amos Yong (Bloomington: Indiana University Press, 2010), pp. 192-208.

[59]Thus even a generation ago, the prescient Jacques Ellul wrote: "Enclosed within his artificial creation, man finds that there is 'no exit'; that he cannot pierce the shell of technology to find again the ancient milieu to which he was adapted for hundreds of thousands of years." See Ellul, *The Technological Society*, trans. John Wilkinson (New York: Vintage Books, 1964), p. 428; cf. Ellul's *The Technological Bluff*, trans. Geoffrey W. Bromiley (Grand Rapids: Eerdmans, 1990).

[60]Thus do the essayists in Michael Breen, Eamonn Conway and Barry McMillan, eds., *Technology and Transcendence* (Dublin: Columbia Press, 2003), strive for transcendent perspective over the ubiquitousness of technology and its grip on human life.

[61]Hence my proposals are meant to complement those of Newbigin's and his eminent missiological colleague David J. Bosch, *Believing the Future: Toward a Missiology of Western Culture* (Valley Forge, PA: Trinity Press International, 1995).

[62]On technology's invisibility in Christian perspective, see Albert Borgmann, *Power Failure: Christianity in the Culture of Technology* (Grand Rapids: Brazos, 2003), chap. 1; in this text, Borgmann refracts his expertise in philosophy of technology, about which he has published extensively, through a Christian lens.

nology's promise to produce what in premodern times had been the preserve of God? To the degree that bio-agricultural technologies, for instance, have harnessed and produced food to alleviate hunger around the world (the hindrances to distribution of political economies notwithstanding), thereby lifting the urgency of prayer for rain or for holding back the floods that could destroy the harvest; to the degree that biomedical technologies have made possible the repair and even enhancement of human bodily impairment, dysfunction and frailty, thereby lessening the need for miraculous curing or healing; to the degree that information and engineering technologies have produced a middle class defined by entertainment, leisure and consumption, thereby eliminating the hope of divine intervention for a flourishing quality of life, and so on—to that same degree modern technology has shifted the human gaze from the divine to the immanent sphere. It is not even that there is a need to call on God to defend ourselves against technology, but that a technologically constructed and sustained life minimizes the need to call on God at all. In fact, its pervasiveness has rendered all of us, Christians and otherwise, complicit in enhancing such a way of life, so that there is "a common and tacit agreement to shape the world and conduct one's life according to the technological pattern."[63] Technology is thus not the enemy out there (as scientists and their laboratories can be imagined to be) but is now within us, having redefined our humanity, creatureliness and even finitude.[64] More troublingly, however, it is not just that most of us now think that the many problems human beings confront can be technologically overcome, but that our technological expertise has transformed us into masters of our own fate, bringing with this also our capacity for ultimate self-destruction.[65]

Needless to say, any attempt to develop a naysaying approach that rejects technological advances will be ineffective, not to mention hypocritical, given its reliance on information technologies for dissemination of such an apologetic. A more measured stance will attempt to retain the interpersonal aspects of human interaction in order to ameliorate the universal stranglehold of a technologically ordered way of life. Yet such an approach, while

---

[63]Borgmann, *Power Failure*, p. 44.

[64]Philip Hefner, *Technology and Human Becoming* (Minneapolis: Fortress, 2003).

[65]David J. Hawkin, ed., *The Twenty-First Century Confronts Its Gods: Globalization, Technology, and War* (Albany: State University of New York Press, 2004), although the essayists in this volume tend to treat technology and war as disparate idols rather than explore their interrelated character.

valuable in many important respects, remains ultimately reactionary to modern science and technology. And even if some ground were gained in the meanwhile, in the long run, human life and identity will only be increasingly intertwined with technology (even as we have from our earliest history already been tool-makers and technology-developers).

My proposal, then, is to reorient our posture toward technology so that we are not merely reacting to its potential threats, but consciously engaged with what we might call its Christianization and even redemption.[66] By this, I am referring not to any neo-colonialist takeover of our technological industries, but to a more intentional attempt to reorient and redeem the opportunities and challenges inherent in technology. There are at least three trajectories for such a task: one generic, the second along a more specifically Newbiginian route and, finally, in pneumatological mode toward a trinitarian missiology for contemporary pluralistic and secularistic culture.

More generally, any Christian approach to technology will need to have practical benefits. By this, I mean that a Christian theology of technology in the end empowers more faithful Christian discipleship through the use of technology. Brent Waters, a Christian ethicist, puts it this way: that one noble objective is "to develop and use technologies that enable a faithful exercising of limited dominion,"[67] which, in recognition of our creatureliness, respects the finitude of our technological undertakings. Given the dizzying breadth of technological developments, Christians will need to nurture interdisciplinary expertise so as to be able to bring theological and ethical commitments to bear on the analysis, assessment and discernment of technological advances. If Newbigin decried a one-size-fits-all approach to the plurality of cultures,[68] so also ought we to be wary about any *one* mode of engaging with the diversity of human technologies. How to live as technological pluralists will remain a central question that will require input from as many perspectives as there are technological disciplines and sciences.

---

[66]Here along the lines of the redemption of technology proposed by Brad J. Kallenberg, *God and Gadgets: Following Jesus in a Technological Age* (Eugene, OR: Cascade, 2011), chap. 5.

[67]Brent Waters, *From Human to Posthuman: Christian Theology and Technology in a Postmodern World* (Burlington, VT: Ashgate, 2006), pp. 144-50, quotation at p. 146.

[68]Cogently argued by Nicholas J. Wood, *Faiths and Faithfulness: Pluralism, Dialogue and Mission in the Work of Kenneth Cragg and Lesslie Newbigin* (Waynesboro, GA: Paternoster, 2009).

Yet, second, the goal is not only to develop a practical strategy for controlling technology before it controls us, as essential as such may be. Rather, such a utilitarian approach buys into the instrumentalist premises that spur technological inquiry and development. A more holistic Christian response will spring off Newbigin-ings afforded by his epistemology of indwelling. Here, as in the preceding section, Christians are urged toward what might be considered a mutual inhabitation wherein Christian faith informs interaction with our culture of technology on the one hand, and responsible participation in our technological world shapes Christian practice on the other hand. The goal here is a prioritization or privileging of Christian commitments in engagement with technology, even while acknowledging that technological knowledge can also enhance and empower a more authentic Christian faith and robust Christian witness.

Newbigin's proposal of the "congregation as hermeneutic of the gospel"[69] invites further consideration of how such a redemption or Christianization of technology might unfold. Newbigin's focus in this matter was on providing the communal, traditioned and interpersonal framework for reading, interpreting and understanding the Scriptures on the one hand, and for communicating the gospel to a watching world on the other hand. This is because any truth claims are sustained and convincing not on their own as logical arguments but as informed ways of life that coherently address contemporary experiences, questions and anxieties.[70] Thus the practices of Christian congregations—their praise/thanksgiving, truth-seeking/testifying, ministry of edification to those within the congregation, and priestly and compassionate mediation to outsiders—both represent and embody God's "new social order" and provide hope to the world.[71] I suggest that such practices, already technologically mediated, need to be technologically alert, savvy, so to speak. Without explicit attention to the technological dimensions of our worship, prayer, praise, ministry and mission, we will be blind to how each of these activities is already technologically

[69]Newbigin, *GPS*, chap. 18; see also John Flett's chapter in this volume, and compare Darren Cronshaw and Steve Taylor, "The Congregation in a Pluralist Society: Rereading Newbigin for Missional Churches Today," *Pacifica: Australasian Theological Studies* 27, no. 2 (2014): 206-28.

[70]See Newbigin, *Foolishness to the Greeks*, p. 64; the entire third chapter of this book explicates on the interconnections between beliefs and practices.

[71]Newbigin, *GPS*, p. 231.

framed anyway. Thoughtful alertness to the underlying technological mediation of such practices allows both more appropriate modes of indwelling the technology on the one hand and redirection of such technology for missional purposes on the other hand.[72]

This leads, third, to what might be considered a pneumatological missiology of technology. Such a theological vision is pneumatological in extending the pentecostal theology of science proposed above in a performative direction so as to be alert to and pointedly engaged with the full scope and range of technological enterprises that constitute human life. The many tongues of Pentecost not only provide a pluralistic theology and ontology for understanding, interacting with and redeeming the many scientific disciplines, but also empower many practices amidst the technological pluralism of the present age.[73] Such a pentecostal and pneumatological missiology understands the many forms of technology as divine gifts that can be deployed for good or ill, and thereby recognizes the need to nurture proper habits of living technologically *and* faithfully so as to facilitate more accurate discernment about the promise and challenges of technological advance in light of the promise of the coming reign of God. If what we need "is a Spirit-led understanding of the trinitarian life of God that shows us how to be related to the lives of other people,"[74] then nothing less ought to be expected for us to engage with others about what is at stake in a technologically mediated, if not defined, human future so that such is oriented toward the values of the divine reign. This means that the gospel narrative as scripted in the biblical witness provides the template for how the medium shapes the message and does so by reordering human life in accordance with the message of

---

[72]This is also the call of Shane Hipps, *Flickering Pixels: How Technology Shapes Your Faith* (Grand Rapids: Zondervan, 2009).

[73]I elaborate on the "many tongues equal many practices" argument both for engaging religious pluralism and for a pluralistic public square, respectively, in my books *Hospitality and the Other: Pentecost, Christian Practices, and the Neighbor*, Faith Meets Faith series (Maryknoll, NY: Orbis, 2008), esp. chap. 2, and *In the Days of Caesar: Pentecostalism and Political Theology—The Cadbury Lectures 2009*, Sacra Doctrina: Christian Theology for a Postmodern Age series (Grand Rapids: Eerdmans, 2010), esp. chap. 3.

[74]As summarized by Daniel Hardy, "A Response to the Consultation," in *A Prophet: The Way of Mission After Newbigin*, ed. Thomas F. Foust, George R. Hunsberger, J. Andrew Kirk and Werner Ustorf (Grand Rapids: Eerdmans, 2002), pp. 227-33, quote at p. 230.

Jesus.[75] The objective is to live into the promise of technology insofar as it enables more Spirit-imbued life and witness in a pluralistic and secular world, while resisting its insidious power to corrupt Christian belief and practice in the present time.

The call for a teleological and performative mode of engagement with science and technology nevertheless depends on divine initiative rather than on human responsibility. Fortunately, the outpouring of the Spirit in "the last days" (Acts 2:17) inaugurates the eschatological purposes of God and enables our participation in such a venture. In this way the gift of the Spirit is central to the trinitarian *missio Dei* for a pluralistic and secularistic late-modern third millennium.[76]

[75]Murray Jardine, *The Making and Unmaking of Technological Society: How Christianity Can Save Modernity from Itself* (Grand Rapids: Brazos, 2004), esp. pp. 247-51, suggests how Christian liturgical, charismatic and communal practices have the potency of reforming social space, interactivity and life and thereby redeem human technological creativity from its otherwise unanticipated destructive effects.

[76]I am grateful to Veli-Matti Kärkkäinen for his reading of a penultimate draft of this chapter. Also a novice on the interface between Christian theology and modern technology, I am thankful to Dennis Cheek for his feedback on my essay. Last but not least, I appreciate the proofreading of my graduate assistant, Ryan Seow. Of course, any errors of fact or interpretation remain my responsibility.

8

Evangelism in a Pluralistic Society

The Newbigin Vision

Carrie Boren Headington

The crisp, English spring morning began with a brief time of prayer just outside the room where the esteemed Christian theologian Cardinal John Henry Newman had prayed daily over a century ago. As the missioner designated for Oriel College for the Oxford University Christian Union missions week, I was filled with anticipation. The breakfast dining hall was crowded with students ready to start their day, and I sat smack in the middle of a packed table. As we introduced ourselves, it became clear that my table was laden with first-year students, many of them studying science, brimming with ideas and academic acumen.

"I haven't seen you before. Are you visiting?" one student asked.

"Yes, in fact, I am. I am a graduate student at Wycliffe Hall down the road," I replied.

"What brings you here?"

"Well I am part of a group on campus this week which is engaging students in discussions about the meaning of life."

"Let me know when you figure it out," said Dan, the evident leader.

"We are available so people can ask any question about life and spiritual issues."

"Spiritual? Are you here to talk about God?"

"Yes," I replied.

"Good luck with that!" Dan quipped.

Laughter erupted from the entire table except for three female students adorned in hijabs. I exchanged a quick glance with them but they kept their heads down and did not engage the conversation.

"Surely you have some questions about God," I said with a smile.

At that prompting, the questions flew.

They began asking how anyone can know there is a God at all. They were science majors who sought proof and evidence.

We began discussing how there are very few things one can actually prove in an airtight manner. I argued that I couldn't prove, for example, that my mom loves me but I know it to be true more than anything on this earth. So how do we come to know anything?

As science majors, they countered by discussing the value of inductive reasoning.

For the next hour we discussed reasons for God's existence: the fact of the universe, the design of the world, the creativity of humanity and the sense of global values.

We were having fun bantering with each other. Then I asked, "And what about the fact of religion around the world?"

"Religion is what has caused all of the wars and messes in the world," one student replied.

"Yes, part of that is true but much good has come out of religion too—hospitals, schools, care for the poor, to name a few. But think about this for a moment: Doesn't it seem that all people have an instinctual desire to worship something beyond themselves? There is an innate spiritual impulse to connect with the divine. This impulse cannot be squelched by communism or persecution. It is a universal instinct."

"Maybe. I am not sure," one of the students said quietly.

I had one more point to share.

"I believe that the greatest pointer to the existence of God is the reality that God has actually revealed himself to humankind in the person of Jesus Christ. God came to earth and walked among us."

Dan looked at me with disdain and said, "Ohhh, I see, you are a Christian. So you are not really here to have an open discussion about God. You want to convert us. Not going to happen."

At this point the students peeled off. They "suddenly" had to go to class.

A couple of students stayed behind asking questions about Jesus, the cross and the Bible. I was astonished that citizens of a country that has an established state church could have no sense of Christianity, even to the point of total ignorance about the symbol of the cross.

To my surprise, when I exited the dining hall, the three Muslim women were waiting for me. They invited me to their dorm room for tea and more discussion. They said they were praying for me as I discussed God with such a hostile (albeit jovial) group of students. They were proud of me for my perseverance. We sat for a number of hours getting to know one another. I invited them to the evening talk where there would be a presentation of the gospel. They agreed.

This was the first morning of the mission.

When Lesslie Newbigin wrote his groundbreaking work *The Gospel in a Pluralist Society*,[1] he prophetically defined the situation I faced that morning around the breakfast table: a pluralistic world where the gospel of Jesus Christ would be one of many competing voices in the public square and where Christianity would be diminished to private belief and rejected as public truth. Newbigin wrote on the cusp of a post-Christian era in the West, when Christians were grappling with how (if at all) to proclaim the Christian message. Today marks an even more diverse landscape of competing and often clashing worldviews. Newbigin's diagnosis of Western culture and the church's mission to share the gospel in the public arena is a call to reexamine how evangelism is done in and through our churches today.

In this chapter, I engage Newbigin's *The Gospel in a Pluralist Society*, examining its implications for evangelism in our world today. It is my contention that twenty-five years after its publication, Newbigin's insights serve as a compass for how the church should undertake evangelism in the West. While Newbigin serves as a foundational resource for challenging the church to embrace its missional identity,[2] the specific practice of evangelism has not played a major role in the discussion. That being said, *The Gospel in a Pluralist Society* has much to say about evangelism. Newbigin, in fact, provides an evangelism commitment, one that maps a plan regarding

[1]Lesslie Newbigin, *The Gospel in a Pluralist Society* (Grand Rapids: Eerdmans, 1989).

[2]See Darrel Guder et al., *Missional Church: A Vision for the Sending of the Church in North America* (Grand Rapids: Eerdmans, 1998). A basic introduction to this conversation from a Newbigin perspective is Alan Roxburgh and M. Scott Boren, *Introducing the Missional Church* (Grand Rapids: Baker, 2009).

the message, the messenger and the method the church is to take in the work of evangelism.

I write as an evangelism practitioner serving in a mainline Protestant denomination that is in rapid decline in the West. In a sincere, impassioned attempt to reach people with the gospel in our contemporary culture, some within my denomination and other mainline churches have been on the forefront of defining evangelism in terms of how the gospel can best absorb much of the Western pluralistic mindset in both theology and ethics.

For the past decade, I have served as missioner for evangelism for the Episcopal Diocese of Dallas. My task has been to do the work of an evangelist and apologist, proclaiming the gospel in word and deed, and to equip congregations to share our faith as individuals in their everyday lives and as local church communities. We have seventy-five churches in our diocese that include churches in rural areas, the inner city, Spanish-speaking-only areas, rich, poor and mixed-income areas, universities, suburbs, and new immigrant communities such as Bhutanese, Nigerian, Kenyan, Sudanese and Korean, to name a few. Additionally, I have had the opportunity to work with ecumenical partners through various citywide and global evangelistic movements and missions in the UK, Africa, Latin America, Europe and the US. Alongside evangelistic teams, we have struggled together in seeking to grasp our respective cultural contexts and how to express the good news we have in Jesus Christ.

In my context, not unlike other parts of the West, the topic of evangelism elicits strong reactions, both positive and negative. Theologians, practitioners and the lay faithful alike have views of how evangelism should be done (if at all). The term itself stems from the Greek word *euangelion*, meaning good news. Evangelism is the act of sharing the good news of Jesus Christ in word (proclamation) and deed (actions) and inviting people to become a follower of him. Missiologists have various emphases when defining evangelism, but the three elements of evangelism involving words, actions and invitation are central. Christopher Wright emphasizes the proclamation aspect of evangelism. Wright notes, "The work of the 'gospel' (Phil 2:22), then, seems to refer primarily to this task of making the good news known by all means of communication possible and at whatever cost. There is an intrinsically verbal dimension to the gospel. It is a story that needs to be told in order that its truth and significance may be understood."[3] The words must be accompanied by actions in evangelism. Missiologist David Bosch defines evangelism "as that dimension of activity of the church's mission which seeks to offer every person, everywhere, a valid opportunity to be directly challenged by the gospel of explicit faith in Jesus Christ, with a view to embracing him as Savior, becoming a living member of his community, and being enlisted in his service of reconciliation, peace and justice on earth."[4] Evangelism today, as in centuries past, echoes the disciple Andrew sharing with his brother, "We have found the Messiah" (John 1:41) and inviting him to meet and to follow Jesus. As Scott Sunquist highlights, "Evangelism is, at heart, introducing Jesus Christ to others and inviting them to become partakers in his Kingdom."[5]

Newbigin's Diagnosis of Evangelism in the West

What does evangelism look like in the pluralistic context of Dallas? To answer this question well and to properly equip people for the work of evangelism, we must follow Newbigin's emphasis on understanding the cultural landscape and diagnose the role that evangelism has played in our culture. He observed, "In the past two hundred years European missionaries have given much attention to studying the cultures of non-European people with a view to communicating the gospel to them. They have unfortunately not given so much time to understanding this (Western) culture within which

---

[3]Christopher Wright, *The Mission of God's People* (Grand Rapids: Zondervan, 2010), pp. 192-93.

[4]David Bosch, "Evangelism: Theological Currents and Cross-Currents Today," in *The Study of Evangelism: Exploring a Missional Practice of the Church*, ed. Paul W. Chilcote and Laceye C. Warner (Grand Rapids: Eerdmans, 2008), p. 17. See also, within this same volume, Orlando E. Costa's definition, which focuses on the call to invite one to make a commitment to follow Jesus Christ, pp. 33-42; Ron Sider focuses on evangelism as an announcement through both words and actions and the invitation to be part of the reconciling community of Christ followers, p. 200; George R. Hunsberger focuses on evangelism as being companions to others on the spiritual journey, pp. 67-68; and last but not least, Walter Brueggemann: "Evangelism is an invitation and summon to reinstate our talk and our walk according to the reality of this God, a reality not easily self-evident in our society. The call of the gospel includes the negative assertion that the technological-therapeutic-militaristic consumer world is false, not to be trusted or obeyed, and the positive claim that an alternative way in the world is legitimated by and appropriate to the new governance of the God who is back in town" (p. 233). Beyond this, I also draw attention to Michael Green who in his *Evangelism Through the Local Church* (London: Hodder & Stoughton, 1993), p. 9, cites his favorite definition of *evangelism* from Archbishop William Temple as follows: "To evangelize is so to present Jesus Christ in the power of the Holy Spirit, that men shall come to put their trust in God through him, to accept him as their Saviour, and serve him as their King in the fellowship of his church."

[5]Scott W. Sunquist, *Understanding Christian Mission: Participating in Suffering and Glory* (Grand Rapids: Baker Academic, 2013), p. 312.

the gospel has been so long domesticated. And this is a very, very difficult undertaking, a very painful undertaking."[6]

The *Gospel in a Pluralist Society* commences with a direct confrontation of the way evangelism is being done and has been done in the Western church. Newbigin rattles the slumbering church, saying that evangelism in the Western context can no longer follow the strategy of "revival" and "calling one back to their Christian roots."[7] The context has changed.

Serving in the Bible Belt region of America, where it seems there is a megachurch on every corner,[8] Newbigin's challenge is especially poignant to us. For the past fifty years, the national Episcopal Church's evangelistic campaign was to place a sign in the middle of every town, which read, "The Episcopal Church Welcomes You" with an arrow pointing to the church location. We truly thought that this was all we had to do in Texas in order to fill our pews. Other denominations would say the same. Our region in the American South was perhaps the last bastion of Christendom in the West. This is no longer true. Even here, roughly sixty percent of the people in our region say they do not attend church regularly.[9] *The Gospel in a Pluralist Society* alerts the church that we are in a post-Christian pluralistic reality, which calls into question the continued use of past evangelism strategies.

Newbigin's depiction of Western culture as one of doubt and suspicion, where all truth is seen as subjective and relative, is even more pronounced today than it was twenty-five years ago. Any claim to absolute truth, except in the scientific arena, is viewed as untenable, haughty and naive. Knowledge is bifurcated into belief and fact. The world of beliefs and values has been relegated to the private sphere of personal opinion. The world of facts, mainly scientific, are the only ones allowed in the public sphere as objective truth. "One is free to promote [Christianity] as personal belief but to affirm it as fact

---

[6]Lesslie Newbigin, *Signs Amid the Rubble: The Purposes of God in Human History* (Grand Rapids: Eerdmans, 2003), p. 117.

[7]Newbigin, *GPS*, p. 4.

[8]As of 2013, the Dallas area has five of the top fifty largest churches in America. "2013 100 Largest Churches in America," *Outreach Magazine*, accessed November 22, 2014, www.outreachmagazine.com/2013-outreach-100-largest-churches-america.html.

[9]Michael Lipka, "What Surveys Say About Worship Attendance—and Why Some Stay Home," Pew Research Center website, September 13, 2013, www.pewresearch.org/fact-tank/2013/09/13/what-surveys-say-about-worship-attendance-and-why-some-stay-home.

is simply arrogance."[10] A Western free society is "not controlled by accepted dogma but characterized by the critical spirit which is ready to subject all dogmas to critical (and even skeptical) examination."[11] As a result, very little is accepted as public truth. Most beliefs are relativized to private subjectivity.

I will never forget a conversation about sin I had with a highly intelligent, affable, seemingly reasonable college student. He said he didn't believe in sin because there is no objective, supreme moral law or moral lawgiver to define right and wrong. For this young man, all truth and morality was subjective, except perhaps scientific law. I said, "Well surely you cannot say the horrific Holocaust of the Jewish people is morally acceptable." The young man thoughtfully paused and said, "Well, I did not live during that time. I was not in the mind of the SS. Who am I to judge their actions?" The young man was not trying to be provocative. He was expressing the relativism that Newbigin analyzed. Morality, religion and all that comes with them are siloed to personal preferences. They have nothing to do with truth.[12]

Western culture especially embraces this relativistic worldview in our burgeoning pluralistic and increasingly urban culture, where various secular and religious beliefs interact and sometimes collide.[13] This is evident in our own context in Dallas, Texas, which reported the highest influx of refugees in the past year of any city in the United States.[14] Newbigin noted that the leading Western approach to managing globalization and diverse communities is to embrace all voices and never affirm one truth over another for the sake of peace and unity. "Pluralism is conceived to be a proper characteristic of the secular society, a society where there is no officially approved pattern of belief or conduct."[15]

---

[10]Newbigin, *GPS*, p. 5.

[11]Ibid., p. 1.

[12]About Newbigin's home country, he writes in his book *The Other Side of 1984* (Geneva, Switzerland: World Council of Churches, 1983), p. 23, "It would be hard to deny that contemporary British (and most Western) Christianity is in an advanced case of syncretism. The Church has lived so long as a permitted and even privileged minority, accepting relegation to the private sphere in a culture whose public life is controlled by a totally different vision of reality, that it has almost lost the power to address a radical challenge to that vision and therefore to 'modern Western civilization' as a whole."

[13]See Diana Eck's Pluralism Project at Harvard University: www.pluralism.org.

[14]"The Vision" Movement Day Greater Dallas, http://movementdaygreaterdallas.com/the_vision.php.

[15]Newbigin, *GPS*, p. 1.

Newbigin deploys the work of Michael Polanyi and places the Western relativistic and pluralistic society in the context of what Polanyi, sociologist Peter Berger and others term "a plausibility structure." "Every society depends for its coherence upon a set of . . . 'plausibility structures,' patterns of belief and practice accepted within a given society, which determine which beliefs are plausible to its members and which are not."[16] This plausibility structure becomes the public truth, the contours of how one should live. In the current Western plausibility structure, the gospel plays a limited role, relegated to private belief.

Newbigin illustrates how the church in large measure has bowed to this plausibility structure and relegated evangelism in the West to a relativistic, privatized spirituality. While there are plenty of examples where the gospel is winsomely presented and demonstrated in communities throughout the West, Newbigin's diagnosis of the way the Western church has become infected by the prevailing culture is sobering. Newbigin warns of three conditions in particular:

1. *Evangelism is not to be done with those practicing other faiths.* Christians use the term evangelism when speaking of neighbors who are like them but with those practicing other religions they speak of "dialogue." "This reluctance to use the language of evangelism in a multi-faith context is a symptom of something very fundamental in our contemporary culture."[17] In this context, religion in general plays a role in private, personal beliefs, and Christianity is just one truth among many.

2. *Evangelism focuses on individual conversion.* Evangelistic methods center on private conversion and often ignore the public arena. "The affirmation that the truth revealed in the gospel ought to govern public life is offensive."[18]

3. *Evangelism has been diminished in both message and action.* The evangelistic message has been domesticated into either a set of propositions capitulating to modernity, or relativized to one of the many ways to know God, capitulating to postmodernity. This diminishment of gospel proclamation directly affects evangelistic actions. When proclamation is

[16]Ibid., p. 8.
[17]Ibid., p. 4.
[18]Ibid., p. 7.

> missing from evangelistic action, the church then becomes relegated to one of the many social agencies doing good works. Message and action no longer go hand in hand.

The Gospel in a Pluralist Society offers more than a creative analysis of Western culture; it also offers solutions for Western Christians to break out of the evangelistic traps where we have placed ourselves. Newbigin invites the Western church to see the gospel afresh as public truth and thereby leads the church to rethink the evangelistic message, the evangelistic messenger and the evangelistic methods.

The Message

The gospel is not some good news or a bit of good news—it is *the* good news that God has revealed himself and redeemed the world in and through the life, death and resurrection of Jesus Christ. Evangelism is the proclamation of this good news in word and deed, affecting the whole of life. Before launching into the way we evangelize, it is crucial to look at the gospel message itself. Newbigin firmly expresses a particular view of the message we are to proclaim.

In an effort to uphold the Christian faith in the face of post-Enlightenment modernity, Christian evangelism and apologetics sought to define the Christian message in the rational terms of the day. Evangelists explained that Christianity, like science, is reasonable. Newbigin contends that the eighteenth-century Christians onward were misguided in their articulation of the faith. Christianity was relegated to a mere system of "timeless metaphysical truths about God, nature, and man. The Bible was a source of information about such eternal truths as could be discovered by direct observation of nature or by reflection on innate human ideas."[19] As a result, the Bible was viewed more as a list of facts rather than a narrative. Newbigin counters, "We do not defend the Christian message by domesticating it within the reigning plausibility structure. This was surely the grand mistake of the eighteenth-century defenses of the reasonableness of Christianity."[20] The defenders of Christianity accepted "the assumptions of their assailants."[21]

---

[19]Ibid., p. 12.
[20]Ibid., p. 25.
[21]Ibid., p. 3.

"The eighteenth century was, above all, the time when the attempt was made to show that Christianity was acceptable within the limits of reason and without recourse to revelation."[22] This has played out into two ways, one modern and one often labeled as postmodern.

The modernist evangelistic message became an affirmation of Christianity's logicality according to the terms of modernity. Cru's (formerly Campus Crusade for Christ) primary evangelistic tool for many years, *The Four Spiritual Laws*, is an example depicting Christian propositions according to the patterns of scientific and natural laws. Christianity is diluted when defined only in terms of its "reasonableness."[23] Often as a result, those who assent to mere propositional truths become followers of an intellectual ideology that does not permeate the whole of life.

At the Third Lausanne Congress on World Evangelization 2010 in Cape Town, South Africa, I remember vividly when Antoine Rutayisire, the dean of Anglican Cathedral of Kigali, Rwanda, posed the question regarding his country, "How is it that a country whose population was cited as 90 percent Christian could collapse into genocide?" I thought the answer would entail a lack of discipleship. To my surprise, the dean rooted the problem in how Christianity was initially presented and then subsequently taught in Africa by many Western missionaries. The difficulty originated with the evangelistic message itself. He said that because the gospel was presented as a set of propositional truths, the fullness of the gospel was not grasped. The Rwandans were given Christian information but neither the message nor the tools for transformation. As a result, when it came to facing tribal battles, the Rwandans resorted to their traditional tribal way of thinking and handling conflict. To use Newbigin's terminology, the Rwandans were given a gospel in narrow, modernistic, propositional terms that did not incorporate the whole of life. The way we evangelize is not only a matter of eternal life; it is a matter of life and death, here and now.

The current evangelistic message has also been shaped by the ruling worldview of postmodernity, centering on subjective personal experience. Sincerity and authenticity have become the test of the gospel's relevance. In this postmodern scenario, the Christian message becomes one of the

---

[22]Ibid., p. 52.

[23]Ibid., p. 3.

many choices from which to choose in the smorgasbord of philosophical and ideological options.

> There are on the one hand those who seek to identify God's revelation as a series of objectively true propositions, propositions which are simply to be accepted by those who wish to be Christians. And on the other hand there are those who see the essence of Christianity as an inward spiritual experience, personal to each believer, and who see Christian doctrine as formulated during church history as symbolic representations of these essentially inward and private experiences.[24]

This too results in the gospel remaining privatized and open to subjective interpretation. In this scenario, Christianity is not public truth; it is merely one of many paths on an individual's experiential spiritual journey. This mitigates the purpose and therefore the fervor to evangelize in a pluralistic world. The urgency is lost.[25]

Furthermore, evangelism under these strictures centers on personal conversion and often omits communal and public life. When this individualistic Western style of evangelism is exported to other, more communally-oriented countries, like Rwanda, the impact can be devastating. When truth is privatized, the communal ethics can easily become lost, and havoc can ensue. Perhaps the destruction that can result from the privatization of the gospel is not as overt in the West as it is in other contexts, but it is no less destructive.

In today's postmodern context, one could argue that the prevailing "plausibility structure" in the West is free-market capitalism. The goal in life for Westerners is material security, happiness and prosperity. Newbigin explores this in *Truth to Tell*, a subsequent work to *The Gospel in a Pluralist Society*. While capitalism was designed as a way to balance supply and demand, it has become a system that operates independently of ethical boundaries. Financial gain and growth are ends in and of themselves, and the laws of the market dictate the way common life works. The gospel itself has no bearing on financial questions from a public point of view, as they operate in separate domains.[26] Within this plausibility structure, the evangelistic message

---

[24]Ibid., p. 24.

[25]Ibid., p. 25.

[26]See Lesslie Newbigin, *Truth to Tell: The Gospel as Public Truth* (Grand Rapids: Eerdmans, 1991), pp. 76-77. Also note that Alexis de Tocqueville made similar observations in the 1830s; see his *Democracy in America*, trans. and ed. Harvey C. Mansfield and Delba Winthrop (Chicago: University of Chicago Press, 2000).

is often presented as God sending Jesus Christ to fill the personal inner void that material goods will not fill. It can easily turn the gospel into some kind of panacea for the "God-shaped hole"[27] in individuals, to give us a better life, a fulfilled spirituality and, in some circles, even material success. The gospel in this context remains privatized and domesticated.[28]

In an effort to contend with dominant Western plausibility structures, Newbigin shows how Christian theologians have wrangled over the nature of the Christian gospel, soteriology, and the role and authority of Scripture. A divide between "fundamentalists" and "liberals" has resulted in radically different perspectives on which evangelistic message to proclaim (if one is to proclaim at all). From the gospel message being defined as a series of propositions to transactional penal substitution to a subjective personal spiritual experience that will bring personal fulfillment, the evangelistic message has been a source of contention. Newbigin's proposal for the evangelistic message cuts through this quandary. He not only provides a way forward for Christians to engage the non-Christian world, he potentially provides a bridge between Christian "fundamentalists" and "liberals."[29]

The evangelistic message, according to Newbigin, should center on the cosmic narrative of God's purposes for the world. Above all else, evangelism should be rooted in the telling of the biblical story of God creating the world, revealing himself to the world, and redeeming the world in and through his Son, Jesus Christ. "The dogma, the thing given for our acceptance of faith, is not a set of timeless propositions: it is a story."[30] The evangelistic message is the particular biblical story rooted in the life, death and resurrection of Jesus Christ. This christocentric story of God's purpose and historical ac-

---

[27]See Blaise Pascal, *Pensées* (London: Penguin, 1995), 10.148.

[28]N. T. Wright makes an overt argument along these lines; see his *Surprised by Hope: Rethinking Heaven, the Resurrection, and the Mission of the Church* (New York: HarperCollins, 2008), p. 217.

[29]With regard to the debate between fundamentalist versus liberal strategies, Newbigin writes, "I believe that this is an unnecessary quarrel arising from the fact that both sides have been seduced by the unquestioned assumptions of our culture. We shall prove our faithfulness to the gospel by being both fundamentalist and liberal; fundamentalist in the sense that we acknowledge no other foundation upon which to build either our thinking or our action, either our private or our public life, than the Lord as he is known to us through the Scriptures; and liberal in the sense that we are ready to live in a plural society, open to new experience, ready to listen to new ideas, always pressing forward toward fuller understanding in the confidence that Jesus is indeed the true and living way, and that when we follow him we are not lost" (*Truth to Tell*, pp. 87-88).

[30]Newbigin, *GPS*, p. 12.

tions is singularly distinctive, unlike any other worldview. It ushers in a new reality. "What is unique about the Bible is the story it tells, with its climax in the story of the incarnation, ministry, death and resurrection of the Son of God. If this story is true, then it is unique and also universal in its implications for all human history."[31]

The narrative is trinitarian in nature, showing how God—Father, Son and Holy Spirit—works in communion to save the world and creates a new heaven and a new earth. In this new creation, God is the God of all people and re-establishes perfect communion between himself and the whole of creation for eternity (Rev 21). This story, which is historical fact, reveals "a truth about the meaning of the whole human story."[32] "It is the beginning of a new creation. . . . Accepted in faith it becomes the starting point for a wholly new way of understanding human experience."[33] By telling the story as public truth for the whole world, we are inviting people into a new way of life, shaped by the life, death and resurrection of Jesus Christ. Evangelism should be about telling the story and inviting people into a new plausibility structure, in which we "indwell" the gospel story. By indwelling the biblical narrative, we receive a new set of lenses in how to view God, neighbors, the world and ourselves. "The lenses of our spectacles are performing exactly the function that lenses of our own eyes are made to perform. In that sense they are part of us. We indwell them. . . . The Christian story provides us with such a set of lenses, not something for us to look at, but for us to look through."[34]

Newbigin shows that this evangelistic message is "a call to conversion. . . . The ministry of Jesus began with such a call 'Repent, for the Kingdom of God is at hand.'"[35] Entering into the Christian story is "radical, a conversion of the mind, which leads to a totally new view of life."[36]

The Messenger

Newbigin defines evangelistic mission as "those specific activities which are undertaken by human decision to bring the gospel to places or situations

---

[31]Ibid., p. 97.

[32]Ibid., p. 92.

[33]Ibid., p. 12.

[34]Ibid., pp. 35, 38.

[35]Ibid., p. 239.

[36]Ibid.

where it is not heard, to create a Christian presence in a place or a situation where there is no such presence or no effective presence."[37] This message is announced by a chosen people who indwell the story of the gospel. But this message is not only something that is announced; it is good news because it is lived. "I suggest the Christian community is invited to indwell the story, tacitly aware of it as shaping the way we understand, but focally attending to the world we live in so that we are able confidently, though not infallibly, to increase our understanding of it and our ability to cope with it."[38]

For Newbigin, the medium of the evangelistic mission is the local church, especially commissioned to share the evangelistic message.[39] The church is not only as vital as the message; in a real sense it is the evangelistic message. The church embodies and incarnates the gospel. It brings the evangelistic message in words to the world and breathes life into the evangelistic message through public action. Newbigin suggests, "The church is not so much the agent of mission as the locus of mission."[40]

The agent of mission and the ultimate messenger is God himself. God is the great evangelist. Newbigin emphasizes that "it is God who acts in the power of his Spirit, doing mighty works, creating signs of a new age, working secretly in the hearts of men and women to draw them to Christ."[41] It is evident throughout the Bible that God is the great missionary who comes to redeem a broken world. It is equally clear that when Jesus ascended into heaven, he left his followers a mandate to go into the world to share the good news of himself (Mt 28:18-20; Mk 16:15; Lk 24:48; Acts 1:8). The commission to the Christ-followers is clear and unmistakable. Jesus said, "As the Father has sent me, so I send you" (Jn 20:21). "You did not choose me but I chose you. And I appointed you to go and bear fruit, fruit that will last" (Jn 15:16). The church is the body of Christ on earth, which indwells his life, death and resurrection. The gospel is heralded to the world in and through the church, which is the hermeneutic of the gospel.

[37]Ibid., p. 121.

[38]Ibid., p. 38.

[39]Newbigin on the church as the messenger: "The Church lives in the midst of history as a sign, instrument, and foretaste of the reign of God" (*The Open Secret: An Introduction to the Theology of Mission*, rev. ed. [Grand Rapids: Eerdmans, 1995], p. 110).

[40]Newbigin, *GPS*, p. 119.

[41]Ibid.

The Method

Newbigin challenges the church to reject the competing plausibility structures of the West and calls on the church to evangelize by living and telling the story as God's elect people. The evangelistic message of the life, death and resurrection of Jesus Christ will not reach the world fully, unless the Christian community indwells it as an elect people.

This election of the church to bear the message of God should in no way engender pride for being specially chosen. Followers of Jesus are not those whom God loves above others. We are sinners saved by grace called to bear the gospel story. It is a cruciform witness and life. As Christians, we bear the gospel to a hurting world. The church should be on the front lines of entering the wounds of the world, taking the gospel to the most broken. We take the good news into the pain of society. As we engage in evangelistic witness, there is a corresponding journey along the path of suffering and self-denial that reflects the love exhibited by Christ crucified (Lk 9:23). "A church which preaches the cross must itself be marked by the cross."[42]

Newbigin highlights that the spirit in which the church shares the evangelistic message is crucial. "God's electing grace, his choosing of some to be the bearers of his salvation for all, is a matter of awe and wonder and thankfulness: it can never become the ground for making claims against God which exclude others. God does not choose to save some and exclude others."[43]

The church should also not bring the good news in a coercive manner. With the not-too-distant memory of Western imperialism, Christians have become cautious about appearing as gospel bullies. While we should heed the failings of our past misuse of power, the church must not shrink from sharing the public truth of the Christian story. "When coercion of any kind is used in the interest of the Christian message, the message itself is corrupted. . . . We must affirm the gospel as truth, universal truth, truth for all peoples and for all times, the truth which creates the possibility of freedom; but we negate the gospel if we deny the freedom in which alone it can be truly believed."[44] We are "not a new imperialism, not a victorious crusade.

---

[42]Christopher Wright, "Calling the Church Back to Humility, Integrity, and Simplicity," http://conversation.lausanne.org/en/resources/detail/11484#.VSK41ZTF_-U.

[43]Newbigin, *GPS*, p. 85.

[44]Ibid., p. 10.

Its visible embodiment will be a community that lives by this story, a community whose existence is visibly defined in regular rehearsing and reenactment of the story which has given it birth, the story of the self-emptying God in the ministry, life, death and resurrection of Jesus."[45]

Equipping the Messenger for the Method

"To be elect in Christ Jesus, and there is no other election, means to be incorporated into his mission to the world, to be the bearer of God's saving purpose in the world, to be the sign and agent and the first fruits of his blessed kingdom which is for all."[46] This is the call of the followers of Jesus the world over. The Lausanne Covenant describes it well: "the whole church, taking the whole Gospel, to the whole world."[47] It is ecumenical, local, global and public.

Yet today many in the Western church, illustrated in Newbigin's diagnosis above, have lost this sense of purpose and evangelistic call. In reaction to the contemporary climate, the church does not want to impose the Christian message on others or bring faith into the public arena. The church shrinks from a proactive proclamation of the biblical story.

Perhaps most troubling is that the Western church has lost its sense of mission. Many congregations truly do not know they have been elected to proclaim and indwell the Christian story. When I started my job as an evangelist, many earnest followers of Jesus commented that they did not know our denomination did evangelism. They were not trying to be amusing; they truly thought evangelism was a peculiar strategy some denominations (primarily Baptist and nondenominational evangelicals) deployed in order to woo new members. To share the Christian story with others was not what one does in modern church life. The residue of this mindset calls for a new kind of equipping God's people, one that focuses on two themes: embassy and ambassador as defined by Newbigin.

The Archbishop of Canterbury William Temple was known to say, "The church is the only society that exists for the benefit of those who are not its members." Evangelism is at the very heart of who we are as followers of Jesus.

---

[45]Ibid., p. 120.

[46]Ibid., p. 86.

[47]"Reflections of the Lausanne Theology Working Group," Lausanne Movement 2014, www.lausanne.org/content/twg-three-wholes.

We have been elected to bear the biblical story. Newbigin's framework assists the church in recapturing God's mission vision for his people.

God's embassy. In *The Gospel in a Pluralist Society*, Newbigin provides an evangelistic strategy by defining the church as an embassy. Newbigin says the church is "God's embassy in specific places."[48] God's embassy is "a community that does not live for itself but is deeply involved in the concerns of the neighborhood."[49] This unique embassy, the local church, placed throughout the world, represents the kingdom of God on earth bearing the story of Jesus' life, death and resurrection. It is "the visible foretaste" of what is to come.[50]

By viewing the church as the embassy of the kingdom of God, Newbigin provides an evangelistic paradigm for how we strategically and intentionally equip the messengers for evangelistic mission. God has tactically placed churches throughout the world to be his salt and light in the context of specific locals (Mt 5:13-16). "The gospel has to be communicated in the language of those to whom it is addressed and has to be clothed in symbols which are meaningful to them."[51] The gospel must be contextualized, that is, lived, spoken and made manifest in ways that are meaningful to local situations. There is no abstract gospel. The story of God is truly translatable in any context. "True contextualization happens when there is a community which lives faithfully by the gospel and in that same costly identification with people in their real situations as we see in the earthly ministry of Jesus."[52]

If the local church is the embassy for God's kingdom, the minister should function like the commander and chief equipper of the ambassadors. The ambassadors (i.e., members of the congregations) in turn represent God's kingdom and carry the Christian story beyond the walls of the church into the world. "The business of leadership is precisely to enable, encourage and sustain the activity of all of its members."[53] Since the primary activity for members of the congregation is to be "ambassadors for Christ, since God is making his appeal through us" (2 Cor 5:20), the primary task of the minister

---

[48]Newbigin, *GPS*, p. 229.
[49]Ibid.
[50]Ibid., p. 123.
[51]Ibid., p. 141.
[52]Ibid., p. 154.
[53]Ibid., p. 235.

is to help his or her people grasp this call and to provide tools to carry out this evangelistic mission.

For ministers to perform this teaching charge, they need to first be trained in evangelism. When *The Gospel in a Pluralist Society* was written, ministerial training was "almost entirely conceived in terms of pastoral care of existing congregations."[54] The focus was on maintenance, not mission.[55] Even today very few seminaries have specific teaching in evangelism and mission, and there are even fewer who train pastors from the perspective outlined by Newbigin. Now that we are living in a new post-Christendom era in the West, we need clergy who comprehend this missional reality and are able to engage their local context with the gospel. Pastors cannot train others in what they themselves have not experienced. Seminaries need to commit as much teaching in evangelism as they do on pastoral care and administration of the sacraments. There is much discussion today in seminaries about being missional, but actual training in personal and parish proclamation evangelism is sadly lacking.

Missional education is usually centered on being a presence in the community and engaging in social justice. As Newbigin affirms, "Action for justice and peace in the world is not something which is secondary and marginal to the central task of evangelism. It belongs to the heart of the matter. Jesus' action in challenging the powers that ruled the world was not marginal to his ministry; it was central to it. Without it there would be no gospel."[56] For Newbigin, evangelism is both proclamation of the story and living out the story in public action. Newbigin rightly cites that "to set word and deed, preaching and action against each other is absurd. [Word and deed] mutually reinforce and interpret one another. The words explain the deeds, and the deeds validate the words."[57] There is "an indissoluble nexus" between deeds and actions in evangelism.[58]

Newbigin argues that most of the proclamations in the book of Acts were prompted by questions. People saw something different in the way followers

---

[54]Ibid.

[55]Michael Green, *Evangelism Through the Local Church* (London: Hodder & Stoughton, 1993), p. 397.

[56]Newbigin, *GPS*, p. 137.

[57]Ibid.

[58]Ibid., p. 131.

of Jesus lived and loved, and they were motivated to ask what caused the transformation. In response, the messengers gave "an accounting for the hope that is in [them]" (1 Pet 3:15). Newbigin says followers of Jesus need to live in such a way that people will ask about our faith, and then we must be ready to give a reason for the hope that we have in Christ.[59] If our chief commanders and equippers of the local church do not know how to engage in sharing the biblical narrative in proclamation because they themselves have not been trained, how can they teach their congregations to take the story to others? Adding training in articulating the evangelistic message to seminary education is vital.

God's ambassadors. Paul says in Romans 10:14-15, "How are they to call on the one in whom they have not believed? And how are they to believe in one of whom they have never heard? And how are they to hear without someone to proclaim him? And how are they to proclaim him unless they are sent? As it is written, 'How beautiful are the feet of those who bring good news!'" The church's members are the kingdom ambassadors out in the world. Members of the congregation who witness in their local communities, the workplace, with families and friends are the ones on the frontline of evangelistic mission. "The major impact of such congregations on the life of society as a whole is through the daily work of the members in their secular vocations and not through pronouncements of ecclesial bodies."[60] Newbigin emphasizes that the local church "has to be a place where members are trained, supported, and nourished in the exercise of their parts of priestly ministry in the world."[61]

Many church systems, however, remain confined to a maintenance model. Ministry for the laity centers on how they can best serve within the walls of the church as volunteers—greeters, choir members, coffee-hour servers, Christian formation teachers, nursery workers and stewards. While these are needed and important, equipping for evangelism is frequently missing from Christian formation. At best, it is a tangential program that frequently falls through the cracks, succumbing to the inner demands of caring for the flock. Training the ambassadors for the evangelistic call should be at the heart of the entire life of the church.

---

[59]Ibid., p. 119.
[60]Ibid., p. 234.
[61]Ibid., p. 230.

A Model for Evangelistic Equipping Using Newbigin's Embassy Framework

Step 1: Preparing the embassy. We cannot give what we do not have. Newbigin astutely observed that Paul in the New Testament never had to tell the followers of Jesus to evangelize. The gospel bubbled out of them with ebullient joy. After their encounter with the resurrected Jesus, they could not stop talking about what they had seen and heard (Acts 4:20). Michael Green defines evangelism as "overflow."[62] Evangelism results from the exuberant overflow of sharing about our encounter with Christ. This stands in contrast to the predominant way evangelism is defined in churches, "as an obedience to a command";[63] thus evangelism becomes a task, a duty and a program. Evangelism should be the result of an encounter with Jesus Christ that propels ambassadors to share this good news. As Paul said, "for the love of Christ urges us on" (2 Cor 5:14).

Hence, the first step of preparing the embassy for mission is to nourish a daily Christ-encounter for the ambassadors through worship, Christian formation and education, retreats, prayer gatherings, and other faith-building activities. "To the extent that we nourish ourselves on Christ and are in love with him, we feel within us the incentive to bring others to him: Indeed, we cannot keep the joy of the faith to ourselves; we must pass it on."[64] As the church gathers, the people of God encounter the presence of Christ and are filled with his presence. Ambassadors are priests to the world, but if there is no consistent Christ-encounter, there will be no evangelism. We will revert to evangelism as a duty or obligation.

Step 2: Cultivating the call. As stated above, many Christians do not know that they have been called to be ambassadors, and they do not know how to evangelize. Throughout our diocese, we have encouraged all parishes to do a preaching series on the imperative to evangelize. We have also provided workshops and adult education series, which cover the following:

---

[62]Green, *Evangelism Through the Local Church*, p. 8.

[63]Newbigin, *GPS*, p. 116.

[64]Pope Benedict XVI, Papal Address to Rome Diocesan Congress, June 23, 2006. See also John Paul II, *Redemptoris Missio* [Encyclical Letter on the Permanent Validity of the Church's Missionary Mandate], December 7, 1990, http://w2.vatican.va/content/john-paul-ii/en/encyclicals/documents/hf_jp-ii_enc_07121990_redemptoris-missio.html.

- *Teaching* on the mission of the church and the evangelistic call of all ambassadors.
- *Strategy* that uses Jesus' words to his disciples in Acts to be his witnesses "in Jerusalem, in all Judea and Samaria, and to the ends of the earth" (Acts 1:8). We encourage all members of the congregation to assess where God has strategically placed them as his ambassador in
  - "Jerusalem": friends and family
  - "Judea": workplaces, hobbies, special-interest groups and areas the ambassador frequents
  - "Samaria": the poor and outcasts in the community
  - "Ends of the earth": we are especially focused on refugees and immigrant populations in our city; as Tim Keller emphasizes, God is bringing the nations to Western cities[65]
- *Prayer* for the unreached individuals in the ambassador's strategic mission field. Martha Grace Reese, in a grant from the Lilly Foundation, analyzed the top five hundred fastest growing, most evangelistic churches in America. She found the one common denominator in all of them was prayer, which cultivated a Christ-encounter and a heart for his lost sheep.[66]
- *Reaching out in love* as each ambassador analyzes his or her mission field and develops a particular strategy for each unreached person. We, as the embassy, support the ambassadors in their mission. For example, if an ambassador wants to reach the workplace, the church works with the ambassador to run a lunchtime Alpha course, or we hold a breakfast where we have a speaker talk about what Christianity says about their respective vocation. If the ambassador is involved with sports the church might have a sports-watching party with an invitation to church at the end. An example of a church that has grasped the embassy model is Holy Trinity Brompton in London. It holds a weekly commissioning for ambassadors (laypeople) in specific mission fields from stay-at-home moms to cor-

[65]Tim Keller, "What Is God's Global Urban Mission?," Cape Town 2010 Advance Paper, May 18, 2010, http://conversation.lausanne.org/en/resources/detail/10282.

[66]See GraceNet, Inc., www.gracenet.info.

porate executives. This ministers of the church pray for and commission the lay ambassadors and send them out in their local missions fields.

- *Storytelling,* in which all ambassadors are trained in how to tell the gospel story, how to tell their own faith story and how to begin faith conversations. We intentionally do this through workshops and Christian education.
- *Embassy in mission,* in which we engage in collective evangelistic mission as an embassy. We engage seekers through the offering of courses such as Alpha, Christianity Explored, Explore God and others. We hold public events at local pubs, coffee shops, and so on, where we have presentations of the Christian story in all sorts of ways through the arts, sports and personal testimonies. We also hold seeker Bible studies.[67] In all settings, the churches seek to provide spaces where spiritual seekers can ask questions. We also collectively care for the poor through various outreaches. Just like the organic evangelistic method in Acts (Acts 2:41-47), we meet corporately at the embassy for spiritual sustenance through the breaking of bread and the apostles' teaching, and then we go out as Christ's ambassadors and care for our local community. As a result of this model, we grow.

Because of our intentionality in developing an evangelistic strategy in the Episcopal Diocese of Dallas, our parishes are reaching their communities for Christ. They see the mission vision with their new set of missional lenses. Their joy and energy is infectious. They too "cannot keep from speaking about what [they] have seen and heard" (Acts 4:20). As we have stepped out and shared the gospel in our communities, new life and energy have rushed into our parishes. One of my greatest joys is hearing testimonies of our local ambassadors who have evangelized in their respective community. Often these are people who had never considered sharing their faith but have now caught the mission vision. I think of a twentysomething, Steve, who brought his neighbor to the church outreach at the local Gingerman pub, which we called "Ale and the Almighty." His neighbor went to meet new people, and upon hearing the personal testimonies and how the pastor answered questions regarding the

[67]Rebecca Manley Pippert, Saltshaker Resources Set (Downers Grove, IL: InterVarsity Press, 2003). Titles include *How to Lead a Seeker Bible Discussion*, *Looking at the Life of Jesus*, *People Who Met Jesus*, *Spirituality According to Jesus*, *Talking About Jesus Without Sounding Religious* and *The Way of Jesus*. To equip for evangelism we use Canon J.John's Natural Evangelism Course; see J.John, *Natural Evangelism* (Chorleywood, UK: PhiloTrust, 2014).

Christian faith, he started attending church and told Steve he wanted to know this Jesus. Steve was astonished and overjoyed. I think of one of our churches in McKinney, Texas, that asked the ambassadors of the embassy to pray for one person each with whom they would share Jesus, and on Palm Sunday 2013, the church had literally doubled. Not only are the new Christians elated, the ambassadors who shared the good news were amazed how God worked through them. I think of three people in one of our inner-city churches that started a community garden and went door to door to pray for people. To their surprise, many people needed food, and the embassy and its ambassadors were able to provide it. They told story after story of how God had cared for the needs of people through their local embassy. I think of a woman in Richardson, Texas, who started a seeker Bible study at a local coffee shop. She invited the teller at her local gas station, the local librarian, her son's teenage friend and her neighbor. To her astonishment, they all said yes, and she has watched firsthand as they have come to know the irresistible Jesus. She said, "I see the change in them from week to week as they understand God's unconditional love, grace, and forgiveness." I think of an ambassador in Plano, Texas, who held a weekly pizza night with his guy friends. Once he caught the mission vision, he invited Christian speakers to share at his pizza group. He watched as some of his best buddies came to know Jesus. I think of the local embassy near a park that started providing free water to runners on the local running path. As they consistently cared for people, curiosity arose and some runners joined seeker courses and have come to know the source of living water himself.

As embassies and ambassadors reach beyond the church walls, the Christian life becomes a great adventure. The gospel comes alive not only for the new hearers but also for the sharers. We are reminded time and again that the gospel is life transforming, and the source of life itself. As we evangelize, we experience the heart of God to reach all people through his chosen embassy and its ambassadors. As we evangelize, some hearers will doubt, some will want to know more and some will believe. We will not carry out the mission perfectly, but in our weakness he is strong (2 Cor 12:9-11). As we do our work of being his ambassadors, God draws people to himself. And as Newbigin ends *The Gospel in a Pluralist Society*, "God is faithful, and he will complete what he has begun."[68]

---

[68]Newbigin, *GPS*, p. 244.

Newbigin gave the church a great gift in *The Gospel in a Pluralist Society*. With laser-sharp analysis he diagnoses why we shy away from evangelism in the West today and provides followers of Jesus with a renewed confidence to share the gospel in the public square. The evangelistic message rooted in the story of the life, death and resurrection of Christ is the good news for all humankind. The West is on a spiritual search. As Augustine said, "For Thou hast made us for Thyself and our hearts are restless till they rest in Thee."[69] We are the public mouthpiece and the hands and feet of God in earth.

When I sat down for breakfast that morning at the Oxford University Mission, I had no idea how people would respond. The two people who had questions about Jesus after breakfast never followed through with interest. I continued to meet with the Muslim women for the better part of the year. I read the Qur'an and shared the gospel while they read the Bible and shared their beliefs. We found common ground in many areas except the most important tenets of our faith. We remained friends throughout. Dan, the staunch vocal atheist, joined an Alpha course in order to prove the Christians wrong and ended up committing his life to following Jesus. He is now an ambassador in a local Christian embassy seeking to glorify God.

[69]Augustine, *Confessions*, trans. F. J. Sheed, ed. Michael P. Foley, 2nd ed. (Indianapolis: Hackett, 2006), book 1, chap. 1.

9

What Does It Mean for a Congregation to Be a Hermeneutic?

John G. Flett

For all its epigrammatic force, Newbigin's phrase "the congregation as hermeneutic of the gospel" is odd. With "congregation," his focus falls not on the church catholic and the institutions associated with such but on the local and concrete body of people gathered in a certain place. Nor is this body an "interpretation," a translation of the message into local idiom. Though perhaps the more common term, Newbigin avoids it, one might suggest, due to its potential alignment with a federal model of Christian unity—a model he describes as in "vain" because it leaves "each sect free to enjoy its own particular sort of spirituality, merely tying them all together at the center in a bond which does not vitally and costingly involve every member in every part of his [or her] daily life." It leaves untouched "the heart of the problem—which is the daily life of men and women in their neighborhood."[1] In other words, while his point of concentration is this local and particular body, precisely due to its locality and particularity this body is one, and this determines also its local behaviors.

The congregation is not then an interpretation, but the "only" hermeneutic of the gospel.[2] A hermeneutic, simply stated, is a set of rules that assist

[1]Lesslie Newbigin, *The Household of God: Lectures on the Nature of the Church* (London: SCM Press, 1953), p. 14.

[2]Lesslie Newbigin, *The Gospel in a Pluralist Society* (Geneva: World Council of Churches, 1989), p. 227.

the faithful interpretation of a text. Hermeneutics examines how human beings communicate, investigates the conditions of symbolic interaction, observes the ground of all thought within a cultural and historical context, and recognizes the effect social structures, political institutions and economic order have on the reading of a text. As a hermeneutic, in other words, the congregation is the method of the gospel's interpretation. What Newbigin means by this is the subject of this essay.

We begin by examining the problem Newbigin develops in *The Gospel in a Pluralist Society* for which the congregation as hermeneutic is the solution, namely, how in a post-Christendom context can the gospel be seen as it is: public truth. Following this is an interpretation of Newbigin's position using the language of visibility, and so through the ecclesial lens of word, sacrament and office. While this approach has much to commend it, especially given the focus on the local and the concrete, it reduces an external mission to a secondary action contingent on the church as a settled body. The argument advances by using Karl Barth's description of the church's "special visibility" as a way of summarizing the relationship Newbigin forms between the cross and the resurrection. The cross is a historical event visible to all. The resurrection is and remains an act of God because knowledge of the resurrection constitutes knowledge of God himself. Newbigin, in other words, develops the congregation as hermeneutic of the gospel in this dialectic of visibility and invisibility. Newbigin accomplishes this, the penultimate section argues, because he defines mission in terms of history, not geography. Jesus Christ is the center of history, and the church exists only as it is participant in this history, in the new reality of the coming kingdom. This gives mission its congregational shape, while locating the identity of that community beyond itself and in the pressing to visibility of the kingdom. The final section applies this logic to the six characteristics of the congregation as hermeneutic of the gospel developed by Newbigin.

The Background Problem

Though theologically normative in Newbigin's thinking, the chapter on "the congregation as hermeneutic of the gospel" concludes an extended discourse concerning the form of pluralism characterizing secular Western culture. This discourse establishes a problem, namely, the Christian gospel becomes "one element in a society which has pluralism as its reigning ideology."[3] The gospel becomes a personal value, and discipleship is reduced to the private and the domestic. To follow this path, Newbigin argues, constitutes a fundamental betrayal of the message of Jesus Christ, of him crucified and raised, and of the coming kingdom.

Newbigin counters by first questioning the notion of neutrality. The secular state is not without ideological intent. A public truth exists, one that shapes public debate, and this "is either in conformity with the truth as it is given in Jesus Christ, or it is not." It is the responsibility of Christians and the church to refuse the space consigned to the gospel within secular liberal democracy and to "claim the high ground of public truth."[4] The old forms by which the gospel was seen to be public, those of a "pre-Constantinian innocence" or of "Constantinian authority," cannot today accomplish this. So the question occupying Newbigin is "How is it possible that the one who was nailed to a cross should be seen by society as the ultimate source of power?"[5]

The first part of the answer denies that this can be a human work. No evangelistic technique will assure success; the conversion of the world is not a human achievement.[6] Newbigin turns to the story of Jesus feeding the multitude in John 6 and his refusal to follow the urging of the crowd. Only the Father draws people to the bread of life. Potential followers leave as a result of this message, and the whole pericope ends with a warning of treachery even among his closest disciples. This story, for Newbigin, combines both "tender compassion and awesome sovereignty."[7] The gospel serves the world, but does so by fixing its attention on God and his kingdom, by recognizing that such service is only an act of God. In terms of the church representing the kingdom of God to society, it excludes, first, the way of political power and coercion; second, the way of reflecting in the church the popular aspiration of the people; and third, conceiving "the Church in the style of a commercial firm using modern techniques of promotion to attract members."[8] This last caution needs to be taken seriously because it goes to the heart of Newbigin's concern.

---

[3]Ibid., p. 222.
[4]Ibid.
[5]Ibid., p. 224.
[6]Ibid.
[7]Ibid., p. 226.
[8]Ibid.

The church represents God's reign not because it has a technique but because it is a body of people shaped by the gospel.

The point is christological and stems from the simple observation that Jesus "did not write a book but formed a community." This community is gathered with Jesus Christ at its center and takes its character from him. Basic is the "remembering and rehearsing of his words and deeds, and the sacraments given by him through which it is enabled both to engraft new members into its life and to renew this life again and again through sharing in his risen life through the body broken and the lifeblood poured out." What this short formulation means for Newbigin is a question we will ponder. Nevertheless, when this community is "true to its calling, it becomes the place where men and women and children find that the gospel gives them the framework of understanding, the 'lenses' through which they are able to understand and cope with the world."[9] Notable here is the direction of the hermeneutic: living in the gospel, the congregation develops a way of interpreting the world. The gospel interprets creation and history for the people of God.

As soon as he makes this point, however, Newbigin inverts the direction: in answer to the question of how the church might claim the gospel as public truth, how "it is possible that the gospel should be credible, that people should come to believe that the power which has the last word in human affairs is represented by a man hanging on a cross," he states that "the only hermeneutic of the gospel is a congregation of men and women who believe it and live by it."[10] With this direction, the acting subject is not first the gospel but the congregation. It is this group of people gathered and formed by the gospel who embody the gospel for the world. As hermeneutic of the gospel, the congregation is the "central reality" by which the gospel might become "credible," might claim to be public truth.

Hermeneutic as Visibility

How might one interpret this position? One way, following Murray Rae, is to use the language of visibility. Given the ecumenical significance accompanying this term, the choice is an interesting one. Rae reads Newbigin through an established ecclesial lens, conceiving the church as hermeneutic of the gospel in terms of word, sacrament and office.

---

[9]Ibid., p. 227.
[10]Ibid.

Rae begins his exposition with Newbigin's *The Household of God.* As a methodological move it is interesting, for it trades on a continuity through Newbigin's corpus, using a more ecclesial argument found elsewhere to buttress what is not so strongly stated in *The Gospel in a Pluralist Society.* To quote from *The Household of God,* "The divinely willed form of the Church's unity is at least this, a *visible* company in every place of all who confess Jesus as Lord, abiding together in the Apostles' teaching and fellowship, the breaking of bread and the prayers. Its foci are the word, the sacraments, and the apostolic ministry."[11] The church is this "*visible* fellowship," it is "humanity in every place re-created in Christ."[12] Via the term *visible,* Newbigin links word, sacrament and office to the re-creation of humanity. By implication, this re-creation constitutes the congregation as hermeneutic.

Visibility concentrates on the body of people shaped by this order. Word, sacrament and office supply the template. As a consequence of this, Rae argues, that visibility refers to the church as a concrete body in a particular place and time. Second, because the gospel is the good news of human reconciliation with God and so with one another, a reconciled community is "simply the content of the gospel."[13] The community shaped by this gospel becomes a "new order."[14] Third, it is the form of Newbigin's "mission imperative," because "the visibility of the community is the means of God's self-presentation."[15] In this people "God makes himself available."[16] The first two elements, I suggest, are indeed central to what Newbigin means by the congregation as hermeneutic. The third is an issue to which we shall return.

As his argument progresses, Rae turns to the shape of this new order, to what it looks like after Christendom. In Christendom, the church allied with state power and assumed a type of privilege that reflected the "faults and failings of the old order."[17] It was "often visible in the wrong way," taking the

[11]Newbigin, *Household of God,* p. 14. Rae supplied the emphases; see Murray Rae, "The Congregation as Hermeneutic of the Gospel," in *Theology in Missionary Perspective: Lesslie Newbigin's Legacy,* ed. Mark T. B. Laing and Paul Weston (Eugene, OR: Pickwick, 2012), p. 190.

[12]Newbigin, *Household of God,* p. 14.

[13]Rae, "Congregation as Hermeneutic of the Gospel," p. 192.

[14]Ibid., p. 193. Rae takes this position from Lesslie Newbigin, *Truth to Tell: The Gospel as Public Truth* (Grand Rapids: Eerdmans, 1991), p. 85.

[15]Rae, "Congregation as Hermeneutic of the Gospel," p. 191.

[16]Ibid.

[17]Ibid., pp. 193-94.

"form of political power and privilege, accumulated wealth, and the availability of its ministers sometimes to bless the sinful institutions and endeavors of a fallen world."[18] After Christendom, by contrast, this new order constitutive of the church's visibility is cruciform. In defining the problem of Christendom as primarily a problem of power, the solution lies in shifting the church's focus from power located in state institutions to the power located in the cross. This, in Rae's estimation, strengthens the case for defining visibility in terms of the church's institutions.

Citing Newbigin's 1967 *Honest Religion for Secular Man,* Rae confirms the central thrust of his argument. In the local congregation, the word is preached, the Eucharist is celebrated, and a new social order develops.[19] Preaching the word and administering the sacraments is, in Rae's estimation, "more public" than other activities of the church (such as small groups reading the Bible together), and the "life of the church depends on their faithful execution by ministers of word and sacrament."[20] From this point, the final sections of his text serve as an apology for a traditional church order. The church becomes "visible only in and through the formation of a differently ordered community,"[21] and it is the liturgy that so forms this people, because through the order of word and sacrament the community takes "to heart the pattern of death and new life."[22]

As to mission, this is

> grounded in a particular set of practices—the practice of worship, the practice of faithful transmission of that which has been received, the practice of participation in a community brought into being by the redemptive and liberating work of God. Participation in these practices week by week, in answer to God's call upon us, is the necessary antecedent condition of our being able to tell truthfully in mission the story that Scripture tells.[23]

Mission, by this definition, is essentially internal to the church's order, and the regular occurrence of this constitutes the "necessary antecedent condition" of any external movement because it is basic to our being able to tell

---

[18]Ibid., p. 194.
[19]Ibid., p. 196.
[20]Ibid.
[21]Ibid., p. 193.
[22]Ibid., p. 200.
[23]Ibid.

the story. Or, the externality of the gospel lies in the visibility of the congregation constituted by word, sacrament and office.

What to make of this position? Newbigin, without doubt, stresses the importance of church order through his corpus. He can affirm that the "first priority . . . is the cherishing and nourishing of such a congregation in a life of worship, of teaching and mutual pastoral care so that the new life in Christ becomes more and more for them the great and controlling reality."[24] In *The Household of God,* Newbigin rejects Johannes Hoekendijk's apparent reduction of the church as a body to a mobile missionary unit. In opposition, he describes the church as both "a means and an end," because the nature of salvation determines the form of mission: as salvation is a "healing of all things in Christ," so the church can undertake this task only "insofar as she is herself living in Christ, a reconciled fellowship in Him."[25] Within *The Gospel in a Pluralist Society,* Newbigin takes clues from Alasdair MacIntyre concerning the socially embodied nature of rationality,[26] and talks of the community as "visible embodiment" of the "new reality" in the Spirit, of which the "visible center as a continuing social entity is that weekly repeated event in which believers share bread and wine as Jesus commanded."[27] He conceives mission as an activity of "response to questions asked by others, questions prompted by the presence of something which calls for explanation. . . . Where the Church is faithful to its Lord, there the powers of the kingdom are present and people begin to ask the question to which the gospel is the answer."[28] There is much to commend in Rae's reading. I suspect, however, that it is not quite full enough.

Given that Newbigin does, time and again, return to the themes of word, sacrament and structure, why do these not take center stage when he defines the congregation as hermeneutic of the gospel? His concluding chapter, "Ministerial Leadership for a Missionary Congregation," illustrates that ministry is central to Newbigin's thinking, but it includes the critical observation that "we have lived for so many centuries in the 'Christendom' situation that ministerial training is almost entirely conceived in terms of the pastoral care

---

[24]Lesslie Newbigin, "The Pastor's Opportunities: VI. Evangelism in the City," *Expository Times* 98 (1987): 357.

[25]Newbigin, *Household of God,* p. 169.

[26]Newbigin, *GPS,* p. 87.

[27]Ibid., p. 120.

[28]Ibid., p. 119.

of existing congregations."[29] One should include here Newbigin's own critical reference to congregational life as hindering the church's mission, his concern that established patterns were so steeped in a Christendom mentality that the church found it difficult to move beyond itself. One could refer to the distinction Newbigin draws between mobile and settled ministries, and his lament concerning the disappearance of the former.[30] In positive terms, Newbigin conceives the sacrament of baptism as incorporation "into the dying of Jesus so as to become a participant in his risen life, and so to share his ongoing mission to the world. It is to be baptized into his mission."[31] Likewise, in *The Household of God* Newbigin states that the church should "understand that participation in Christ means participation in His mission to the world, and that therefore true pastoral care, true training in Christian life, and true means of grace will precisely be in and for the discharge of this missionary task." That is, mission is not first participation in certain practices as a necessary antecedent condition for telling the story: "A newly baptized congregation will not be trained first in churchmanship and then in missionary responsibility to neighbouring villages. It will receive its training in churchmanship precisely in the discharge of its missionary responsibility."[32] The congregation as hermeneutic of the gospel is called to be visible, a concrete and historically continuous society, but this visibility does not rest in a simple repetition of what already belongs to the church. Newbigin is at once critical of its received Christendom shape, while consistently locating word, sacrament and office in the church's movement beyond itself.

Rae's point regarding reconciliation as the content of the gospel, and the visibility of a reconciled community as basic to Christian witness, is correct. However, while Newbigin does regard the presence of the new reality in the Spirit, the new reality by which the body of Christ lives as the "locus of witness," one doubts that his "mission imperative" can be identified with "the visibility of the community [as] the means of God's self-presentation."[33] The difficulty with this position lies in the failure to include the movement

---

[29]Ibid., p. 235.

[30]Lesslie Newbigin, "Cross-Currents in Ecumenical and Evangelical Understandings of Mission," *International Bulletin of Missionary Research* 6, no. 4 (1982): 150.

[31]Newbigin, *GPS*, p. 117.

[32]Newbigin, *Household of God*, p. 146.

[33]Rae, "Congregation as Hermeneutic of the Gospel," p. 191.

of reconciling, the movement toward those "far off" (Eph 2:13), as itself belonging to being reconciled, the necessary human response to God's act of grace. Missing in Rae's reading, in other words, is the missionary externality that Newbigin ties to the cross and so to the new order determinative of the church's cruciform life. Newbigin maintains an important tension between valuing the church as something in and for itself and affirming that the church's identity lies beyond it—that the church witnesses to, that is, engages in movement toward, something beyond it, but something which nonetheless determines its life now.

"Special Visibility" and the Question of History

Nor is this missionary absence theologically benign. Though one might welcome the community emphasis (as opposed to individual effort or successful technique), a danger lies in linking the credibility of the gospel with the faithful action of the congregation. Such action comes to rest fully in "remembering and rehearsing" in the repetition of socializing practices and institutions that produce a *habitus*, an ingrained way of reading and responding to the world. While God may be considered basic, the process itself follows quite natural anthropological rules of maturation within a culture. The congregation as hermeneutic of the gospel becomes a wholly human act.

The problem with this should be clear. Because true knowledge of the gospel is knowledge of God himself, nothing can make the gospel credible except God acting to reveal himself. Newbigin makes a similar type of point when referring to the New Testament's use of Isaiah 6:9-10, "Go and say to this people: 'Hear and hear but do not understand; see and see but do not perceive.'" Newbigin's conclusion: "The conversion of the nations is, and can only be, the supernatural work of God."[34] This leaves us with a twofold concern. First, the congregation as hermeneutic of the gospel is a concrete and ordered body of people who indwell the story of the gospel. But, second, Newbigin affirms that the community as this visible reality is not known for what it is as a general datum of history.

Karl Barth proves instructive here. As part of his discussion on the Holy Spirit and the active participation of the human in the divine act of recon-

[34]Newbigin, *GPS*, pp. 224-25.

ciliation, Barth states that it is essential to the church to be visible because "the work of the Holy Spirit to which it owes its existence is something which is produced concretely and historically in this world."[35] The church as the creature of the Spirit is a matter of historical human actions, including ecclesial order, institution, cultus, teaching, theology, hospitality and so on. Nor is it possible to look through this form to find a real church behind it.[36] Barth rejects any form of "*ecclesiastical Docetism*." The church is a "definite human fellowship; in concrete form, therefore, and visible to everyone."[37]

However, and this is the important point, the visibility of the church cannot be other than that which is true now of Jesus Christ himself. It corresponds to the manner in which "the glory of the humanity justified in Him is *concealed*."[38] Or, Jesus Christ's resurrection from the dead, though a historical fact—indeed, the center of history—is not visible to everyone. The visibility of the resurrection, the visibility of Jesus Christ as the Lord of all creation, is and remains an act of God. The cross, by comparison, is generally visible. For the church to live in the resurrection, to be visible as participant in the new reality inaugurated by Jesus Christ in the power of the Spirit, is to be seen in history as the people of the cross. It is only because of the resurrection that the church can have this cruciform visibility—the cross is not the end. For this reason, even while stressing the essential visibility of the church and the imperative of the visible attesting the invisible, Barth describes the truth of the Christian community's earthly historical existence as "not a matter of a general but a very special visibility."[39] The church is visible for what it is only as an act of God. Barth's position is interesting here because in *The Gospel in a Pluralist Society* Newbigin articulates an identical position.

In his discussion "Christ, the Clue to History," Newbigin conceives the church in terms of Jesus Christ's own earthly ministry. The church lives now after the cross but before the final revelation of Jesus Christ in his glory. This time, Newbigin argues, is "marked by suffering, and by the presence of the signs of the kingdom."[40] This "double character," which forms the "substance

---

[35]Karl Barth, *The Doctrine of Reconciliation* (Edinburgh: T&T Clark, 1956), p. 652.
[36]Ibid., pp. 653-54.
[37]Ibid., p. 653.
[38]Ibid., p. 656.
[39]Ibid., p. 658.
[40]Newbigin, *GPS*, p. 107.

of the mission to the nations," is related "in the same way as cross and resurrection were related to each other in the ministry of Jesus (cf. 2 Cor. 4:10). The cross was a public execution visible to all—believers and unbelievers alike. The resurrection was as much a fact of history as the crucifixion, but it was made known only to the chosen few who were called to be the witnesses of the hidden kingdom."[41] This dialectic of cross and resurrection, of the church's special visibility, is central to Newbigin's understanding of the congregation as hermeneutic of the gospel.

In terms of suffering as the first element in this "double character," as "Jesus in his earthly ministry unmasked the powers and so drew their hostility on himself, so the Spirit working through the life and witness of the missionary Church will overturn the world's most fundamental beliefs, proving the world wrong in respect of sin, of righteousness, and of judgment (John 16:8)."[42] The context is important. Suffering is not its own good. "Once the gospel is preached and there is a community which lives by the gospel, then the question of the ultimate meaning of history is posed and other messiahs appear."[43] The church encounters the cross as it exposes the false claims made by the principalities and powers. The church encounters the cross as part of its missionary witness.

In terms of the signs of the kingdom, as Jesus' ministry was "marked by mighty works which, for those with eyes to see and ears to hear, were signs of the presence of the kingdom of God in power, so in the life of the Church there will be mighty works which have the same function."[44] The church should expect these mighty works within its own life because the signs of the kingdom accompany the preaching of the kingdom. Herein lies the problem of Christendom. "When the Church tries to embody the rule of God in the forms of earthly power it may achieve that power, but it is no longer a sign of the kingdom."[45] In claiming power for itself, it mistakes its visibility for the truth of the gospel.

To summarize the logic in opposition to the prevailing position, Christendom is the cross without the resurrection. That is, it is a disruption of the necessary relationship between the two with a consolidation of the invisible,

---

[41]Ibid., p. 108.
[42]Ibid., p. 107.
[43]Ibid., p. 122.
[44]Ibid., pp. 107-8.
[45]Ibid., p. 108.

that which is and remains God's own act, into the visible.[46] By contrast, when the church moves beyond itself, impelled by the Spirit to participate in Jesus Christ's own mission to the world, when it unmasks and challenges "the powers of darkness and bearing in its own life the cost of their onslaught, then there are given to the Church signs of the kingdom, powers of healing and blessing which, to eyes of faith, are recognizable as true signs that Jesus reigns."[47] Such missionary movement defines the nature of the church's visibility, its being a hermeneutic of the gospel.

History and Mission

As one rather radical consequence of this dialectic of cross and resurrection, history, not geography, becomes the defining category for mission. A number of consequences follow, the most basic of which recognizes that mission is Jesus Christ's own. Mission is the unfolding of the history at which Jesus Christ is the center, the unfolding of his own history. By way of illustration, Newbigin describes Romans 9–11 as Paul's "most fully developed theology of mission."[48] One finds here an eschatological vision of the gathering of the Gentiles and the salvation of Israel. Paul, Newbigin notes, "is not thinking in terms of the individual but in terms of the interpretation of universal history. The center of the picture is the eschatological event in which the fathomless depths of God's wisdom and grace will be revealed."[49] It is a vision of mission set under the majesty of God, one in which the church is and remains its object and not subject.

It means that history, in Jesus Christ, has a goal. This is not immanent within history, an end result of natural forces. The goal of history takes place within history but is itself external to it. It lies in the promise of the Father to

[46]Newbigin's reaction to Albert Schweitzer's 1906 work, *The Quest for the Historical Jesus*, is informative on this point. Schweitzer's argument, which Newbigin describes as "constantly repeated and hardly questioned," holds that Jesus and the early church believed that the end of history was immanent and the New Testament is to be read from this perspective. "But in fact the end of the world did not happen. Jesus was mistaken. The Church had to adjust its thinking to this reality and so learn to settle down" (*GPS*, p. 104). Newbigin grants that the church became an institution, part of the "established order," but rejects reading the New Testament as though Jesus expected history's immediate end. The point is salient. To conceive the church as some form of eschatological detour is to set it apart from the beyondness of the resurrection and its missionary impetus.

[47]Newbigin, *GPS*, p. 108.

[48]Ibid., p. 125.

[49]Ibid.

reconcile all things to himself. It is this goal, Newbigin argues, that "makes possible responsible action in history" and "heals the dichotomy between the private and the public worlds which death creates."[50] Because Jesus Christ is the clue to history, Newbigin develops no fast border between the Christian community and the world, one that demands complex rules for crossing. Quite the contrary, those who reject the gospel rebuild the walls God in Christ Jesus has already destroyed. For this reason all forms of racism, cultural imperialism, gender or economic inequality are inimical to the gospel, and especially so when they assume the guise of preaching the kingdom of God.

With this ground in history, mission, Newbigin observes, "is rooted in the gospel itself."[51] It is so because "the truth about the human story has been disclosed in the events which form the substance of the gospel. . . . These events are the real clue to the story of every person, for every human life is part of the whole human story and cannot be understood apart from that story."[52] The "logic of mission," by extension, derives from this disclosure of the "true meaning of the human story."[53] Newbigin contrasts this with the "long tradition" that conceived mission as "obedience to a command" or a "mandate given to the Church."[54] This ground, in his estimation, "misses the point" because it makes mission "part of the law rather than part of the gospel."[55] The church does not bear a mission. The image Newbigin prefers is that of "the fallout from a vast explosion, a radioactive fallout which is not lethal but life-giving,"[56] "the radioactive fallout from an explosion of joy. . . . Mission is an acted out doxology."[57] It, as such, belongs to the essence of Christian life and spirituality.

One sees again the dialectic shaping Newbigin's thinking. As the act of God, the church has no mastery of this history. It is gathered and exists in the presence of that new reality. It follows that its form is necessarily that of a community "indwelling" the story, to use Newbigin's favored phrase from Michael Polanyi. It means the repeated hearing and reenactment of that

[50]Ibid., p. 108.
[51]Ibid., p. 116.
[52]Ibid., p. 126.
[53]Ibid., p. 125.
[54]Ibid., pp. 116, 117.
[55]Ibid., p. 116.
[56]Ibid.
[57]Ibid., p. 127.

story, the repeated return to the event of the crucifixion, resurrection and ascension. Indwelling this story, the community claims no control over history, but witnesses to its "real meaning and goal."[58] Following 2 Corinthians 4:10, the community is called to bear the dying of Jesus Christ so that his risen life might be "made available for others."[59] Newbigin, however, does not stop with this having, with a simple celebration of what is given to the church in its constitution. "It is this indissoluble unity of having and hoping, this presence now of something which is a pledge of the future, this *arrabon* which is both a reality now and at the same time a pledge of something far greater to come, it is this which constitutes the Church as witness."[60] The hoping in what is real now means that the church is called beyond itself to participate in the history of Jesus Christ.

The church, as Newbigin often states, is "not so much the agent of the mission as the locus of the mission."[61] As a locus, the church becomes the place of God's mission, meaning that the church is itself the entity being converted. Conversion, Newbigin argues, is no simple turning from sins. If this were Jesus' call, he would have been "merely a preacher of revival."[62] His call is to "something much more radical, a conversion of the mind which leads to a totally new view of life."[63] Such participation in the history of Jesus Christ means that the church is the locus of mission in a second sense. It is a "company of travelers" who have the "first rays of the morning sun shining" on their faces.[64] As others see this reflected light, they too turn to face the morning sun. In both these senses, Newbigin maintains the beyondness of the church's identity and links this to its necessary missionary form.

It means, finally, that the church is to be a learning community. It learns through what properly belongs to it, but only insofar as this is not "detached from the Church's missionary journey to all the nations." The two remain together because the life of the church is "a foretaste of what is promised for the end, namely that the nations shall walk in the light of the Lamb and their

[58]Ibid., p. 118.
[59]Ibid.
[60]Ibid., p. 120.
[61]Ibid., p. 118.
[62]Ibid., p. 239.
[63]Ibid.
[64]Ibid., p. 120.

kings shall bring their glory into the Holy City (Rev. 21:24)."[65] The church's mission consists not of a type of cultural purification. Instead, the "fulfillment of the mission of the Church . . . requires that the Church itself be changed and learn new things."[66] This is throughout a work of the Spirit. Newbigin finds Peter's encounter with Cornelius to be representative. In spite of Peter's own reluctance, the gospel calls even a pagan Roman officer to repentance and conversion, and in this process Peter is also converted. "'Christianity' was changed," Newbigin argues. "One decisive step was taken on the long road from the incarnation of the Word of God as a Jew of the first-century Palestine to summing up of all things in him."[67] It means that "the church cannot lay down in advance for such people what commitment will mean but must . . . learn from them new lessons about its own obedience."[68] The church, while it engages in the conversation, cannot dictate the form conversion takes. The point is axiomatic. Until the final revelation of Jesus Christ as the Lord of all creation, "our confession can only be partial, culture-bound, and thus incomplete."[69]

To claim that the church is the locus of mission is, of course, to claim that it shares in and so embodies the center of history. The potential danger with such a position lies in the assumption of privilege. The church becomes the vehicle of God's redemptive mission to the world; it has the gospel in its possession. One need not read too much of the biblical text nor delve too far into Christian history to discover the reality and consequences (especially for witness) of this temptation. Newbigin deals with this problem through the language of election, the idea that "from the very beginning God chooses, calls, and sends particular people."[70] He begins, in conversation with his experience with the Indian context, by rejecting the basic assumption of spirituality as an individual endeavor. The Bible sets the person's relationship with God in the context of the relationship between human beings. Such "mutual relatedness, this dependence of one on another," Newbigin continues, "is not

---

[65]Ibid., p. 123.

[66]Ibid., p. 124.

[67]Lesslie Newbigin, *The Open Secret: An Introduction to the Theology of Mission* (Grand Rapids: Eerdmans, 1995), p. 182.

[68]Ibid., p. 140.

[69]Newbigin, *GPS*, p. 124.

[70]Ibid., p. 80.

merely part of the journey toward the goal of salvation, but is intrinsic to the goal itself."[71] In Romans 9–11, Newbigin finds both confirmation of the social nature of salvation ("In the end the chosen people, the elect, will have to receive salvation through the nonelect"), and the impossibility of election leading to a "privileged status before God."[72] Election means that knowing God includes the reception of the neighbor, and that there is no salvation apart from this neighbor. So construed in these social terms, priority attaches to the church as a gathered people. In its gathering the church moves beyond itself in meeting the stranger. Newbigin reinforces the point by reference to election's christological center. "To be elect in Christ Jesus . . . means to be incorporated into his mission to the world."[73] Election receives its shape from Jesus Christ himself, and the church follows in his train.

Six Characteristics of the Church as Hermeneutic of the Gospel

In this discussion of the relationship between mission and history, it may seem that we have traversed far from the congregation as hermeneutic of the gospel. This is not the case. The penultimate chapter in Newbigin's *The Gospel in a Pluralist Society*, I suggest, is the endpoint to which his argument has been developing. Though it is clear he is describing the church mundane and concrete, the tone is not ecclesiastical. Expected elements, such as overt reference to word, sacrament and office, are absent. Instead, a certain tension is evident in the six characteristics Newbigin develops. Each is marked by an orientation to the community itself and an orientation beyond it. He formulates the church, in other words, through this dialectic between the visibility of the cross and the invisibility of the resurrection.

As hermeneutic of the gospel, the congregation is, first, a community of praise. Newbigin rehabilitates the notion that human freedom, dignity and equality come from standing under someone who is worthy of reverence. Basic to praise is thanksgiving, understanding that we only stand in God's presence by an act of his grace. Such gratitude is not containable. It expands beyond our own horizons to encompass our neighbor, not "as an object of

[71]Ibid., p. 82.
[72]Ibid., p. 84.
[73]Ibid., p. 87.

evangelization," but as an overflow of the joy experienced by those liberated from bondage.[74] Nor is this a first followed by a second move. Without this thanksgiving it is not God before whom we stand.

Second, as a community of truth, the congregation is to be nurtured by the "constant remembering and rehearsing of the true story of human nature and destiny." This, Newbigin argues, supports a "healthy scepticism" concerning the stories the world tells about itself. In other words, being formed in the "plausibility structure" of the gospel includes this engagement with the world and the exposing of the false claims to power. The gospel itself gives shape to this engagement, meaning that the congregation will speak truth not mirroring the "techniques of modern propaganda," but in the "modesty, the sobriety, and the realism which are proper to a disciple of Jesus."[75]

Third, this community "does not live for itself but is deeply involved in the concerns of its neighbourhood." Newbigin reasserts the importance of the church being *local*, for the place in which it is. Insofar as its members "are willing to be *for* the wider community," it is a church for them too.[76] Nor, it must be remembered, is this to be conceived in ideal terms. He has in mind the church mundane. Newbigin warns against the twofold temptation of, first, the church so accommodating to the place that it becomes a religious mirror of the setting and, second, the church so focusing on itself that it ignores its neighbors. Instead, the church is to be "God's embassy in a specific place," meaning that it is and remains a foreign presence, but one for this place.

Fourth, this community prepares and sustains its members "in the exercise of the priesthood in the world."[77] As priests, Christians "stand before God on behalf of the people, and stand before people on behalf of God." To this Newbigin adds a further defining point: priests follow the High Priest as the one who alone fulfills this function, meaning that the "Church is sent into the world to continue that which he came to do, in the power of the same Spirit, reconciling people to God (John 20:19-23)."[78] Priesthood is a worldly task. Newbigin understands the church in terms of this commerce between its internal and external aspects. To isolate either in the economy of salvation

---

[74]Ibid., p. 228.
[75]Ibid.
[76]Ibid.
[77]Ibid., p. 229.
[78]Ibid., p. 230.

is to distort both. As such, he expresses concern regarding established theological patterns and forms of ministerial training that are too much concerned with "the pastoral care of the existing congregation, and far too little oriented toward the missionary calling to claim the whole of public life for Christ and his kingdom."[79] Newbigin advocates the recognition of the wider gifts of the body and the different forms of expression such gifts takes. There exists no uniform style of evangelism or of Christian discipleship.[80] Only in the diversity of gifts can the body fully exercise its royal priesthood.

Fifth, it will be a community of mutual responsibility, meaning that it will embody first in itself the type of social concerns it will see in wider society. If individualism is a malaise burdening Western societies, one should not find its religious confirmation in the church. The church should be "the foretaste of a different social order" and so manifest "relationships of faithfulness and responsibility toward one another."[81] Again, Newbigin values this image of "overflow." No secondary point of connection with those outside the church exists because such is given already with the gospel and its superfluity.

Hope is the sixth and final characteristic. Though Newbigin develops this in the Western context, hope, from my experience, is a key theme in both Africa and Asia. Hope, in the terms developed here, is directed to the reality of the resurrection, a reality not yet generally visible, but a present reality nonetheless. Or, we can hope in the eschatological there and then because it is a reality in the eschatological here and now. The church is grounded and exists within this reality, meaning that the congregation as the only hermeneutic of the gospel is the place where this "new creation is present, known, and experienced, and from which men and women will go into every sector of public life to claim it for Christ."[82] Such is possible, Newbigin continues, only when "local congregations renounce an introverted concern for their own life, and recognize that they exist for the sake of those who are not members, as sign, instrument, and foretaste of God's redeeming grace for the whole life of society."[83] This dialectic of the church being something in and for itself because its identity lies beyond it is, and remains, basic.

---

[79]Ibid.
[80]Ibid., p. 231.
[81]Ibid.
[82]Ibid., p. 232.
[83]Ibid., p. 233.

Conclusion

By describing the congregation as the only hermeneutic of the gospel, Newbigin reminds us that the gospel can only take bodily form. The gospel is no free-floating message, no individual belief system. It creates, shapes and sustains a people, a body. This congregation is a visible entity in history. More than this and as idealistic as it may sound, Newbigin expects the congregation local and mundane, filled with the everyday stumbling Christian, to be a sign of the kingdom—not just called to be so, but given all the necessary gifts in the power of the Spirit. Newbigin includes here, as is clear from his wider corpus, word, sacrament and office. In the liturgy, the community remembers the story within which it lives, moves and has its being.

Alone, however, this paints too flat a picture. Newbigin predicates his discussion of the congregation with an affirmation of God's acting to reveal himself. God acts in history; he does not give himself over to historical course. The necessary visibility of the congregation becomes defined in terms of the cross and the resurrection. We see the crucifixion; God reveals the resurrection. This dialectic determines the church. The community is something in and for itself because its identity exists beyond it in the history of Jesus Christ. The church does not control this history. It follows in its wake, meaning that the congregation is baptized into the mission of Jesus Christ and for this is given the Holy Spirit. As the only hermeneutic of the gospel, the congregation assumes its necessary missionary form, finding its identity in the event of being gathered, in the event of fellowship with our neighbor.

This picture is, of course, eschatological—eschatological not as something reserved for the future and for which the church now is some form of detour or waiting room, but eschatological as living in the reality of the cosmic Christ where he "is all and in all" (Col 3:11). For this, God has chosen the congregation to be the hermeneutic of his gospel for the world.

10

Asian Perspectives on Twenty-First-Century Pluralism

Allen Yeh

Perhaps Asia's greatest contribution to the religious landscape today is pluralism. Every major world religion has its roots in Asia, including Christianity.[1] There is no extant world religion that originates from Africa, Europe or the Americas.[2] The subject of missiology in Asia is unique because Asia is more like three continents: (1) In the case of the Middle East (e.g., Israel), it is like Europe in that it was the cradle of much of early Christianity but is now post-Christian.[3] (2) In the case of Central, South and Southeast Asia (the so-called 10/40 Window),[4] it is like frontier missions where many have yet to hear the name of Jesus but instead are rife with every other religion in the world. (3) Parts of East Asia (e.g., South Korea and China) are representative of world Christianity like sub-Saharan Africa or Latin America, because these are arguably the heartlands of Christianity today. As such, at the very minimum three missiological approaches to Asian Christianity need to be taken. One case that illustrates all three is

[1]Todd Johnson, *Atlas of Global Christianity* (Edinburgh: University of Edinburgh Press, 2010). To qualify as a world religion, at least 5 percent of the world's population must be adherents to it.

[2]Mormonism is perhaps the closest to qualify, but it has less than 5 percent of the world's population.

[3]Philip Jenkins, *The Lost History of Christianity: The Thousand-Year Golden Age of the Church in the Middle East, Africa, and Asia—and How It Died* (New York: HarperCollins, 2008).

[4]A term coined by Luis Bush in 1990 referring to latitude markers: the region between ten degrees and forty degrees north (namely northern Africa, the Middle East, India, Southeast Asia and China) is the least-evangelized and most gospel-resistant area of the world.

China's "Back to Jerusalem" movement in which the Chinese want to bring the gospel westward across the Silk Road to its origin.[5] In this case, number 3 above is making its way across number 2 to bring revival to number 1, which is "reverse mission" at its fullest implications: the coming of age of the majority-world church bringing the gospel to the non-evangelized and the already-evangelized. However, with the variety and breadth of religious practice in Asia, in mission there is always "power encounter," when other deities or powers are believed to be resistant to or in competition against the Christian God; very rarely is it missions to atheists.

This chapter aims to show the symbiotic relationship between Christianity and pluralistic Asia, that it can be a mutually strengthening endeavor and not a contrarian one. Christianity can provide definition and direction to Asia's pluralism, and Asia's pluralism can be a mirror in which Christianity can assess itself aright and regain some of its radical authenticity. Newbigin, having been a missionary in Asia, will speak into the discussion at the end.

What Christianity Has to Offer Pluralistic Asia

What does Christianity have to offer religiously pluralistic Asia? There are several unique characteristics about the Christian faith, even in the midst of a multiplicity of other offerings. First, it is the largest religion in the world, though Islam is presently the fastest growing. Second, it is missionary, unlike Judaism and Hinduism.[6] Third, it is monotheistic, which of course the other two Abrahamic faiths can also claim—this implies exclusivism that does not tolerate other gods. Though Islam can make all three of these claims as well, the distinction is best described by what a Pakistani Muslim once said to me: "Wherever Islam goes, it adapts the culture to the religion. Wherever Christianity goes, it adapts the religion to the culture." Both Islam and Christianity have these three factors, which have moved them to the forefront of the world's religious scene (this is why the Islam-Christianity encounter is

---

[5]Paul Hattaway, Brother Yun, Peter XuYongze and Enoch Wang, *Back to Jerusalem: Three Chinese House Church Leaders Share Their Vision to Complete the Great Commission* (Milton Keynes, UK: Authentic Publishing, 2003).

[6]However, it must be noted that Islam and Buddhism are also missionary. In fact, those two (along with Christianity) are the only three major world religions that qualify as missionary, as their founders all commissioned their followers to spread the faith. See Terry Muck, Harold Netland and Gerald McDermott, eds., *Handbook of Religion: A Christian Engagement with Traditions, Teachings, and Practices* (Grand Rapids: Baker, 2014), p. 46.

not just limited to 9/11 but is the battleground in some of the greatest "hot spots" of the world, such as Nigeria and China).

But despite the similarities, the two religions come from very different points of view regarding pluralism. Islam chafes against it, either trying to deny it or squelch it altogether, denouncing other religions as idolatrous and their followers as infidels. When pluralism develops within Islam itself, such as the Shia, Sunni and Sufi offshoots, then caliphates and Islamic states are formed or wars declared. With Christianity, some react to pluralism (both outside and inside the religion) like Islam does with rigid, nonnegotiable entrenchment. Others, however, take pluralism as an unavoidable reality and perhaps even a boon, ranging from grudging toleration to seeing it as an ally in the spread of the faith. Lamin Sanneh makes this case in *Translating the Message*: "Christianity is remarkable for the relative ease with which it enters living cultures. In becoming translatable it renders itself compatible with all cultures. It may be welcomed or resisted in its Western garb, but it is not itself uncongenial in other garb. Christianity broke free from its absolutized Judaic frame and, through a radical pluralism, adopted the Hellenistic culture to the point of near absolutization."[7] Sanneh's point echoes what the Pakistani Muslim said to me: Christianity is remarkable because it navigates the tension between solid rootedness and wide-bending flexibility, like a skyscraper that does not break precisely *because* it sways in the wind. This is the genius of the missionary enterprise.

How does one discern between contextualization and syncretism, then?[8] This is the difficulty with accepting pluralism as an inherent necessity of the system. Not enough flexibility leads to ghettoization, but too much flexibility leads to syncretism. People who are afraid of heresy end up absolutizing everything about their expression of their faith, including their culture. People who are overly accepting of everything also make culture an idol, except instead of being blind to their culture they worship it knowingly. The

[7]Lamin Sanneh, *Translating the Message: The Missionary Impact on Culture* (Maryknoll, NY: Orbis, 1989), p. 50.

[8]Some have suggested that syncretism is not as negative as it may appear at first, such as Indian theologian M. M. Thomas, who calls for a "Christ-centered syncretism." Lesslie Newbigin did not go so far as to call it that, but admitted that Christianity must inevitably encounter culture that colors people's personal expression of their faith. See M. M. Thomas, "The Absoluteness of Jesus Christ and Christ-Centered Syncretism," *The Ecumenical Review* 37 (1985): 387-97.

key is accepting pluralism in the good sense and not in the bad sense.

The *Oxford English Dictionary* has four definitions of pluralism, two of which are listed below and useful for this discussion:

- The theory that the world is made up of more than one kind of substance or thing; (more generally) any theory or system of thought which recognizes more than one irreducible basic principle. Also: the theory that the knowable world consists of a plurality of interacting entities.
- The presence or tolerance of a diversity of ethnic or cultural groups within a society or state; (the advocacy of) toleration or acceptance of the coexistence of differing views, values, cultures, etc.

Therefore pluralism can either be the doctrine that reality is composed of many ultimate substances or the belief that such a condition is desirable or socially beneficial. David Hume's skepticism at the pinnacle of the Enlightenment took the fact-value distinction as "how things are" versus "how things ought to be."[9] The former can scarcely be denied; the world is made up of multiple cultures and languages and religions. The latter can be either good or bad: it is bad when it is akin to relativism, but it is good when it means diversity. Lesslie Newbigin calls these religious pluralism and cultural pluralism.[10]

Relativism says that truth is rooted in the individual hearer/receiver/observer rather than the source/author/fact. It says that all truths are the same, and all truths are equally valid. However, all religions cannot be right, because they have mutually exclusive truth claims. A pluralism that derives from relativism says that nobody has the truth. Clearly this is not Christianity.[11]

However, Christianity is diverse in its very essence. It is built to be pluralistic in a missionary sense, as proven by four historical and biblical examples: (1) It is the only religion whose Scriptures are not written in the language of its founder. Jesus spoke Aramaic; the New Testament was written in Koine Greek—because that was the lingua franca of the Eastern Mediterranean—to get the message out to as many people as possible. Christianity cares less about its own cultural absolutism and more about reaching the masses.

---

[9]David Hume, *A Treatise of Human Nature: Being an Attempt to Introduce the Experimental Method of Reasoning into Moral Subjects* (1739). Another way to discuss this is using the terms positive vs. normative, or descriptive vs. prescriptive.

[10]Lesslie Newbigin, *The Gospel in a Pluralist Society* (Grand Rapids: Eerdmans, 1989), p. 14.

[11]Ibid., pp. 166-70.

(2) The location of Israel is right at the crossroads of three continents—Africa, Asia and Europe—meaning that it was originally situated to spread multidirectionally. Just as chosenness is always about responsibility and not for resting on your laurels, the Promised Land was not meant to be a final resting place but a launching point to the nations. In fact, today Christianity is the only major world religion without a geographic center. (3) The command to spread is a missionary mandate throughout the Bible, from the Cultural Mandate (Gen 1:28) to the Tower of Babel (Gen 11:8-9) to the Abrahamic covenant (Gen 15:5) to the Great Commission (Acts 1:8). (4) Multiethnicity or multiculturalism is a key characteristic of Christianity. The first time the believers are called Christian was at Antioch (Acts 11), the first multiethnic church in history. The Way was not considered Christianity until the gospel had gone to the nations. Even in Pentecost and Revelation 7:9, Babel was not reversed as if it were a curse; diversity is maintained and celebrated as an essential hallmark of Christianity.

Missions is the mother of theology, as proven by the apostle Paul, who was the greatest missionary of the early church and, not coincidentally, also the author of half the New Testament. Theology is occasional, and who had more crosscultural occasions than Paul, founder of dozens of churches in Jewish and Gentile contexts? This first came to a head after Paul's first missionary journey. His missionary encounter with Gentiles provoked questions about pluralism that led to the Jerusalem Council (Acts 15:1, 19-21) to settle the dispute of whether Gentiles need to live like Jews. The verdict was a qualified no: some rules can be bent (like the need for circumcision), and some rules cannot be broken (like the injunction against sexual immorality). The core cannot shift, but the rest must flex, like the skyscraper designed to give with strong winds and earth tremors. The Jerusalem Council allowed Paul to proceed with confidence into his second missionary journey. Not only did missions give birth to theology, but theology gave birth to more missions. It is a synergistic circle that is the lifeblood of the church.

Henry Venn, general secretary of the Church Missionary Society from 1841 to 1873, coined the phrase "the three-self church," referring to a church that is self-governing, self-sustaining and self-propagating.[12] Paul Hiebert

[12]Max Warren, ed., *To Apply the Gospel* (Grand Rapids: Eerdmans, 1971).

calls the Two-Thirds World churches to a fourth self: self-theologizing.[13] Without this last one, majority world churches could remain in a state of rote copying of the West, mechanical imitation without original ideas suitable to their context. If the confrontation with pluralism leads to "invention" of more theology, then Asia should be the greatest birthplace of self-theologizing in the world today! But most of the self-theologizing is not happening from Asia. Latin America certainly has its share of original theology, especially with liberation theology, which had its heyday in the 1970s and 1980s. Sub-Saharan Africa is arguably the heartland of Christianity today, and it has started producing volumes like the *Africa Bible Commentary*.[14] Whither Asia?

What Pluralistic Asia Has to Offer Christianity

Religious pluralism is good for Christianity because it helps us to know who we are. Just as Americans in the US often do not know what constitutes "Americanness" until traveling abroad or being confronted with it by foreigners, Christianity is best identified when set up side by side with other religions. Thus, Asian Christians know who they are and what they believe, perhaps more than Christians in any other continent, because of persecution and rubbing shoulders daily with others. Most Christians in the Two-Thirds World today are well acquainted with at least one other world religion. With Asian Christians, it's a daily encounter *with two or more* world religions. There are at least four major realities of Asian pluralism that can positively affect Christianity on that continent.

1. Minority status. Asia is the only continent on earth that has never had a Christian majority in its history. It need not be said that Europe, at one point, was. Christianity has now overtaken Islam as the biggest religion in Africa. Both Americas have been mostly Christian since the arrival of Europeans. Oceania is the great missionary success story. But Christianity in Asia, even in the early church where it originated, was always a minority. And today, the great religious pluralism ensures that it will remain so. World

[13]Paul G. Hiebert, *Anthropological Reflections on Missiological Issues* (Grand Rapids: Baker, 1994), p. 97.

[14]Tokunboh Adeyemo, ed., *Africa Bible Commentary: A One-Volume Commentary Written by 70 African Scholars* (Grand Rapids: Zondervan, 2006). This was published simultaneously in Africa by Word Alive, an African publisher. A Latin American version will be released shortly, called the CBC: *Comentario Bíblico Contemporaneo* (San José, Costa Rica: Letra Viva).

Christianity, the shift of the center of gravity of Christianity to the global South (Africa and Latin America), leaves out the global East: Asia. As Aloysius Pieris writes:

> Asia is the cradle of all the scriptural religions in the world, including Christianity, which, however, left Asia very early and forced its way back several centuries later as a stranger and "intruder" whom Asia consistently refused to entertain. Thus, after four centuries of missionary presence, Christians are numerically and qualitatively an insignificant minority. . . . Can a Christianity that has lost its "Asian sense" presume to create an Asian theology? Even the churches of the Oriental rites have frozen their early openness to the Asian reality.[15]

John Stott supports this by pointing out the disadvantage of a Christendom mindset:

> When I was ordained in the Church of England, evangelicals were a despised and rejected minority. . . . Over the intervening 60 years, I've seen the evangelical movement in England grow in size, in maturity, certainly in scholarship, and therefore I think in influence and impact. We went from a ghetto to being on the ascendancy, which is a very dangerous place to be. Pride is the ever-present danger that faces all of us. In many ways, it is good for us to be despised and rejected. I think of Jesus' words, "Woe unto you when all men speak well of you."[16]

Christendom has never existed in Asia as a whole. And this may be a good thing, as Asian Christians largely do not have to struggle with nominalism. Persecution is much more the norm, as was also the norm in the early church.

2. A world of contrasts. Asia, in a sense, could be a self-contained entity and a world within itself, because it has over half the world's population on a single continent,[17] often with the greatest polarizations. But the polarizations are what give it strength and authenticity. Addressing the realities of urbanization is more pressing in Asia than anywhere else, because of the twenty-five largest cities in the world, fourteen of them are in Asia.[18] Yet it is also rich in farmland and has vast rural swaths that ought not be ignored. Partially due to this urban-rural dichotomy, economic pluralism is also rife. The richest of the

---

[15]Aloysius Pieris, *An Asian Theology of Liberation* (Edinburgh: T&T Clark, 1988), p. 74.
[16]Tim Stafford, "Evangelism Plus," *Christianity Today*, October 2006, p. 96.
[17]A population of 4.43 billion out of 7.13 billion.
[18]See www.worldatlas.com/citypops.htm.

rich and the poorest of the poor reside in Asia, sometimes side by side—there may be no greater economic contrasts in any other continent on earth. Three of the world's BRIC nations are in Asia.[19] When the poor can prophetically confront the rich, some of the authentic textures of Christianity can be seen more clearly. This is in contrast to a nation like the United States, where Christianity and wealth have often been strange bedfellows, a concept which would have been so foreign to the early Christians that they probably would have had to convene another Jerusalem Council to address this singular juxtaposition—how can one serve both God and mammon?

With Asia having the largest population on earth, this also means potentially the greatest missionary force in world history if they could be converted and mobilized. David Aikman recounts:

> "Muslims prefer Chinese to Americans. They don't like Americans very much," one Chinese Christian said bluntly. He outlined several reasons why Chinese Christians can succeed where Westerners have failed. A major advantage is that the Chinese government supports the anti-American objectives of some political groups in the Middle East "so the Muslim nations support China." He added, "Besides, we have a lot of experience of persecution."[20]

And with a rise in missions would come a rise in self-theologizing, as theology often arises from missionary encounters. One very interesting battleground is Indonesia, the largest Muslim country, which also has a significant Chinese Christian minority who happen to own most of the businesses and capital.[21] Another is the aforementioned Back to Jerusalem movement, which aims to reclaim Central Asia. India is itself a unique situation in that it has just about every religion within its borders, so crosscultural missions does not even have to involve leaving the country.

3. ***Holistic worldview.*** It is not just religious and economic and ethnolinguistic diversity that is plentiful, it is also a pluralism of worldviews. With all the debates of modernism versus postmodernism in the West, it is Asia that

[19]Brazil, Russia, India, China, a term coined in 2001 by economist Jim O'Neill in a paper titled "Building Better Global Economic BRICs," Global Economics Paper No. 66, November 30, 2001, www.goldmansachs.com/our-thinking/archive/archive-pdfs/build-better-brics.pdf.

[20]David Aikman, *Jesus in Beijing: How Christianity Is Transforming China and Changing the Global Balance of Power* (Washington, DC: Regnery, 2003), pp. 12-13.

[21]Allen Yeh, "The Chinese Diaspora," in *Global Diasporas and Mission*, ed. Chandler H. Im and Amos Yong (Oxford: Regnum, 2014), pp. 89-98.

combines these while also including premodern views. Sri Lankan Vinoth Ramachandra of International Fellowship of Evangelical Students lamented at the Edinburgh 2010 missionary conference that the Western view of Asia is one dimensional: "India and China together produce more science and engineering graduates every year than North America and Europe combined. But Asian mission studies dissertations and the bulk of articles in mission studies journals focus on historical studies of religious sects and denominations, traditional tribal cultures or exotic new religious movements."[22]

Part of the reason for Asia's technological boom and the West's postmodern shift is that East and West have exchanged educational philosophies. As the West becomes ever more fascinated with Eastern religions like Buddhism and Hinduism, Asia is becoming ever more scientific, and some parts have even absorbed Marxist thought, which derived from Europe. Asian communication, which is known to be more indirect, has been replaced by straight lecture and rote memorization in the classrooms. The West, in contrast, has become more universalistic and "tolerant" along the lines of South Asian religions and encourages more dialogue. Yet, this does not mean that Westerners are more attuned to the workings of the spiritual realm in daily life, what Paul Hiebert calls the "flaw of the excluded middle."[23] Asia has less of a natural-supernatural divide, and this may be a more realistic way of viewing the world.

Worldview also includes the way that culture affects theology, because theology is ultimately an attempt to answer the great questions of life that culture demands. Christianity was originally an Eastern (Semitic) religion, just as the other two Abrahamic faiths are. However, its missionary encounter with the Hellenistic world changed its flavor forever, especially with the injection of an Augustinian Platonism. Yet there is a potential for Christianity to return to its Eastern roots by reabsorbing an Asian mindset, which is the womb where it was originally nurtured and birthed from. For example, the gospel, while about guilt, is perhaps even more about shame.[24] This is also the crux of N. T. Wright's arguments for the new perspective on Paul:

---

[22]Vinoth Ramachandra's reflection, untitled, in the final plenary, in *Edinburgh 2010: Mission Today and Tomorrow*, ed. Kirsteen Kim and Andrew Anderson (Oxford: Regnum, 2011), p. 335.

[23]Paul Hiebert, "The Flaw of the Excluded Middle," *Missiology: An International Review* 10, no. 1 (January 1982): 35-47

[24]Duane Elmer, *Cross-Cultural Connections: Stepping Out and Fitting In Around the World* (Downers Grove, IL: InterVarsity Press, 2002), pp. 171-81.

that to affirm the deep Jewishness of Paul changes things more drastically than if we were to read him simply as a Hellenist.[25] There could be a radical recovery of authentic early Christianity if Asia can contribute its culture to Christian theology, and by scraping off some of the accretions of time, there can be a rediscovery of the original Christian message.

*4. **Redemptive analogies.*** What is the biggest challenge to Christianity: No religion or other religions? Though the 10/40 Window is often touted as the place with the most urgent need, some might make a case for post-Christian Europe as the top of the list of need. Nominalism and passivity and cynicism seem to be the biggest killers of the faith. In contrast, people who are spiritual but not Christian already have an advantage: at least they have no problem believing in a god. As far as we know, the apostle Paul never confronted atheists, but he confronted people of other religions and used their religions to his benefit. This is called the principle of redemptive analogy.[26] The most notable example is in Acts 17 where Paul used the "unknown god" of the Athenians in Mars Hill to point to Jesus. As long as one can gain a foothold using the society's own religion and culture, a link to Christianity may be drawn. Some would level charges of universalism at this, but again, it is the fine line between syncretism and contextualization. The key lies in articulating the name of Jesus. In the view of redemptive analogy, the more footholds the better, but that is insufficient until there is special revelation (either Scripture or preaching)—Paul certainly did not think that the "unknown god" could save, nor was Philip content to let the Ethiopian eunuch read Isaiah without explanation (Acts 8). This is in keeping with Lesslie Newbigin's position:

> The position which I have outlined is exclusivist in the sense that it affirms the unique truth of the revelation in Jesus Christ, but it is not exclusivist in the sense of denying the possibility of the salvation of the non-Christian. It is inclusivist in the sense that it refuses to limit the saving grace of God to the members of the Christian Church, but it rejects the inclusivism which regards the non-Christian religions as vehicles of salvation. It is pluralist in the sense of acknowledging the gracious work of God in the lives of all

[25]N. T. Wright, *What Saint Paul Really Said: Was Paul of Tarsus the Real Founder of Christianity?* (Grand Rapids: Eerdmans, 1997), p. 13.

[26]Don Richardson, *Eternity in Their Hearts* (Ventura, CA: Regal, 1981).

> human beings, but it rejects a pluralism which denies the uniqueness and decisiveness of what God has done in Jesus Christ.[27]

One historical example that illustrates this effectively was Oxonian sinologist James Legge (1815–1897), who was embroiled in the Term Controversy.[28] As any Bible translator will attest, the hardest word in the Bible to translate is "God." When Legge served as a missionary to China, he advocated for the word *Shangdi* as the biblical word for God. Meanwhile, a contemporary American missionary, William Boone, argued for *Shen*.[29] Jesuit Matteo Ricci, who had come several centuries earlier, used the word *Tianzhu*.[30] All of them came loaded with linguistic baggage: the first implies a supreme being who is head of a pantheon of gods; the second suggests ancestral spirits; and the third seemed too accommodating to Confucianism. However, none of the three missionaries ever advocated for *Yehehua*, the transliteration of the Tetragrammaton into Chinese, because it was a foreign word. The one thing they all could agree on was that Christianity had to be couched in indigenous terms for the Chinese, otherwise the locals would not accept it.

With the immense pluralism of the Asian continent, it would seem that this means much more opportunity for redemptive analogies to be employed. There are far more footholds for the gospel in such a scenario than if the continent was mostly atheist, as Europe is. What looks like a challenge may be one of Asia's greatest assets.

Lesslie Newbigin on Asian Pluralism

Lesslie Newbigin, having been a missionary in India, was steeped in the most pluralistic of all Asian nations. India is rightfully called a subcontinent, and the multiplicity of etymologically unrelated languages, and therefore the ironic necessity of English as the binding mechanism, is insightfully explained by Aloysius Pieris:

---

[27] Newbigin, *GPS*, pp. 182-83.

[28] G. Wright Doyle, *Builders of the Chinese Church: Pioneer Protestant Missionaries and Chinese Church Leaders* (Eugene, OR: Wipf & Stock, 2014), p. 78.

[29] James Legge, *The Notions of the Chinese Concerning God and Spirits: With an Examination of the Defense of an Essay on the Proper Rendering of the Words Elohim and Theos into the Chinese Language by William J. Boone* (Hongkong: Hongkong Register Office, 1852).

[30] Ricci (1552–1610) was himself embroiled in a similar controversy about contextualization, namely the Chinese Rites Controversy, as Newbigin alludes to in *GPS*, p. 142.

> The task of Asian theologians is more complex than that of their colleagues in the North Atlantic region and the Southern Hemisphere. After all, do not European theologians communicate in the same Indo-Germanic languages? Latin American liberation theologians think, act, and speak in a common Iberian idiom. They are all within reach of one another by means of a European medium of communication. Such is not the case in Asia. It is therefore regrettable that Asians are not able to consult each other's hidden theologies except in a *non-Asian idiom,* thus *neutralizing the most promising feature in our methodology.* (The same applies to Africans.) We Asians professionally theologize in English, the language in which most of us think, read, and pray. The theological side of language in a "continent of languages" has been grossly underestimated and our stubborn refusal to consult each other's treasures directly in each other's linguistic idioms, or even to be familiar with one's own cultural heritage, will remain a major obstacle to the discovery of a truly Asian theology.[31]

This is illustrative of the downside of pluralism. How is common ground to be found in such a broad spectrum? Often it seems like the outsider, the colonizer, the Westerner, becomes the arbiter and mediator of what is true. In world Christianity, some people take it to mean that there is "cultural" theology, like African theology, Latin American theology and Asian theology, and then there is "pure" theology, meaning Western theology. Or within Indian theology, there is Tamil theology, there is Malayali theology, there is Hindi theology, but Anglo theology is metatheology. This was basically Newbigin's problem with the illustration of the blind men and the elephant: one claims to see all while the others only see a part.[32] In truth, the one who claims to see all is also seeing just a part. But is this relativism?

A better analogy than the blind men and the elephant would be what Andrew Walls calls "the human auditorium." In this metaphor, a crowded theater's numerous guests are all able to see the stage, although none of them can see it in its entirety. As the drama is acted out, each attendee has a different perspective; some can see more of the stage than others, and some can see more clearly than others, but all are watching the same play. Walls writes, "The play we are watching is the drama of life. The whole human race can see the stage on which the drama is enacted; but the focus varies according to the place in

---

[31]Pieris, *Asian Theology of Liberation,* p. 71.
[32]Newbigin, *GPS*, pp. 9-10.

the auditorium."[33] From this framework, Walls argues that, in order to make sense of the "drama" of not only the human race but also the activity of God on earth, one must understand his or her own place in the theater. Every perspective is incomplete, needing other perspectives to form a coherent understanding of reality. Any culture can maintain an orthodox theology; however, if one were to ask each culture to make a list of which aspects of their theology affect their day-to-day lives, there might be a different list for each one. As he continues, Walls writes, "It is necessary that we hear the Gospel under, and in relation to, the conditions of our experiences and relationships, our environment and society—our culture in fact. Others seated elsewhere in the world theatre will see the same action, hear the same words; but their seating will enable them to see parts of the stage that we do not and will obscure some things which may seem to us crystal clear."[34] For this reason, dialogue between cultures is of utmost importance in humanity's attempts to understand God, develop a coherent theology and missiology, and strategize to most effectively reach nonbelievers. The principles behind this analogy suggest that multiple cultural perspectives on the Christian faith are necessary to move toward gaining a complete picture of the truth. Just as experience and perspective differ from person to person, so also they differ from region to region.

In this sense, Walls is advocating the second *OED* definition of pluralism: "Perhaps it is not only that different ages and nations see different things in Scripture—it is that they *need* to see different things."[35] Is this what Newbigin would malign as the false "fact-value dichotomy"?[36] It would only be if Walls were defining it in the bad sense: religious pluralism as relativism, that everyone has their own truth and is content to let that be the only thing they ever see. But Walls takes the definition in the good sense: cultural pluralism, that everyone's perspective is actually true as a small slice of reality, but instead of remaining isolated, we need each other. It is like the apostle Paul's injunction that the various parts of the body are indispensable to each other (1 Cor 12:12-31). Newbigin describes it in these words: "It is essential to the integrity of our witness to this new reality that we recognize that to be its

[33]Andrew F. Walls, *The Missionary Movement in Christian History: Studies of the Transmission of the Faith* (Maryknoll, NY: Orbis, 1996), p. 44.

[34]Ibid., p. 46.

[35]Ibid., p. 12.

[36]Newbigin, *GPS*, p. 7.

witnesses does not mean to be the possessors of all truth. It means to be placed on the path by following which we are led toward the truth. There is indeed a proper place for agnosticism in the Christian life. There is a true sense in which we are—with others—seekers after the truth."[37] This is not atheism, nor is it relativism. It is agnostic pluralism, to follow Newbigin's suggestion. However, that makes the establishment nervous because it seems like a slippery slope to atheistic relativism and heresy and syncretism. But the opposite end of the spectrum, unyielding intractability, is death to contextualization and innovation and discovery. What we need is Martin Luther's *reformata et semper reformanda*: to be reformed and yet always reforming.

The problem with the fact-value dichotomy is ultimately a question of integration. Just like the "flaw of the excluded middle," Western thought is so often black-and-white. For devout Christians, the temptation is great, in an exclusivist faith, to think in such a way. It seems logical that utter devotion would be a mark of fidelity, much as the first two commandments of the Decalogue forbid worship or idolatry of other gods. It seems to be anathema to even consider anything else. But Andrew Walls observes that Christians are subject to both the indigenizing principle and the pilgrim principle: basically, we are in the world but not of it.[38] We cannot escape this world we are placed in, yet that does not mean we need to be beholden to it. Newbigin calls for a reintegration of the subjective and objective poles of religion and science, of the supernatural world and the natural world.[39] The one place where I would challenge Newbigin is in his Reformed replacement theology where he does not see the Semitic framework as relevant anymore.[40] It is possible that Christianity can go so far afield from its roots that Gentiles and the church become the entirety of God's people. Though the apostle Paul does say that faith, not the physical seed of Abraham, constitutes God's people (Rom 2:29), he also charges in the same epistle that Gentiles ought not to be arrogant lest they be broken off too, just as the natural branches were (Rom 11:17-21). *Semper reformanda* means to keep going back to the roots. Jesus exemplified it best in that he was both uni-

---

[37]Ibid., p. 12.
[38]Walls, *Missionary Movement in Christian History*, pp. 7-9.
[39]Newbigin, *GPS*, p. 23.
[40]Ibid., p. 145.

versal and culturally specific: he was a first-century Aramaic-speaking Jew in Roman-occupied Israel, and yet he is the Savior of the world.

A large part of the reason why Christians are uncomfortable in proceeding with what George Lindbeck calls the "third way" or the Cultural Linguistic Model[41] is because there exists confusion about whether nature is created by God to be good or if the fallenness of sin has irreparably tainted the world. Those who hold to the former, the liberals, espouse what Lindbeck calls the Experiential Model, where everything ought to be used, with no discernment as to what may be harmful. Those who lean on the latter, the Fundamentalists, champion the Propositional Model, where stark boundaries need to be drawn between Christian and non-Christian at least in part because of an Augustinian/Reformed lens, which emphasizes the noetic effects of sin. The result is that either missions becomes unnecessary and even offensive as it is couched in postcolonial imperialistic terms, or missions becomes professionalized rather than an action of the laity. The apostle Paul was a tentmaker. Yes he went to synagogue like a devout Jew, but he did not remove himself from the marketplace, because that would go against the absolute nature of the Father's mission who sent the Son into the world rather than keep him apart and untainted by the world. The *missio Dei* demands that God is the initiator, the Prime Mover, and the one who conquers sin and death rather than being afraid of its taint.[42] This is not to make light of God's holiness but to suggest that the missionary nature of Christianity is first exemplified by the Trinity. Christians do missions because of the *imago Dei*, so there is divine precedence.

Asian pluralism has the power to challenge this disjunctive approach. A true, proper integration is the unification of knowledge, both what we can learn from the Bible (special revelation) and all we can discover through the exercise of our own faculties (general revelation). It is not Enlightenment philosophy, which sees reason as the arbiter of faith.

Perhaps one of the greatest needs today due to the fact-value dichotomy is for religion and theology to be reinstated as a required field of study. That

---

[41]Ibid., pp. 24-25.

[42]Ibid., pp. 121-22. The distinction between "mission" and "missions" is also well documented by David Bosch, *Transforming Mission: Paradigm Shifts in Theology of Mission* (Maryknoll, NY: Orbis, 1991), p. 391.

would fill a huge void in this world that sees international relations purely in terms of politics and economics. The West is seeing its engagement with China and the Muslim world as political and economic,[43] but the missing part of the equation is the explosive growth of Christianity in China, which is creating a Copernican revolution in that country, and the West's proper engagement with Islam as a religion and not as a "war on terror." The West has effectively truncated itself from study of religion because it has relegated it to the sidelines of "values"—but with the rise of the Islamic State and a post-9/11 world, obviously religion is still hugely important today to be studied. Newbigin argues that the idea of an increasingly secularized world is a myth.[44] He was correct in 1989 when he wrote this, and he is even more correct today. Religion is a fact of our time, and nowhere more so than Asia.

The Future of Asian Theology

What is Asian theology? Is it even possible to articulate a cohesive "Asian-ness" in the midst of such pluralistic diversity? What positives can be derived from Asian pluralism? So far we have "water buffalo theology"[45] and Minjung theology,[46] but perhaps we need to move beyond these iterations. Like Maoism owing its foundations to Marxism, these are Asian adaptations of European ideologies. In addition to its imported nature, Newbigin chides liberation theology for being anthropocentric rather than acceding to a God-led *missio Dei*.[47] The struggle of the oppressed is surely one theme of Scripture, but it is not the only one.

To bring the conversation full circle, perhaps Asian theology should be grounded in the pluralism of religious expressions. Instead of class or race or gender or language, the unique contribution of Asia is religion. But is this a contradiction, trying to define one religion by using a multiplicity of religions? Not if the other religions are taken simply as culture, much as the West regards Greco-Roman mythology. Asia is so diverse that to link this vast continent with a meta-paradigm, either a foreign structure needs to be im-

---

[43]The three great superpowers of the twenty-first century as predicted by Samuel P. Huntington, *The Clash of Civilizations and the Remaking of World Order* (New York: Touchstone, 1996).

[44]Newbigin, *GPS*, pp. 211-21.

[45]Kosuke Koyama, *Water Buffalo Theology* (Maryknoll, NY: Orbis, 1999).

[46]Ahn Byung-Mu, *Speaking on Minjung Theology* (Seoul: Han Gil Sa, 1993).

[47]Newbigin, *GPS*, pp. 148-52.

ported like Marxism or the English language, or the linking mechanism needs to be found within the continent itself. In the same way that a more indigenous word for God is always preferable to something like *Yehehua*, I want to argue that the native materials of the continent should be the grounding for an indigenous expression of the faith, not an outside arbitrator.

My proposal is this: Despite the fact that Asia is like three continents, we need to use the three religions or philosophies that have historically proven successful in transcending international boundaries in Asia: Islam, Buddhism and Confucianism, which originated in the West, the South and the East of the Asian continent, thus having representation spanning the entirety of its geography. Islam began in Saudi Arabia but has stretched as far southeast as Indonesia. Buddhism began in India but has made its way as far northeast as Japan. And Confucianism has permeated East Asia and even some of Southeast Asia. If Asian Christian theology can use these three raw materials to construct its own indigenous theology, like Muslim C1 to C6 insider movements[48] or employing Confucian and Buddhist philosophy the same way Western theology builds on the pagan Greek philosopher Plato, then there will be the beginnings of a self-theologizing that is authentically true to the Asian context and that is built on the very pluralism of the continent. What initially seemed to be a hindrance could actually be a benefit: Christianity built on a combination of Islamic/Buddhist/Confucian thought, a strategy similar to the Nestorians' in the seventh century who were the first missionaries to China and used Taoism as their basis for communicating the gospel.[49] The difference is this: it will involve hybridity due to the globalized nature of the world, where absolute insularity is nigh impossible. Instead of being content with a multiplicity of Asian theolog*ies*, it may actually be possible to construct an Asian theolog*y* today. Religion can be to Asia as Koine Greek was to the ancient Eastern Mediterranean world: the commonality that all believers in that part of the world can understand.

Linked by religion instead of language, and framed in Eastern rather than Western thought, Asian theology will inevitably take on an expression dif-

[48]John Travis (a pseudonym), "The C1 to C6 Spectrum: A Practical Tool for Defining Six Types of 'Christ-Centered Communities' ('C') Found in the Muslim Context," *Evangelical Missions Quarterly* 34, no. 4 (October 1998): 407-8.

[49]Martin Palmer, *The Jesus Sutras: Rediscovering the Lost Scrolls of Taoist Christianity* (New York: Ballantine, 2001).

ferent from the *logos* of the West. Instead of relying on creeds,[50] the *logos* of the East perhaps will look more like John and less like Paul: more mystical and less propositional. Once Asia has its own voice on par with the West, even on par with the global South, we may see a revolution in theology. This is the kind of pluralism that Lesslie Newbigin would approve of.

[50]Though it is true that the original seven ecumenical councils were all held in Asia, they were in actuality Greek/Western in their culture and framework.

Contributors

William R. Burrows is research professor of missiology at New York Theological Seminary, New York, and the author or editor of a number of books, including *Understanding World Christianity: The Vision and Work of Andrew F. Walls* (Orbis, 2009).

John G. Flett is on the faculty of Institut für Interkulturelle Theologie und Interreligiöse Studien at Wuppertal/Bethel, Germany, and is the author of *The Witness of God: The Trinity,* Missio Dei, *Karl Barth, and the Nature of Christian Community* (Eerdmans, 2010).

Carrie Boren Headington is missioner for evangelism for the Episcopal Diocese of Texas; she has master's degrees from Harvard University (urban poverty policy) and Oxford University (theology).

Michael Karim is a PhD student in the School of Intercultural Studies at Fuller Theological Seminary, investigating the mechanisms of faith development of East Asian American students during their first year of university life; he has served with InterVarsity Christian Fellowship at Fresno State and Rice University.

Veli-Matti Kärkkäinen is professor of systematic theology at Fuller Theological Seminary, Pasadena, California, and the author or editor of many works, including a five-volume *A Constructive Christian Theology for the Pluralistic World* (Eerdmans, 2013–).

Esther L. Meek is professor of philosophy at Geneva College, Beaver Falls, Pennsylvania, and visiting professor of apologetics at Redeemer Seminary in Dallas, Texas. She is the author of a number of books on epistemology.

Wilbert R. Shenk is senior professor of mission history and contemporary culture at Fuller Theological Seminary, Pasadena, California, and the author or editor of many books, including *The Transfiguration of Mission: Biblical, Theological, and Historical Foundations* (Wipf & Stock, 2008).

Steven B. Sherman is assistant professor of Christian Worldview and philosophy at Grand Canyon University in Phoenix, Arizona, and the author of *Revitalizing Theological Epistemology: Holistic Evangelical Approaches to the Knowledge of God* (Wipf & Stock, 2008).

Scott W. Sunquist is professor of world Christianity and dean of the School of Intercultural Studies at Fuller Theological Seminary, Pasadena, California, and the author or editor of numerous books, including *Understanding Christian Mission: Participation in Suffering and Glory* (Baker Academic, 2013).

Allen Yeh is associate professor of intercultural studies and missiology at Biola University, La Mirada, California, and the author of *Expect Great Things, Attempt Great Things: William Carey and Adoniram Judson, Missionary Pioneers* (Wipf & Stock, 2013), among other works.

Amos Yong is professor of theology and mission and director of the Center for Missiological Research at Fuller Theological Seminary, Pasadena, California. He is the author and editor of over three dozen books, including recently *The Missiological Spirit: Christian Mission Theology for the Third Millennium Global Context* (Cascade Books, 2014).

Index

Series Editors: Scott W. Sunquist, Amos Yong and John R. Franke

Missiological Engagements: Church, Theology and Culture in Global Contexts charts interdisciplinary and innovative trajectories in the history, theology and practice of Christian mission at the beginning of the third millennium.

Among its guiding questions are the following: What are the major opportunities and challenges for Christian mission in the twenty-first century? How does the missionary impulse of the gospel reframe theology and hermeneutics within a global and intercultural context? What kind of missiological thinking ought to be retrieved and reappropriated for a dynamic global Christianity? What innovations in the theology and practice of mission are needed for a renewed and revitalized Christian witness in a postmodern, postcolonial, postsecular and post-Christian world?

Books in the series, both monographs and edited collections, will feature contributions by leading thinkers representing evangelical, Protestant, Roman Catholic and Orthodox traditions, who work within or across the range of biblical, historical, theological and social scientific disciplines. Authors and editors will include the full spectrum from younger and emerging researchers to established and renowned scholars, from the Euro-American West and the majority world, whose missiological scholarship will bridge church, academy and society.

Missiological Engagements reflects cutting-edge trends, research and innovations in the field that will be of relevance to theorists and practitioners in churches, academic domains, mission organizations and NGOs, among other arenas.